TREES

VOLUME THREE
THREE FATES

TREES, VOLUME THREE:
THREE FATES. First printing. March
2020. Published by Image Comics, Inc. Office
of publication: 2701 NW Vaughn St, Suite 780,
Portland, OR 97210. Copyright © 2020 Warren Ellis
& Jason Howard. All rights reserved. Contains material
originally published in single magazine form as TREES: THREE
FATES #1–5. "Trees," its logos, and the likenesses of all characters
herein are trademarks of Warren Ellis & Jason Howard, unless
otherwise noted. "Image" and the Image Comics logos are registered
trademarks of Image Comics, Inc. No part of this publication may be
reproduced or transmitted, in any form or by any means (except for
short excerpts for journalistic or review purposes), without the express
written permission of Warren Ellis & Jason Howard or Image Comics,
Inc. All names, characters, events, and locales in this publication
are entirely fictional. Any resemblance to actual persons (living or
dead), events, or places, without satirical intent, is coincidental.
Printed in the USA. For information regarding the CPSIA
on this printed material call: 203-595-3636.
FOR INTERNATIONAL RIGHTS, CONTACT:
foreignlicensing@imagecomics.com.
ISBN 978-1-5343-1509-9

WARREN ELLIS
WRITER

JASON HOWARD
ARTIST

DEE CUNNIFFE
FLATS

FONOGRAFIKS
LETTERING &
BOOK DESIGN

IMAGE COMICS, INC.

ROBERT KIRKMAN
Chief Operating Officer

ERIK LARSEN
Chief Financial Officer

TODD McFARLANE
President

MARC SILVESTRI
Chief Executive Officer

JIM VALENTINO
Vice-President

ERIC STEPHENSON
Publisher/Chief Creative Officer

JEFF BOISON
Director of Publishing Planning
& Book Trade Sales

CHRIS ROSS
Director of Digital Services

JEFF STANG
Director of Direct Market Sales

KAT SALAZAR
Director of PR & Marketing

DREW GILL
Cover Editor

HEATHER DOORNINK
Production Director

NICOLE LAPALME
Controller

IMAGECOMICS.COM

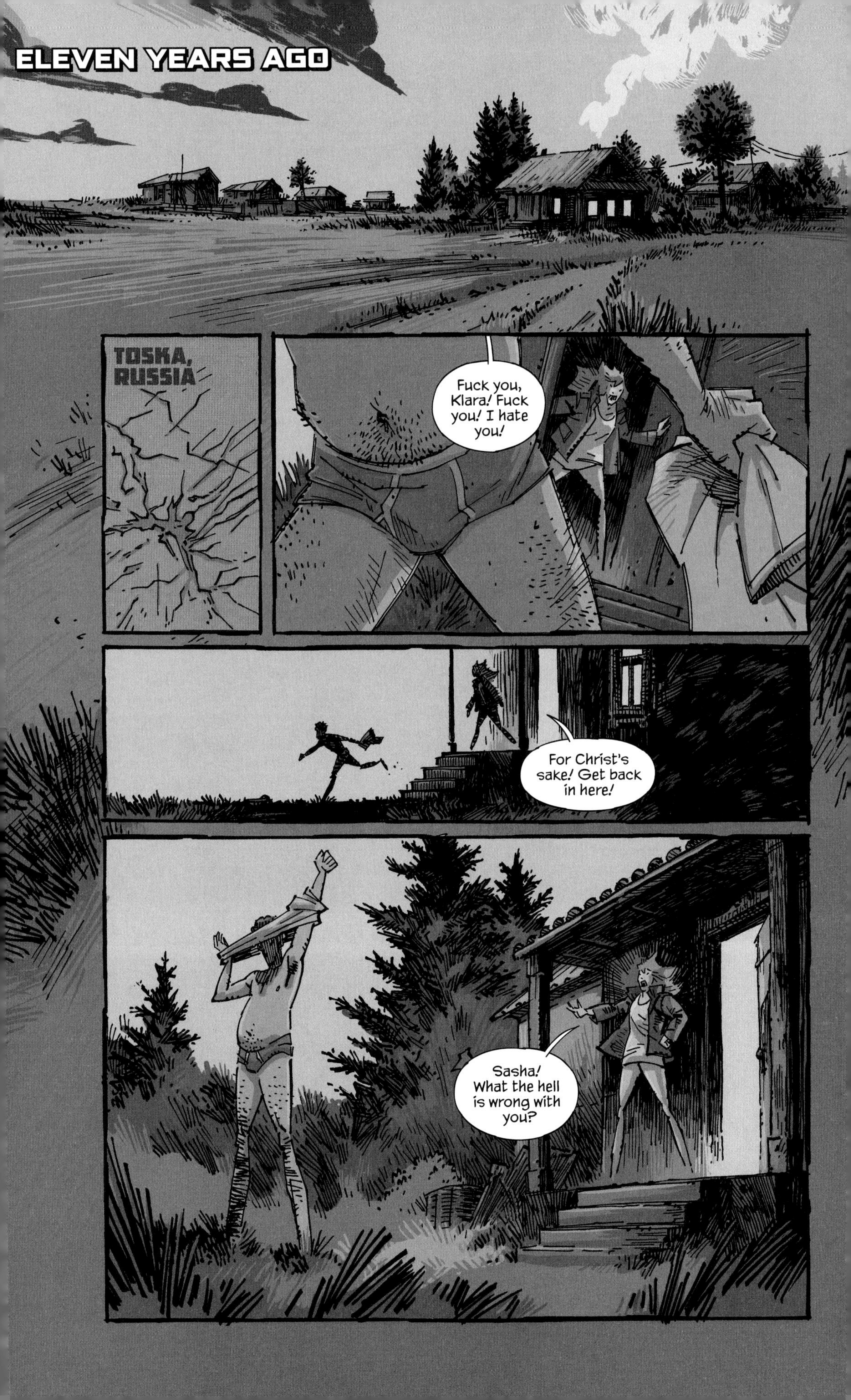
ELEVEN YEARS AGO
TOSKA, RUSSIA
Fuck you, Klara! Fuck you! I hate you!
For Christ's sake! Get back in here!
Sasha! What the hell is wrong with you?

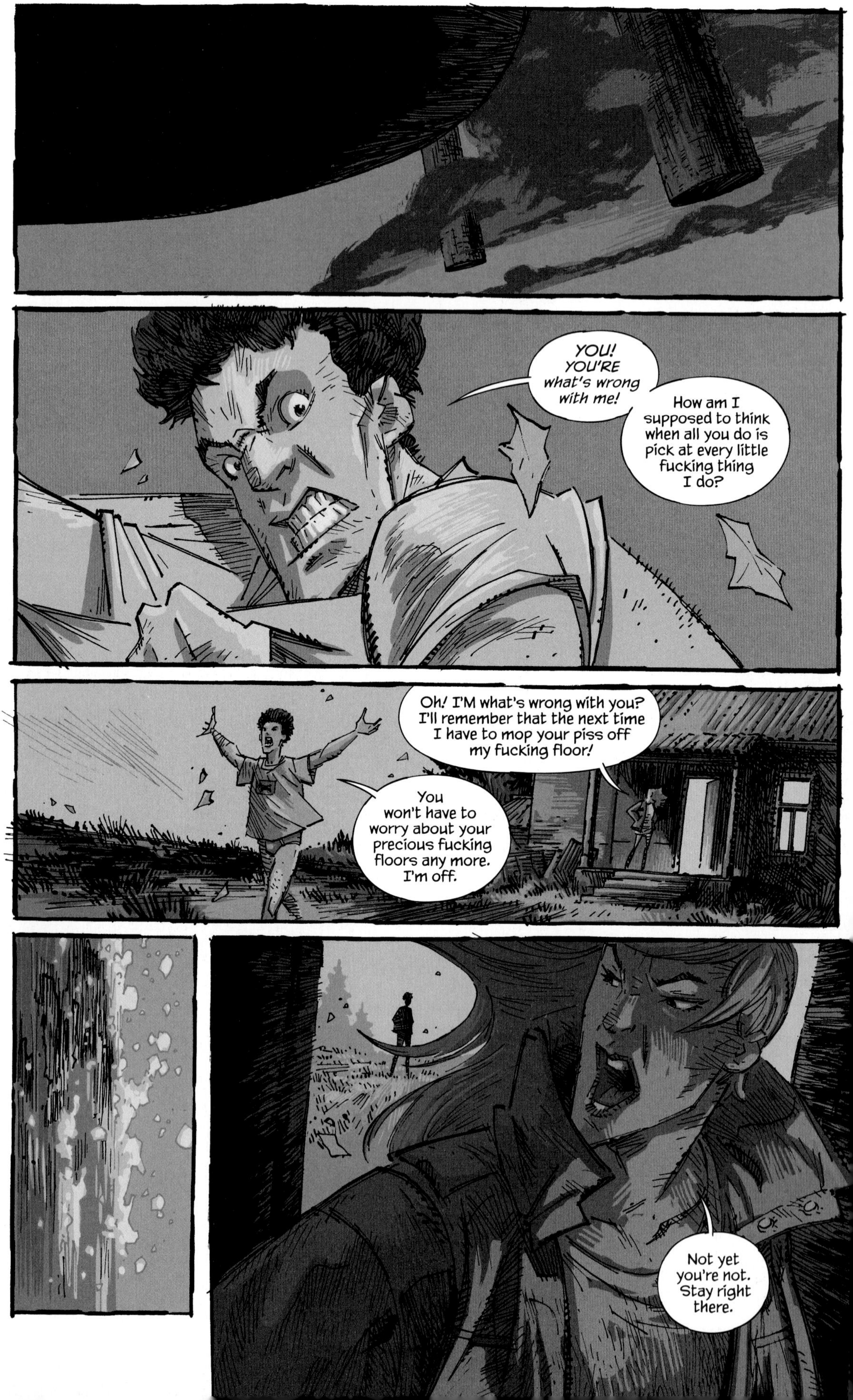
YOU! YOU'RE what's wrong with me!
How am I supposed to think when all you do is pick at every little fucking thing I do?
Oh! I'M what's wrong with you? I'll remember that the next time I have to mop your piss off my fucking floor!
You won't have to worry about your precious fucking floors any more. I'm off.
Not yet you're not. Stay right there.

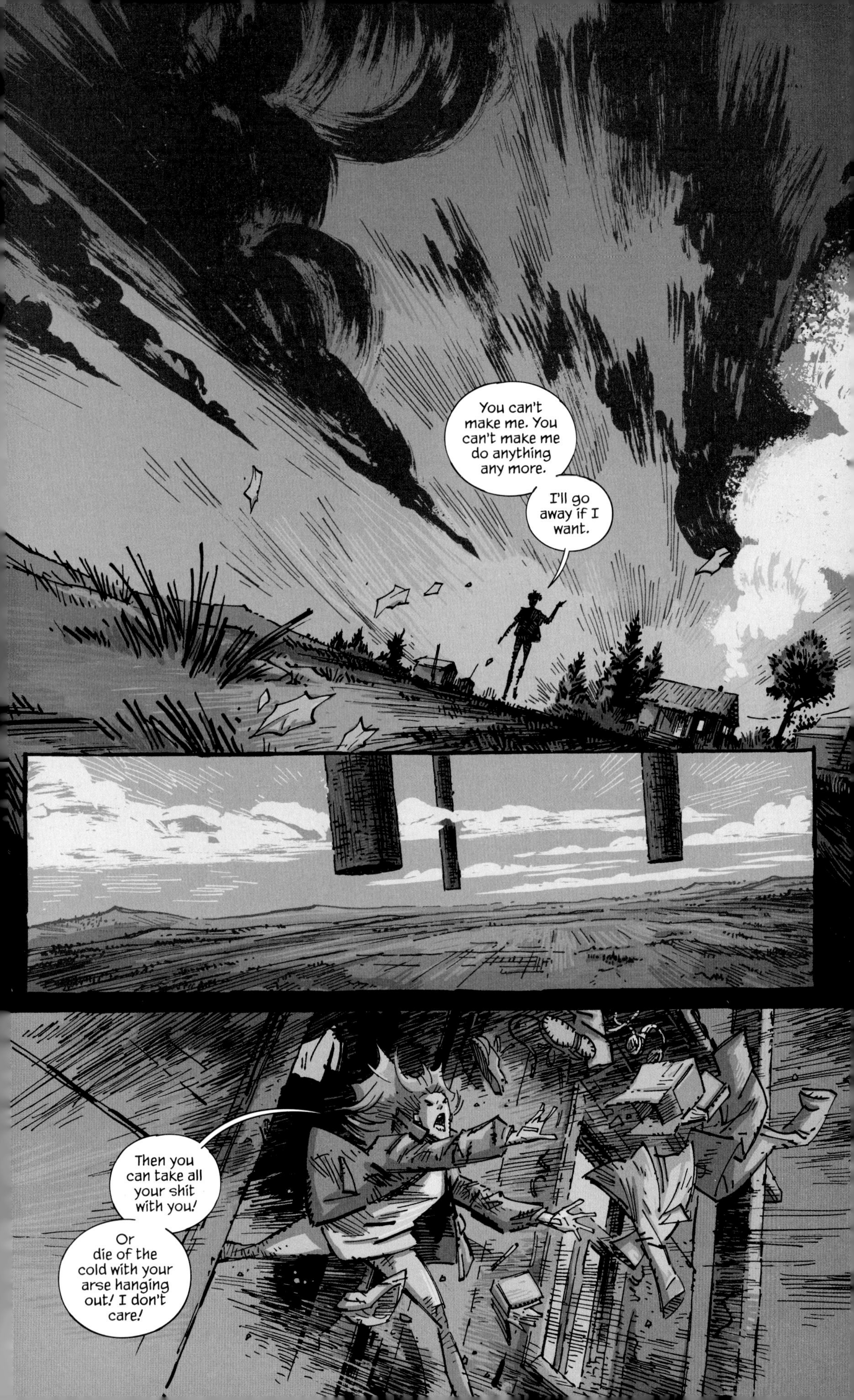
You can't make me. You can't make me do anything any more.
I'll go away if I want.
Then you can take all your shit with you!
Or die of the cold with your arse hanging out! I don't care!

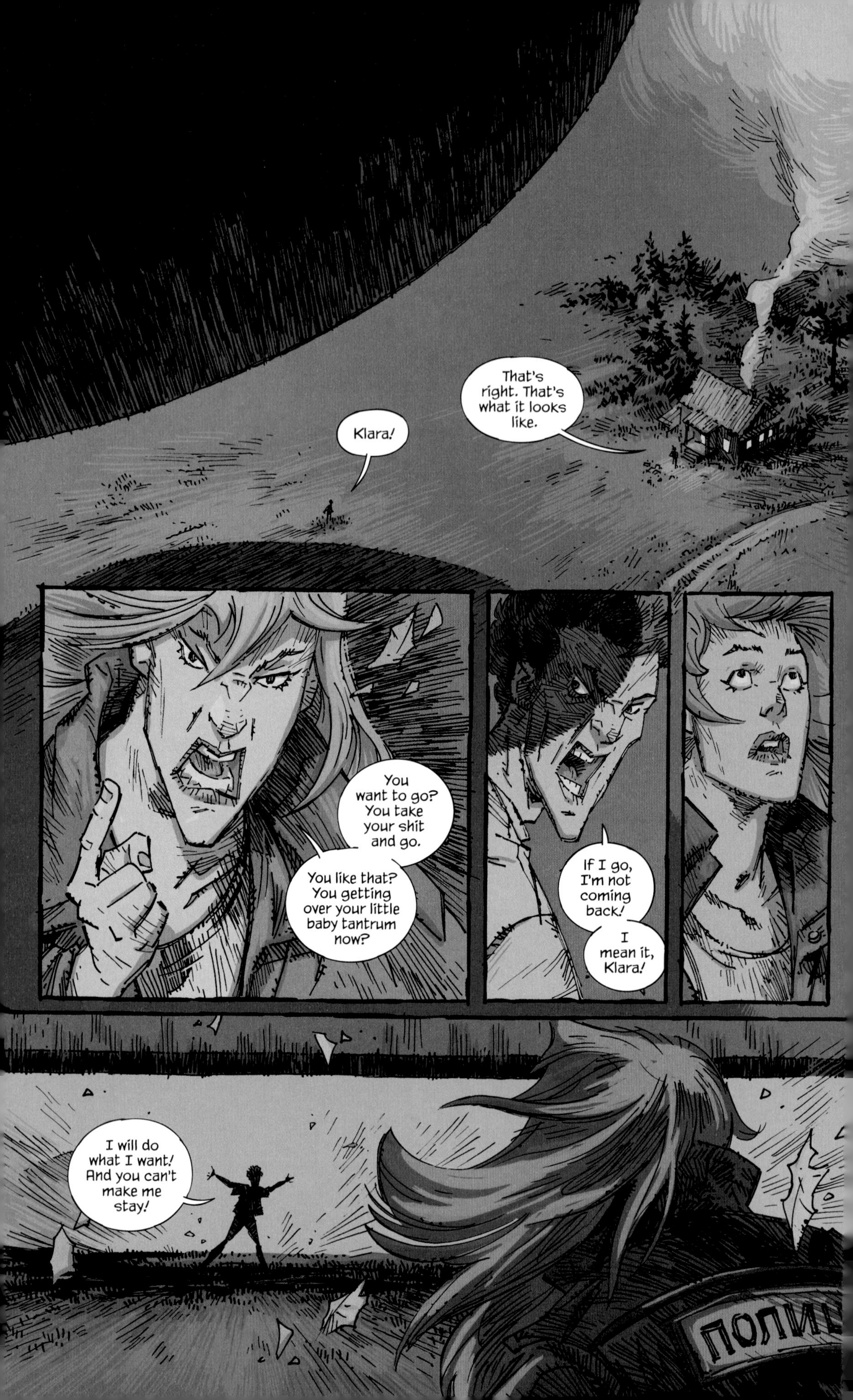
That's right. That's what it looks like.
Klara!
You want to go? You take your shit and go.
You like that? You getting over your little baby tantrum now?
If I go, I'm not coming back!
I mean it, Klara!
I will do what I want! And you can't make me stay!
ПОЛИЦ

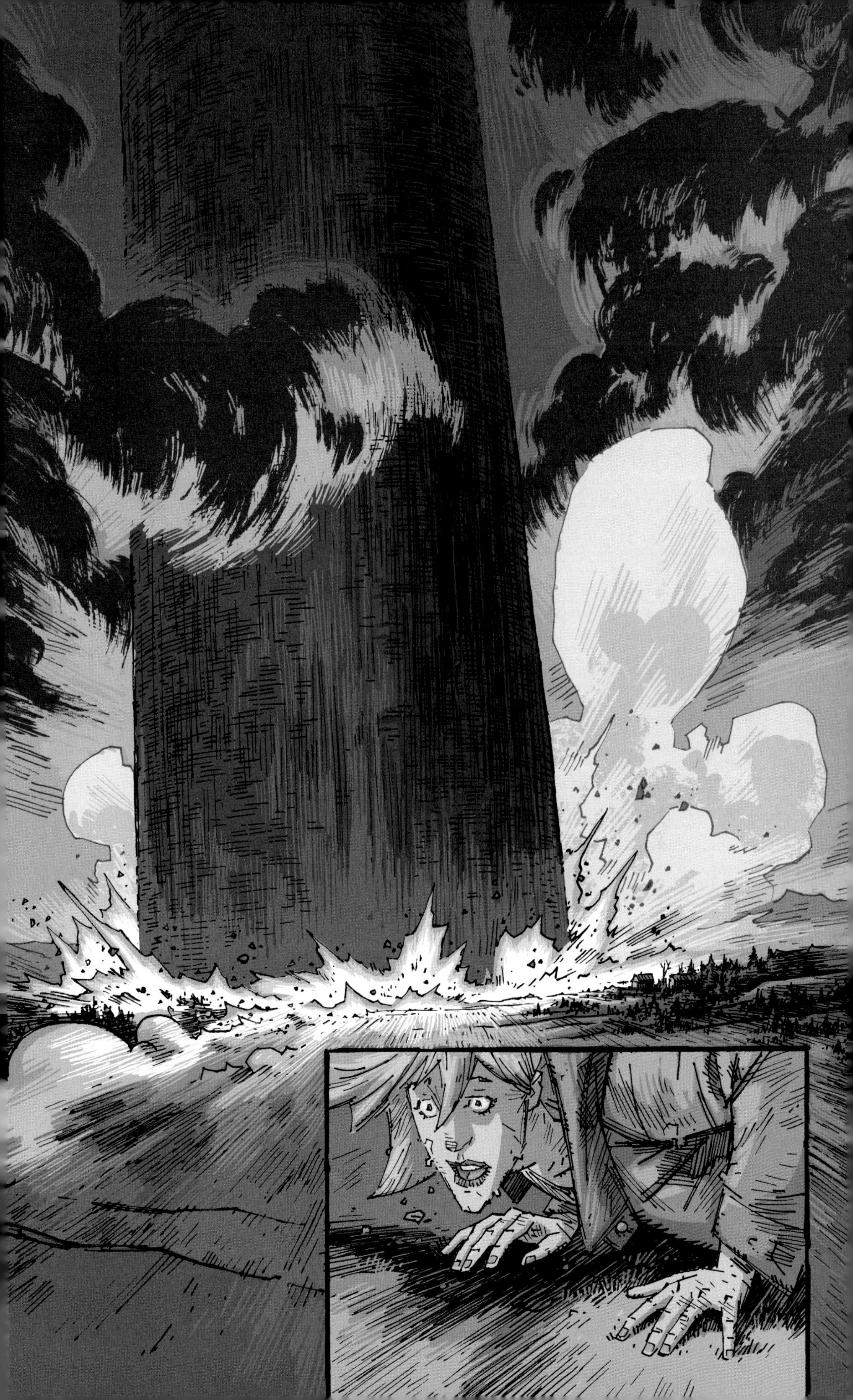

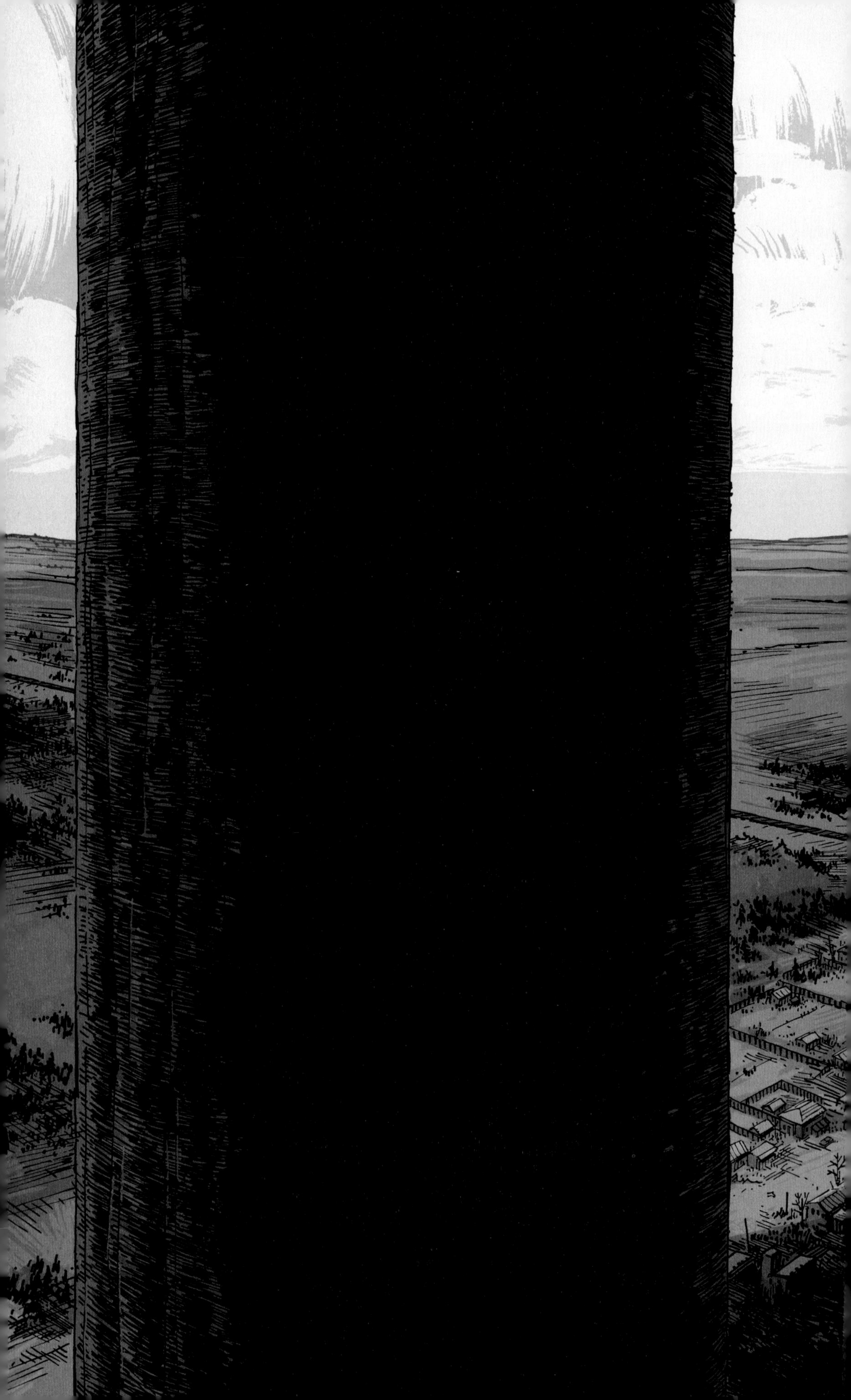

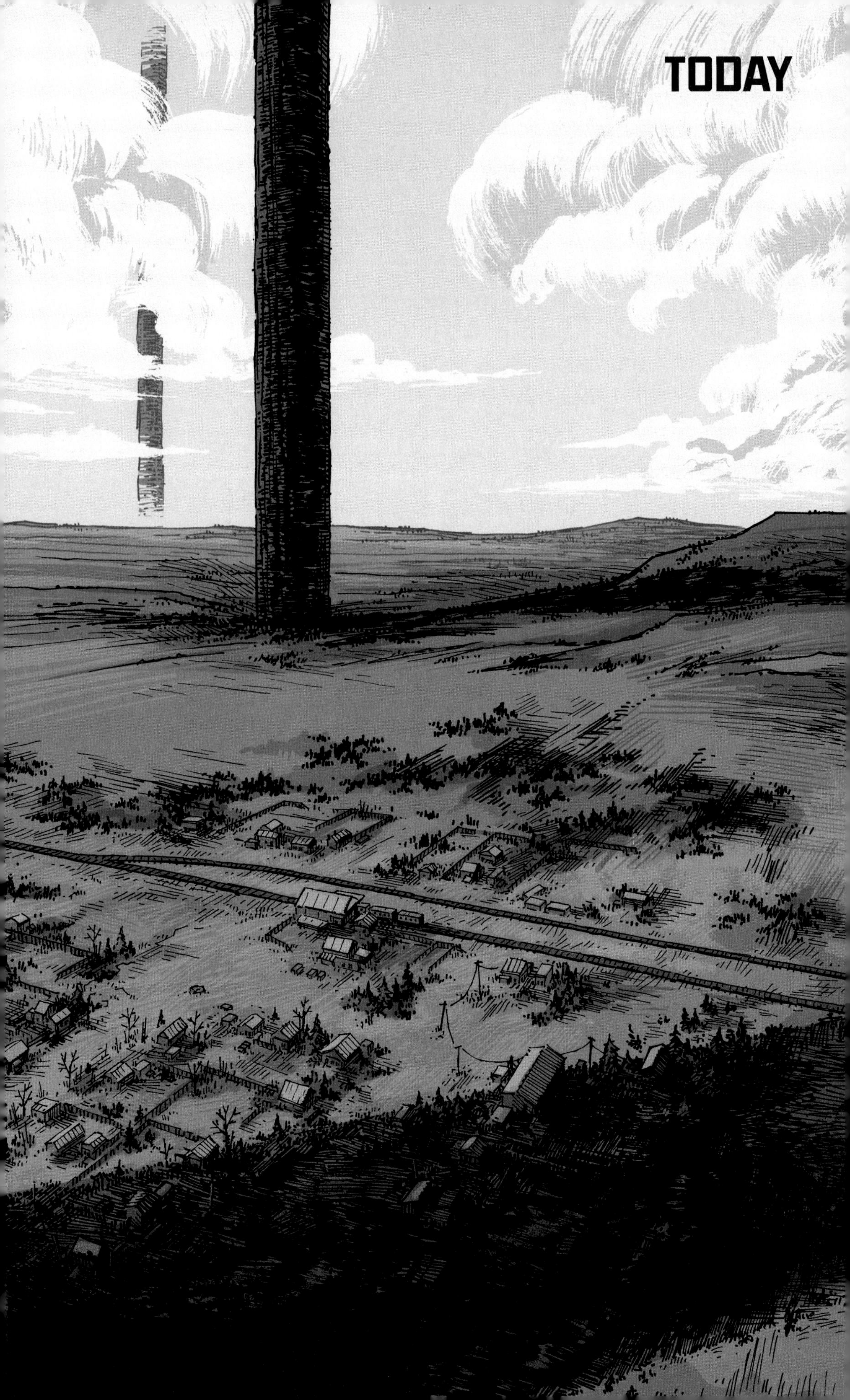
TODAY

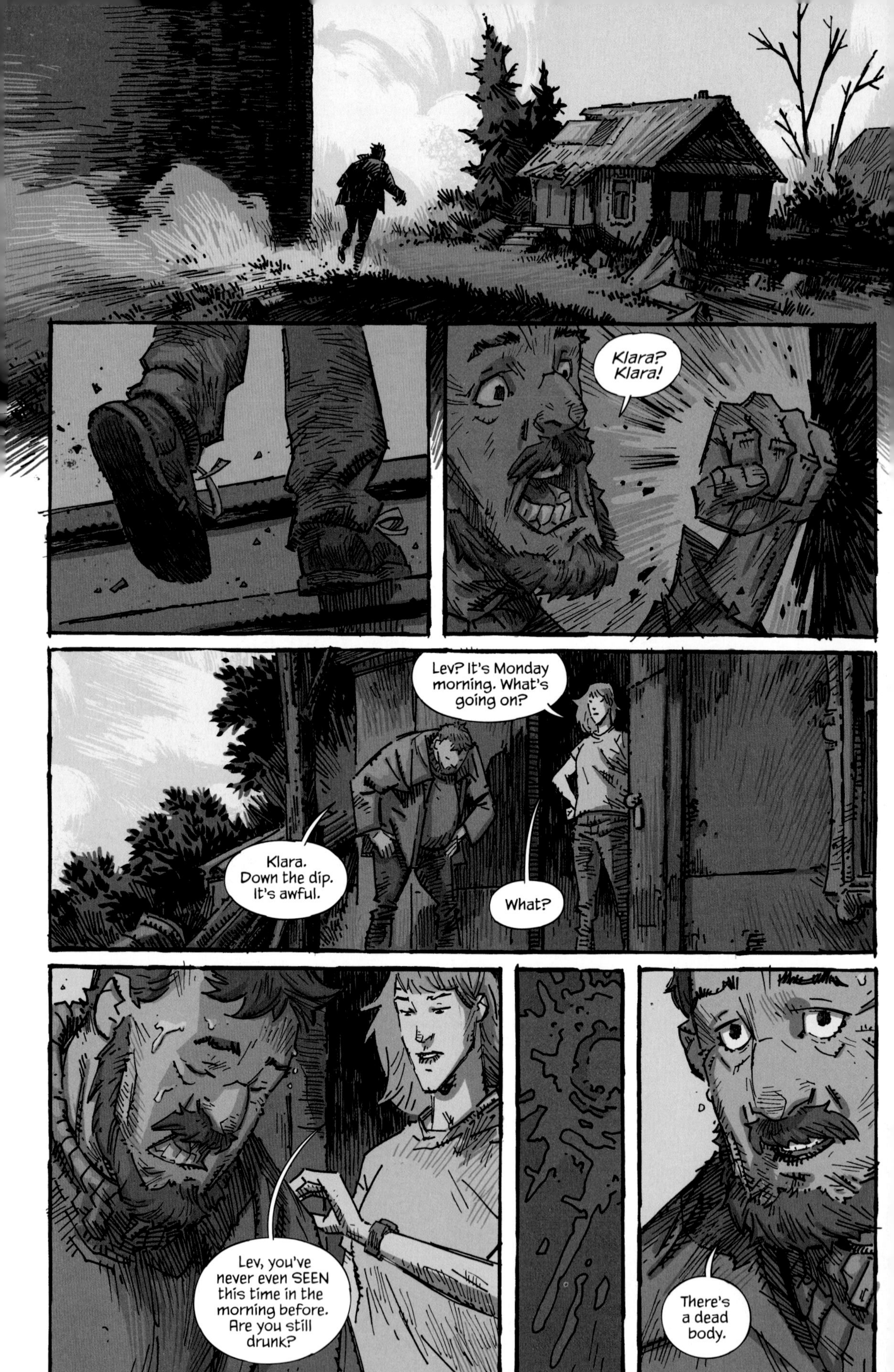
Klara? Klara!
Lev? It's Monday morning. What's going on?
Klara. Down the dip. It's awful.
What?
Lev, you've never even SEEN this time in the morning before. Are you still drunk?
There's a dead body.

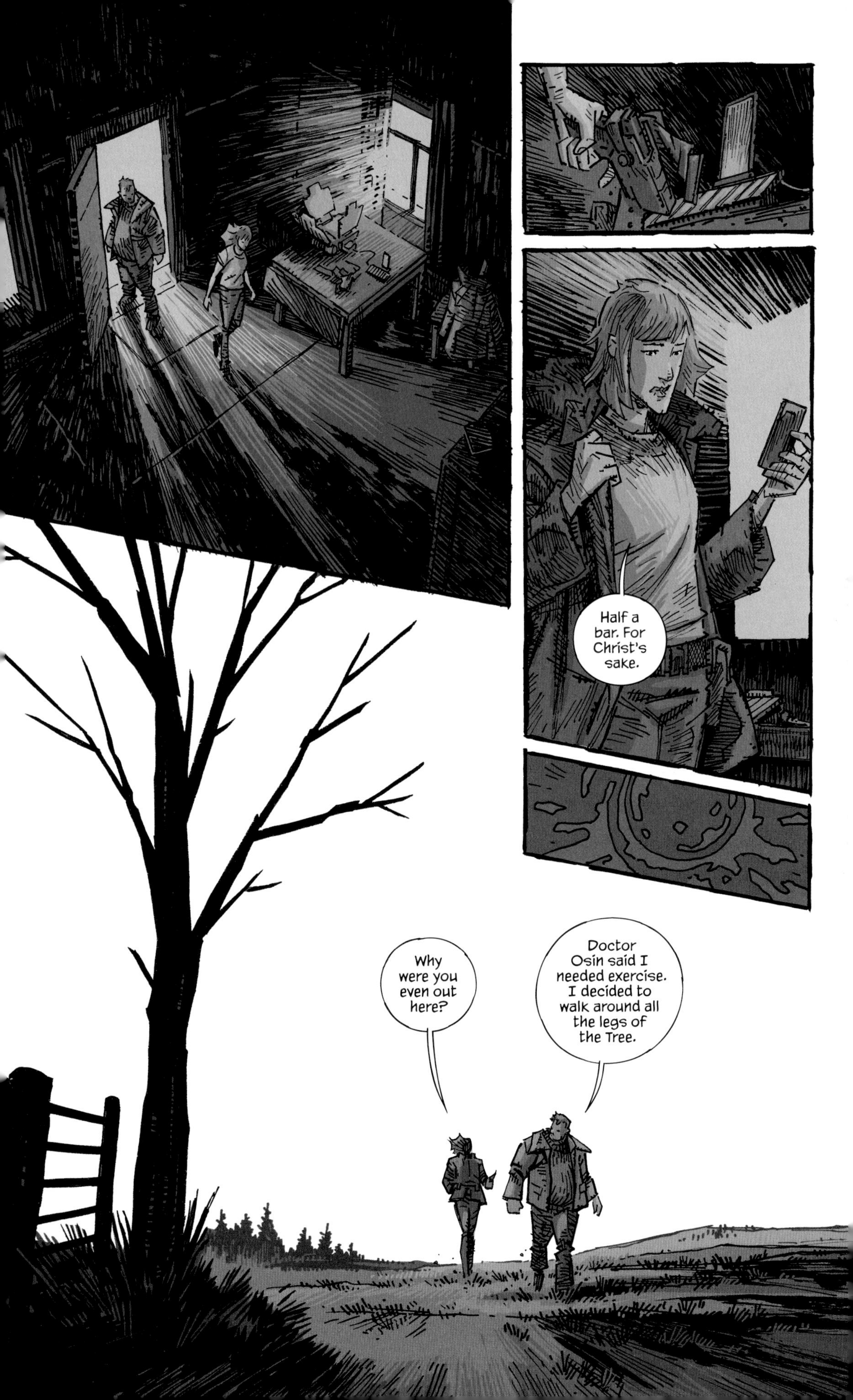
Half a bar. For Christ's sake.
Why were you even out here?
Doctor Osin said I needed exercise. I decided to walk around all the legs of the Tree.

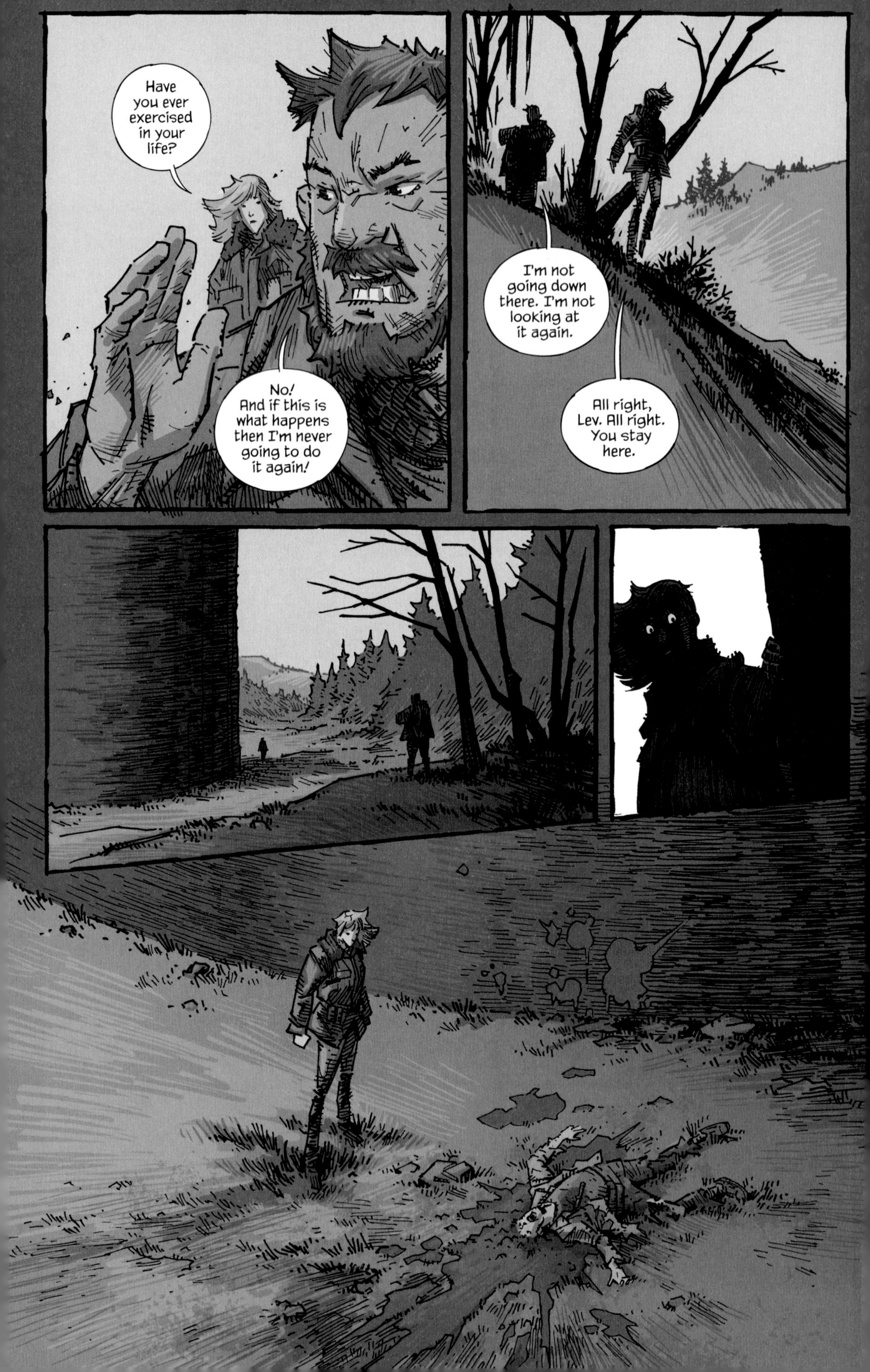
Have you ever exercised in your life?
No! And if this is what happens then I'm never going to do it again!
I'm not going down there. I'm not looking at it again.
All right, Lev. All right. You stay here.

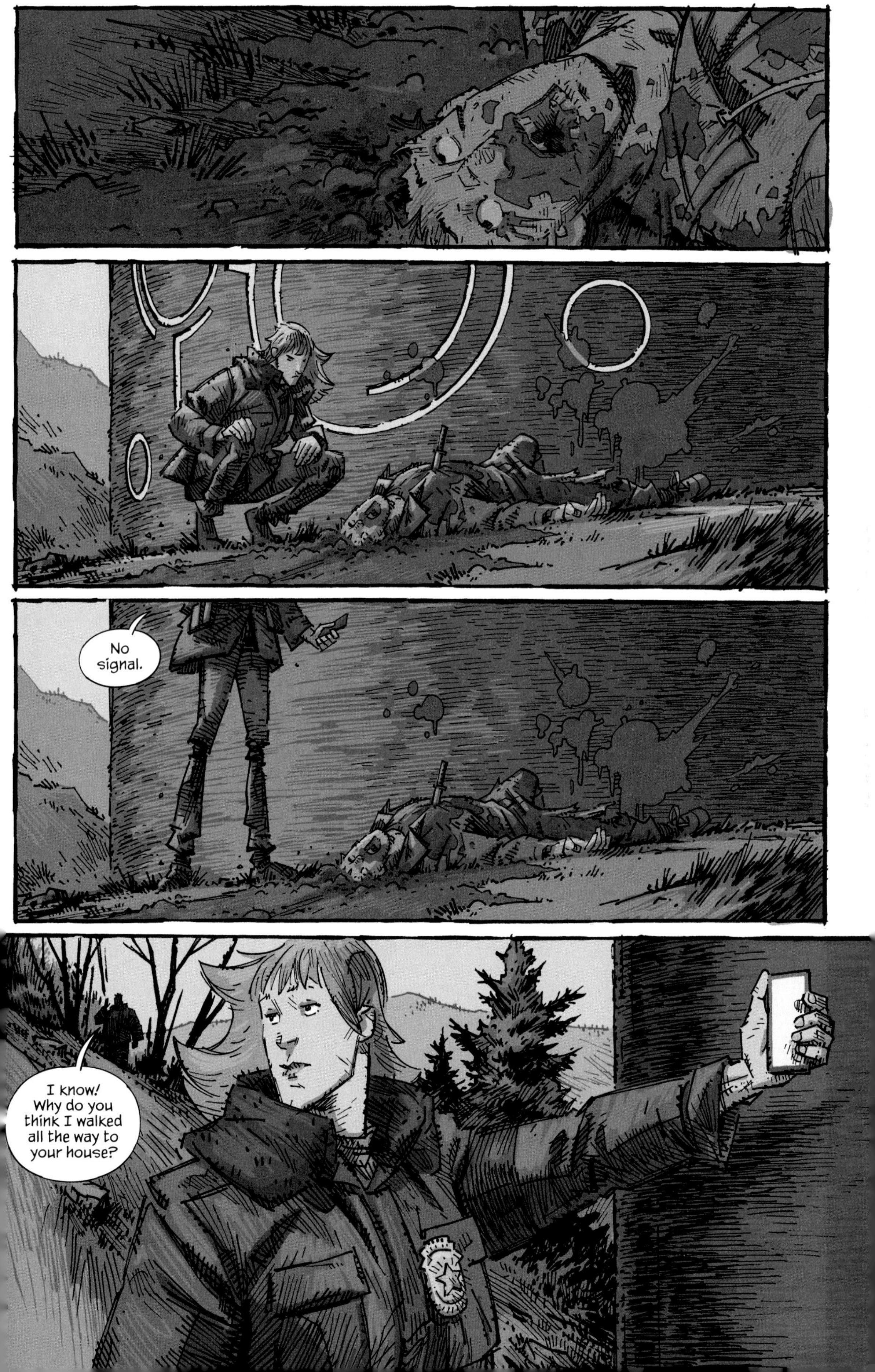
No signal.
I know! Why do you think I walked all the way to your house?

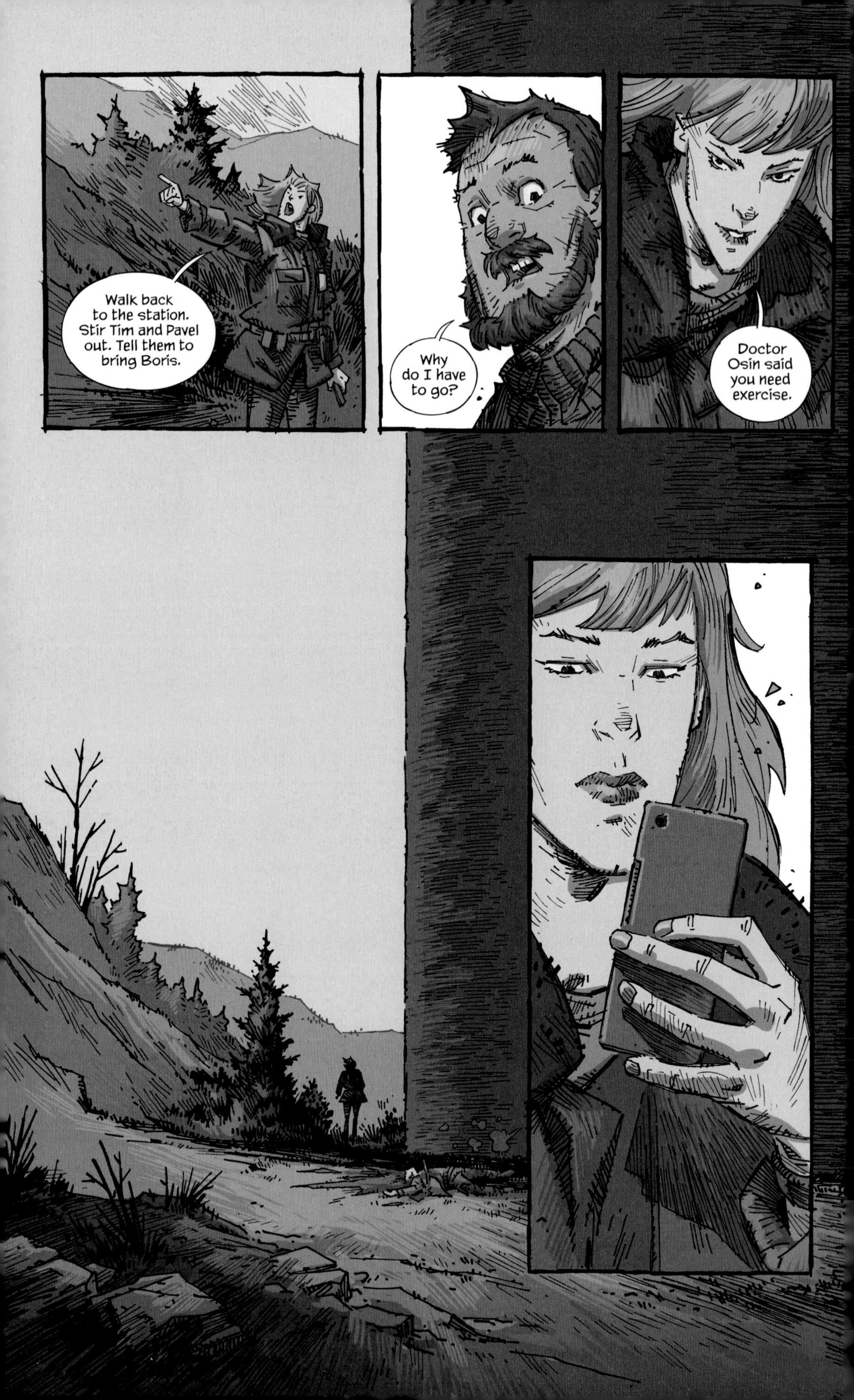
Walk back to the station. Stir Tim and Pavel out. Tell them to bring Boris.
Why do I have to go?
Doctor Osin said you need exercise.

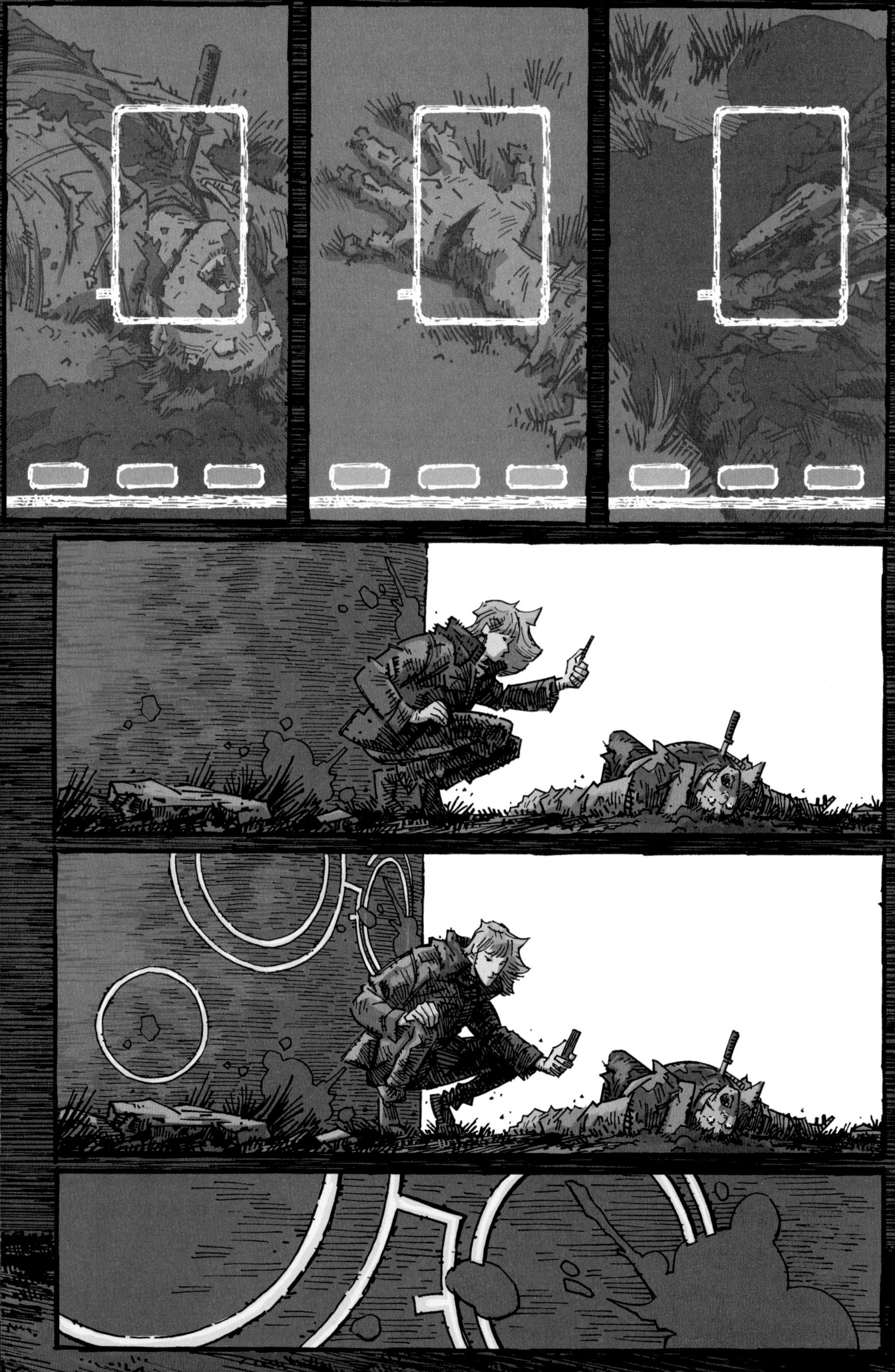

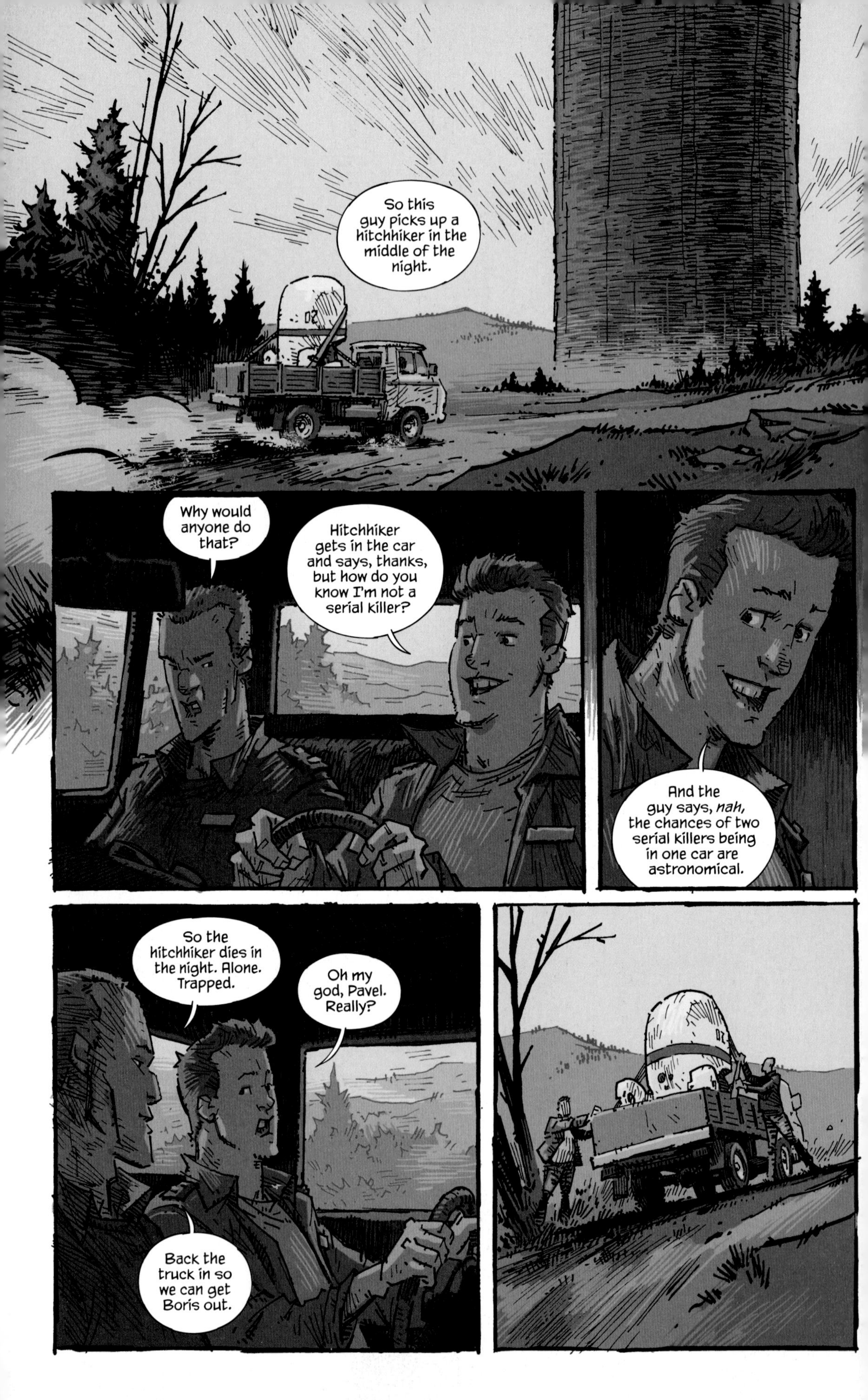

So this guy picks up a hitchhiker in the middle of the night.
Why would anyone do that?
Hitchhiker gets in the car and says, thanks, but how do you know I'm not a serial killer?
And the guy says, *nah*, the chances of two serial killers being in one car are astronomical.
So the hitchhiker dies in the night. Alone. Trapped.
Oh my god, Pavel. Really?
Back the truck in so we can get Boris out.

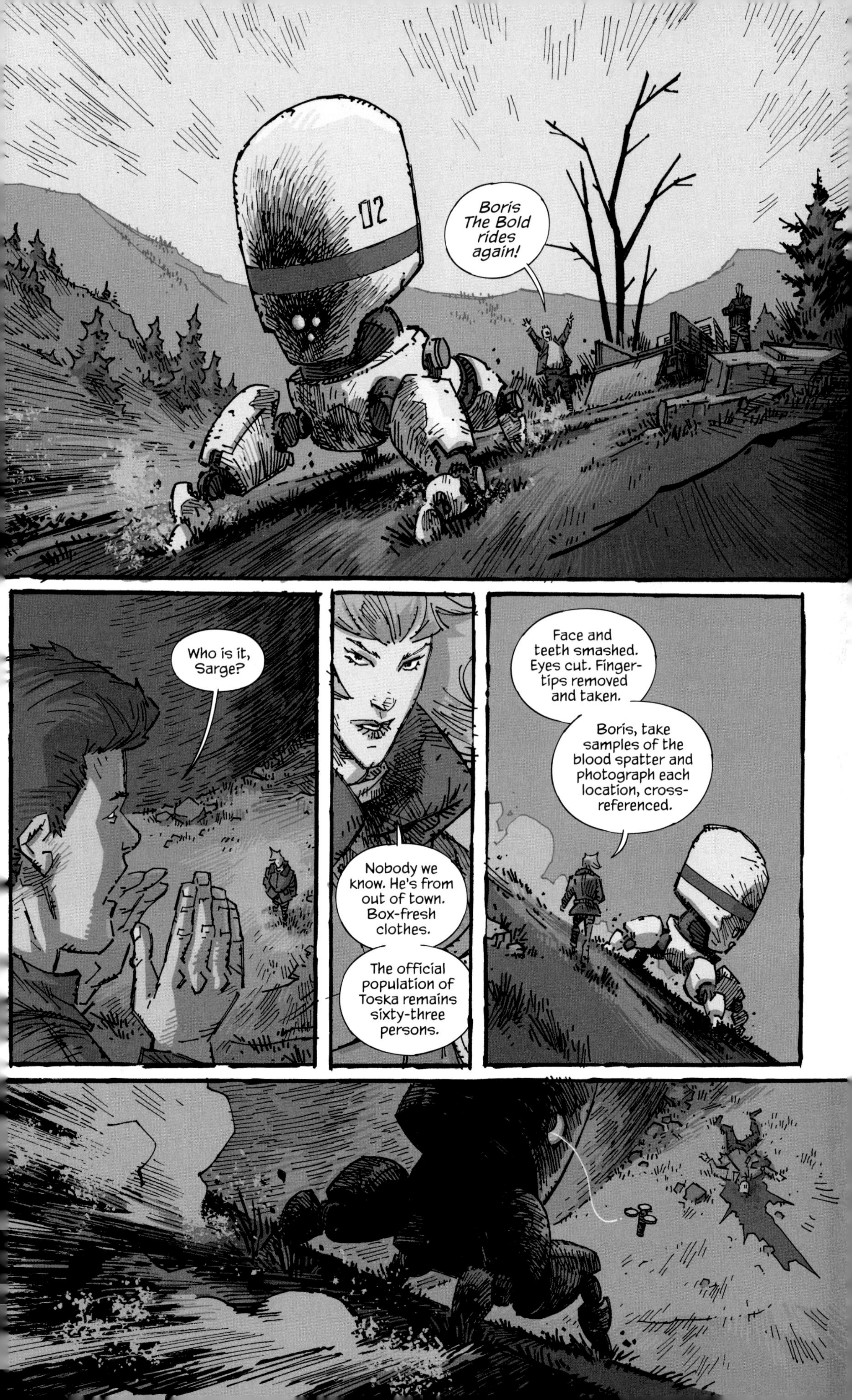
02
Boris The Bold rides again!
Who is it, Sarge?
Nobody we know. He's from out of town. Box-fresh clothes.
The official population of Toska remains sixty-three persons.
Face and teeth smashed. Eyes cut. Finger-tips removed and taken.
Boris, take samples of the blood spatter and photograph each location, cross-referenced.

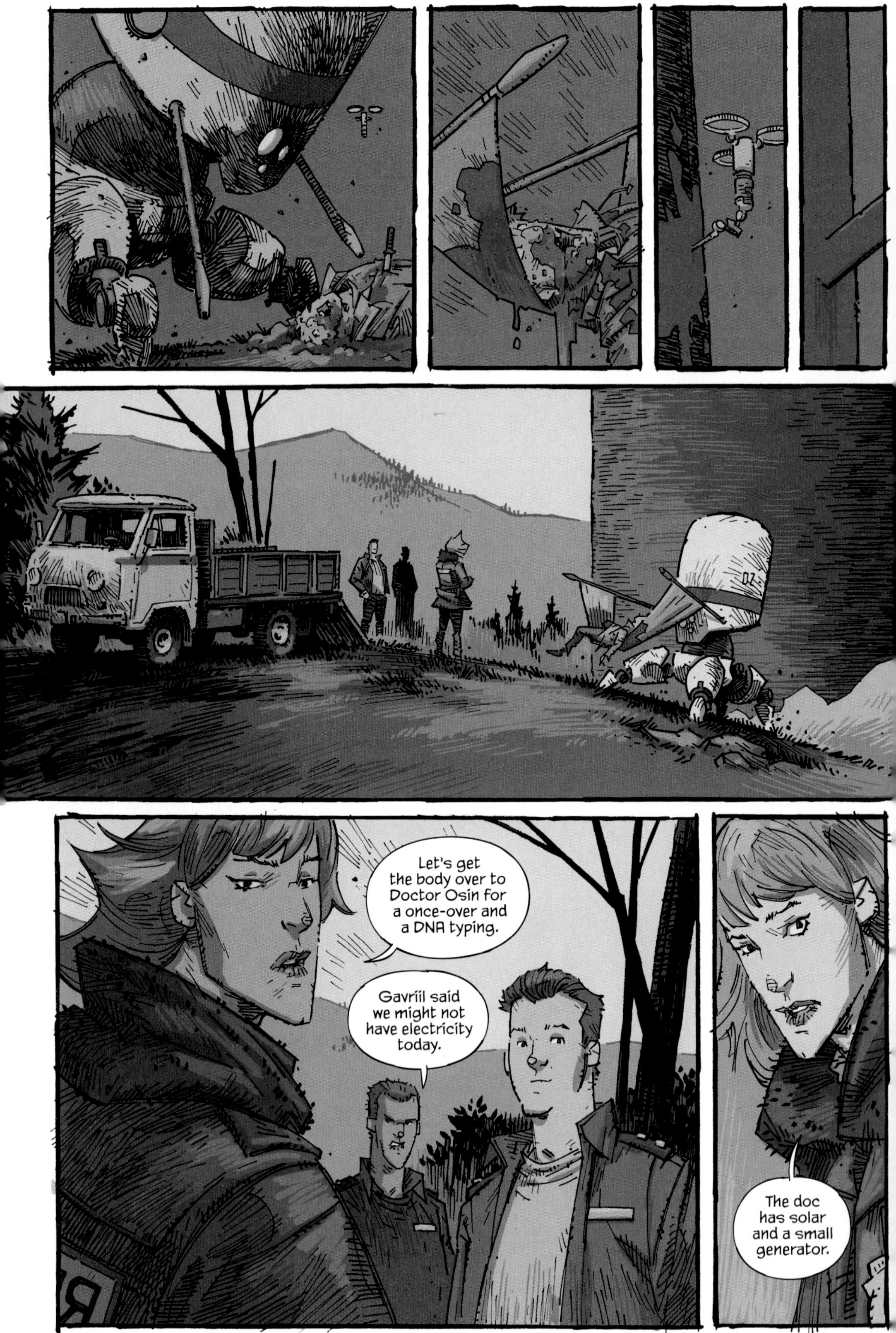
Let's get the body over to Doctor Osin for a once-over and a DNA typing.
Gavriil said we might not have electricity today.
The doc has solar and a small generator.

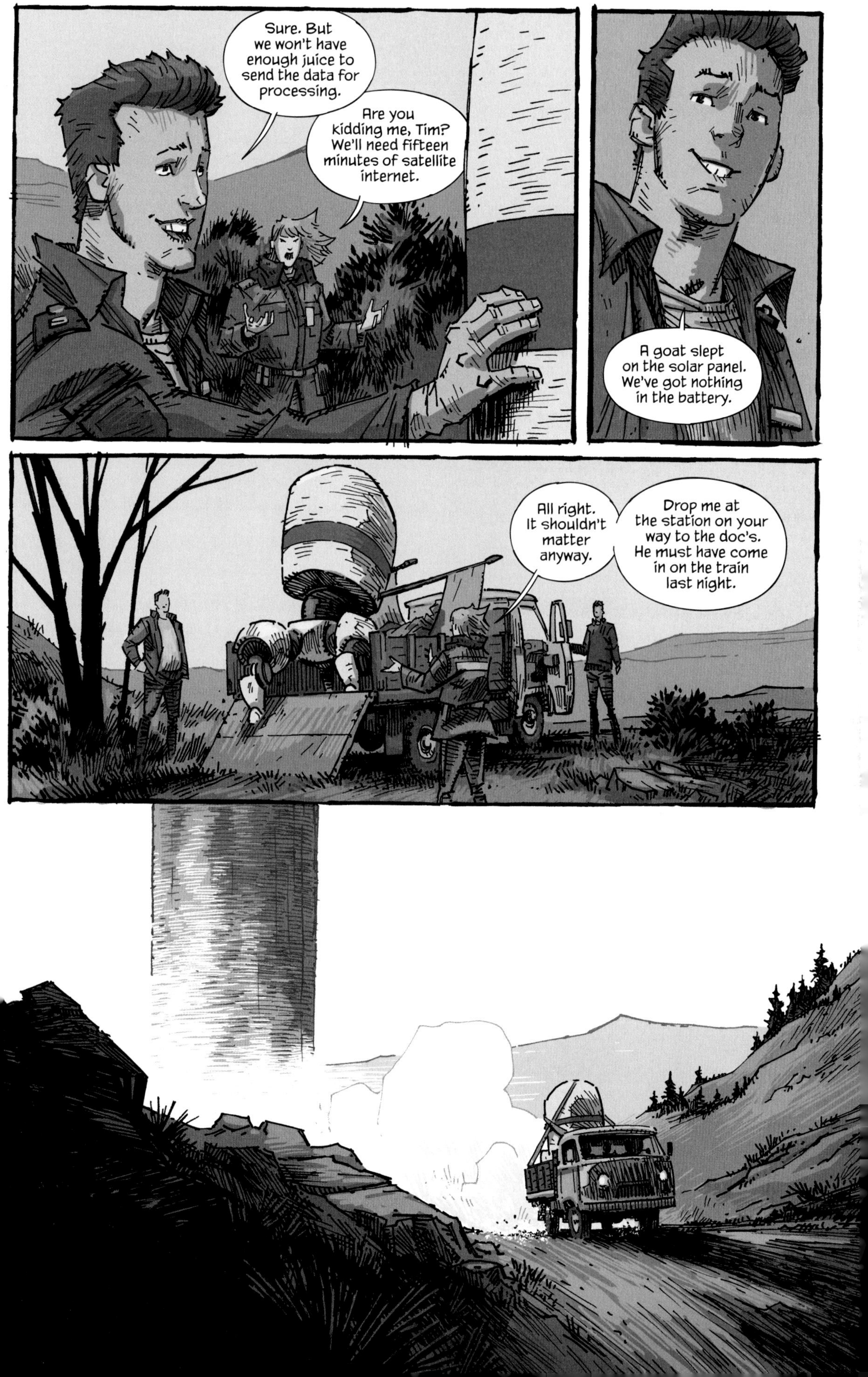
Sure. But we won't have enough juice to send the data for processing.
Are you kidding me, Tim? We'll need fifteen minutes of satellite internet.
A goat slept on the solar panel. We've got nothing in the battery.
All right. It shouldn't matter anyway.
Drop me at the station on your way to the doc's. He must have come in on the train last night.

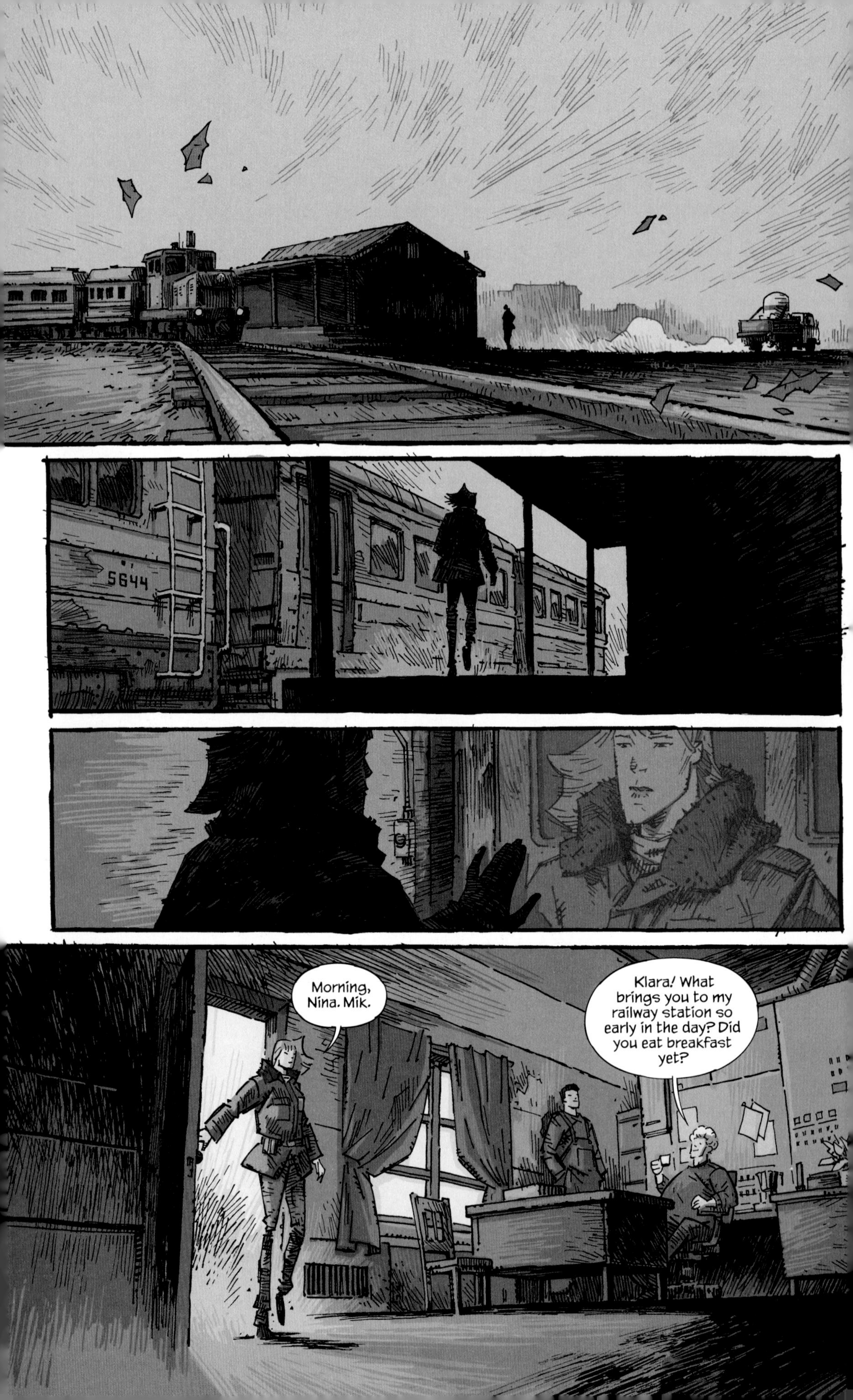
5644
Morning, Nina. Mik.
Klara! What brings you to my railway station so early in the day? Did you eat breakfast yet?

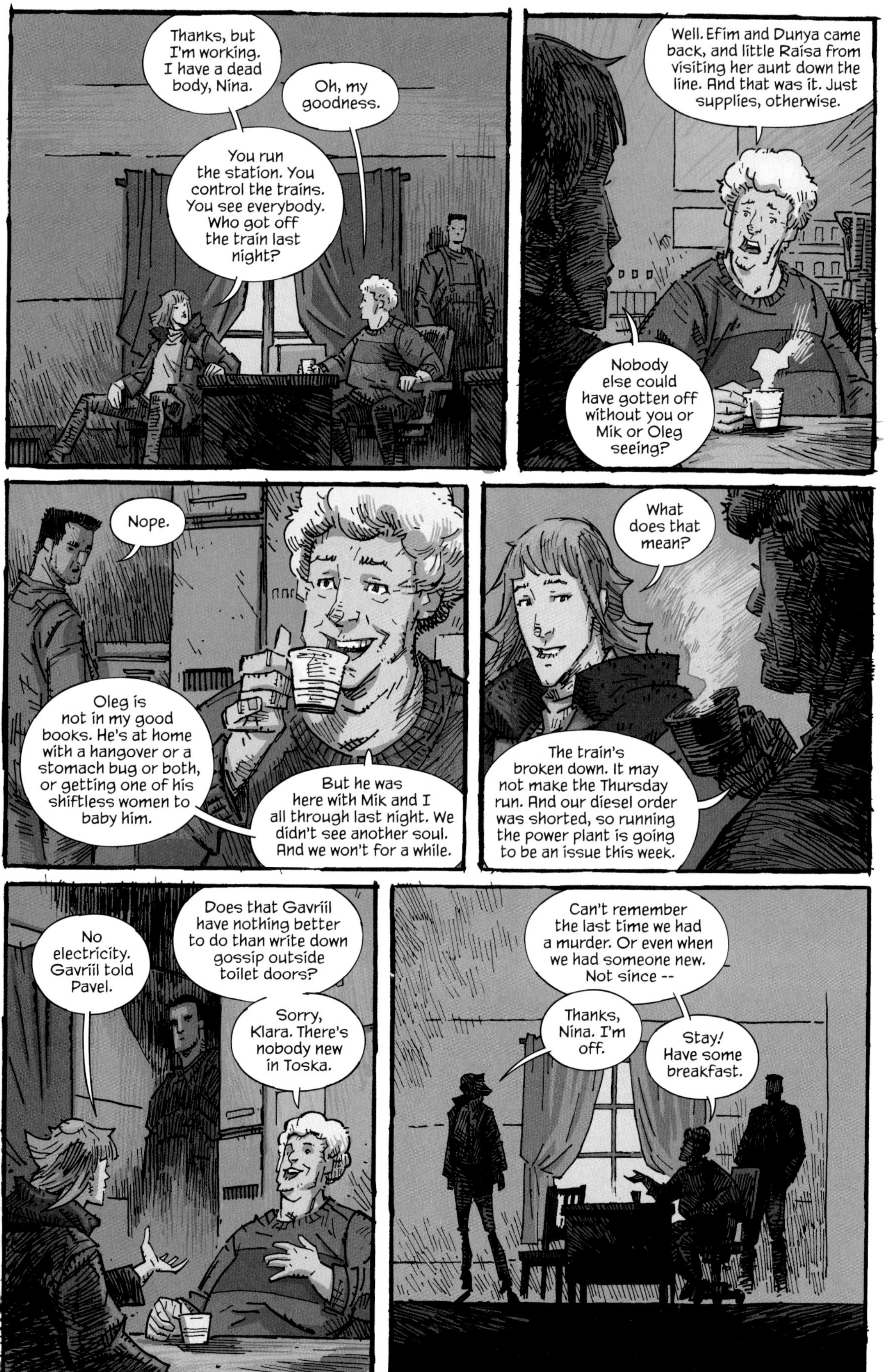
Thanks, but I'm working. I have a dead body, Nina.
Oh, my goodness.
You run the station. You control the trains. You see everybody. Who got off the train last night?
Well. Efim and Dunya came back, and little Raisa from visiting her aunt down the line. And that was it. Just supplies, otherwise.
Nobody else could have gotten off without you or Mik or Oleg seeing?
Nope.
Oleg is not in my good books. He's at home with a hangover or a stomach bug or both, or getting one of his shiftless women to baby him.
But he was here with Mik and I all through last night. We didn't see another soul. And we won't for a while.
What does that mean?
The train's broken down. It may not make the Thursday run. And our diesel order was shorted, so running the power plant is going to be an issue this week.
No electricity. Gavriil told Pavel.
Does that Gavriil have nothing better to do than write down gossip outside toilet doors?
Sorry, Klara. There's nobody new in Toska.
Can't remember the last time we had a murder. Or even when we had someone new. Not since --
Thanks, Nina. I'm off.
Stay! Have some breakfast.

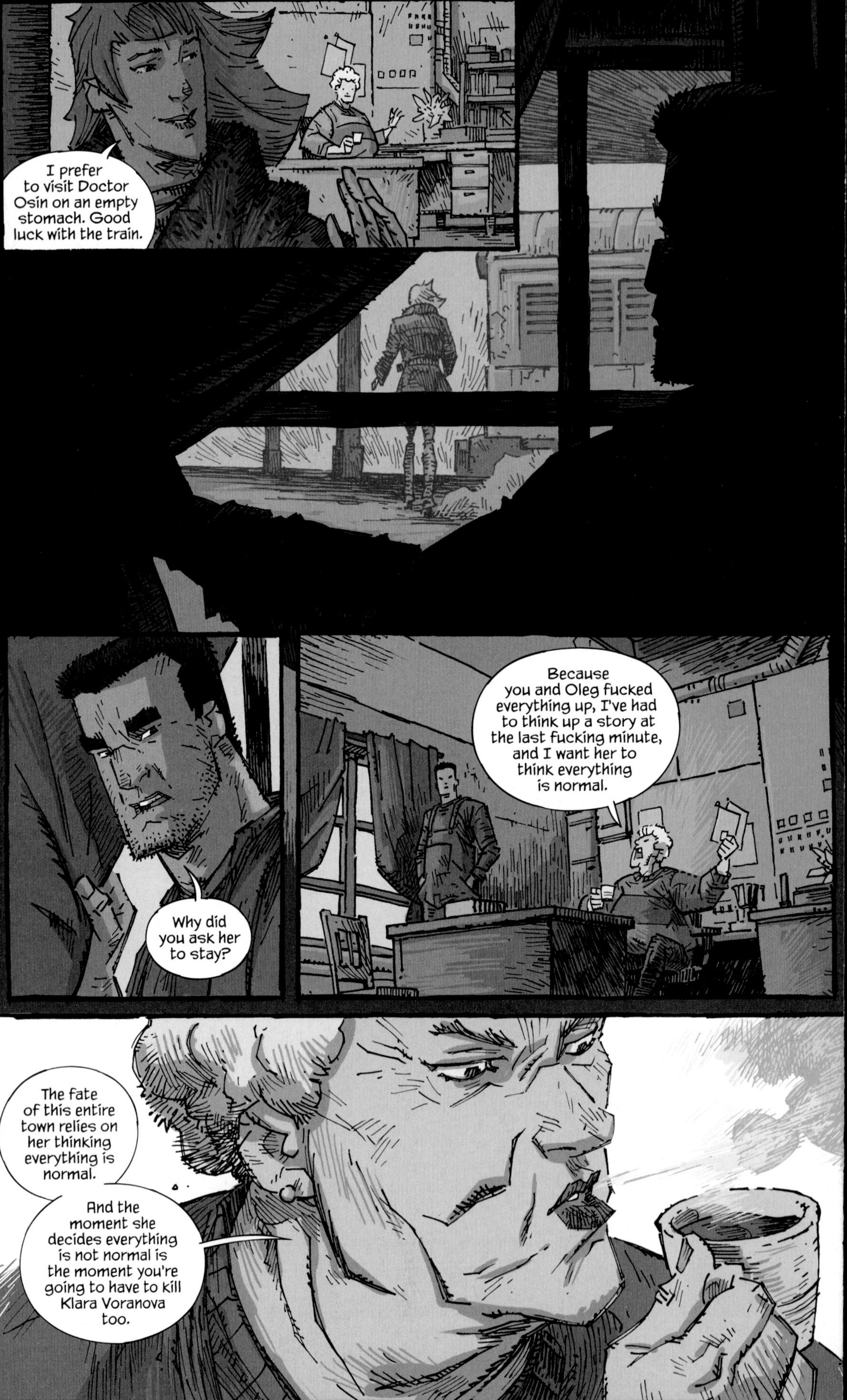
I prefer to visit Doctor Osin on an empty stomach. Good luck with the train.
Why did you ask her to stay?
Because you and Oleg fucked everything up, I've had to think up a story at the last fucking minute, and I want her to think everything is normal.
The fate of this entire town relies on her thinking everything is normal.
And the moment she decides everything is not normal is the moment you're going to have to kill Klara Voranova too.

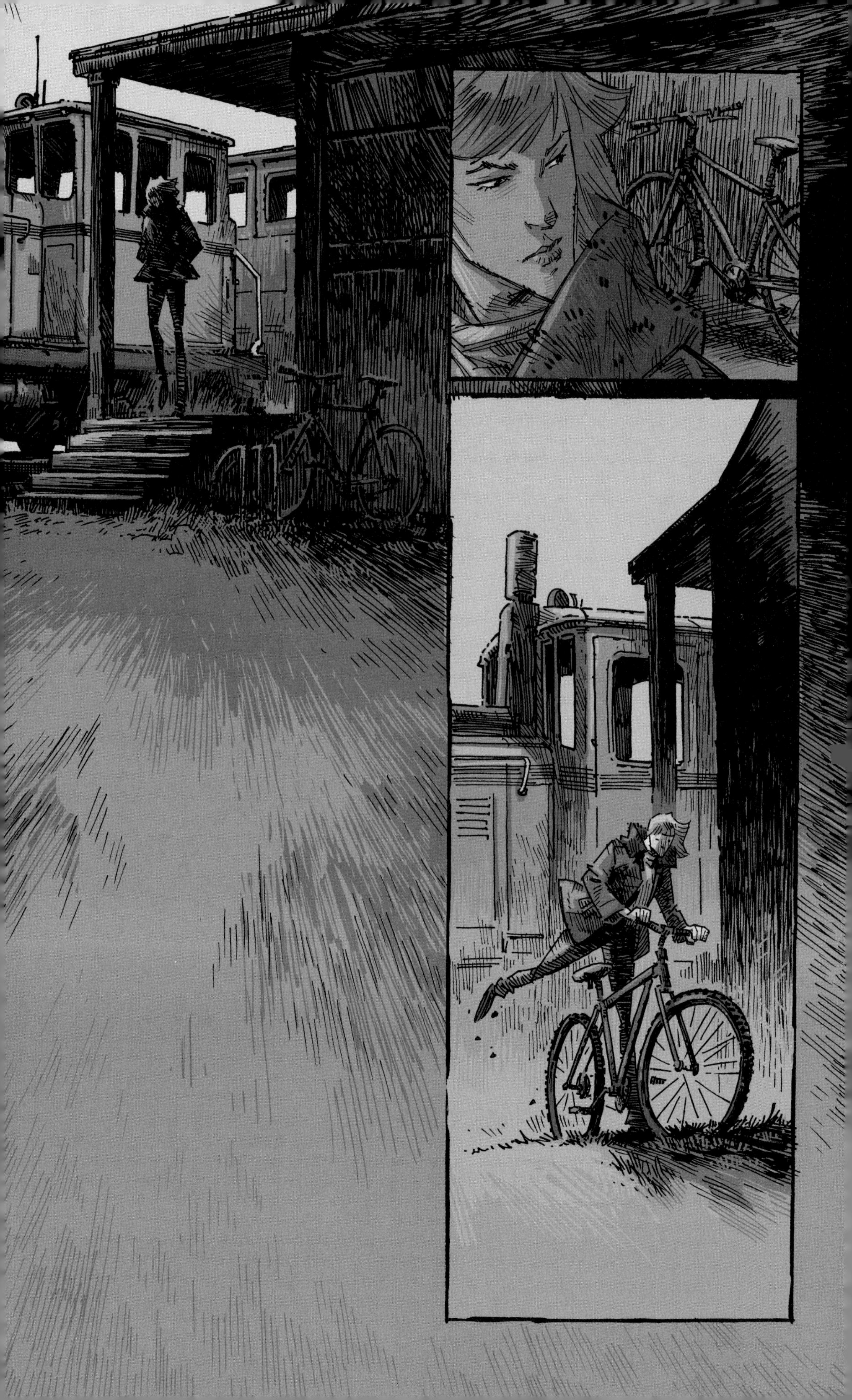

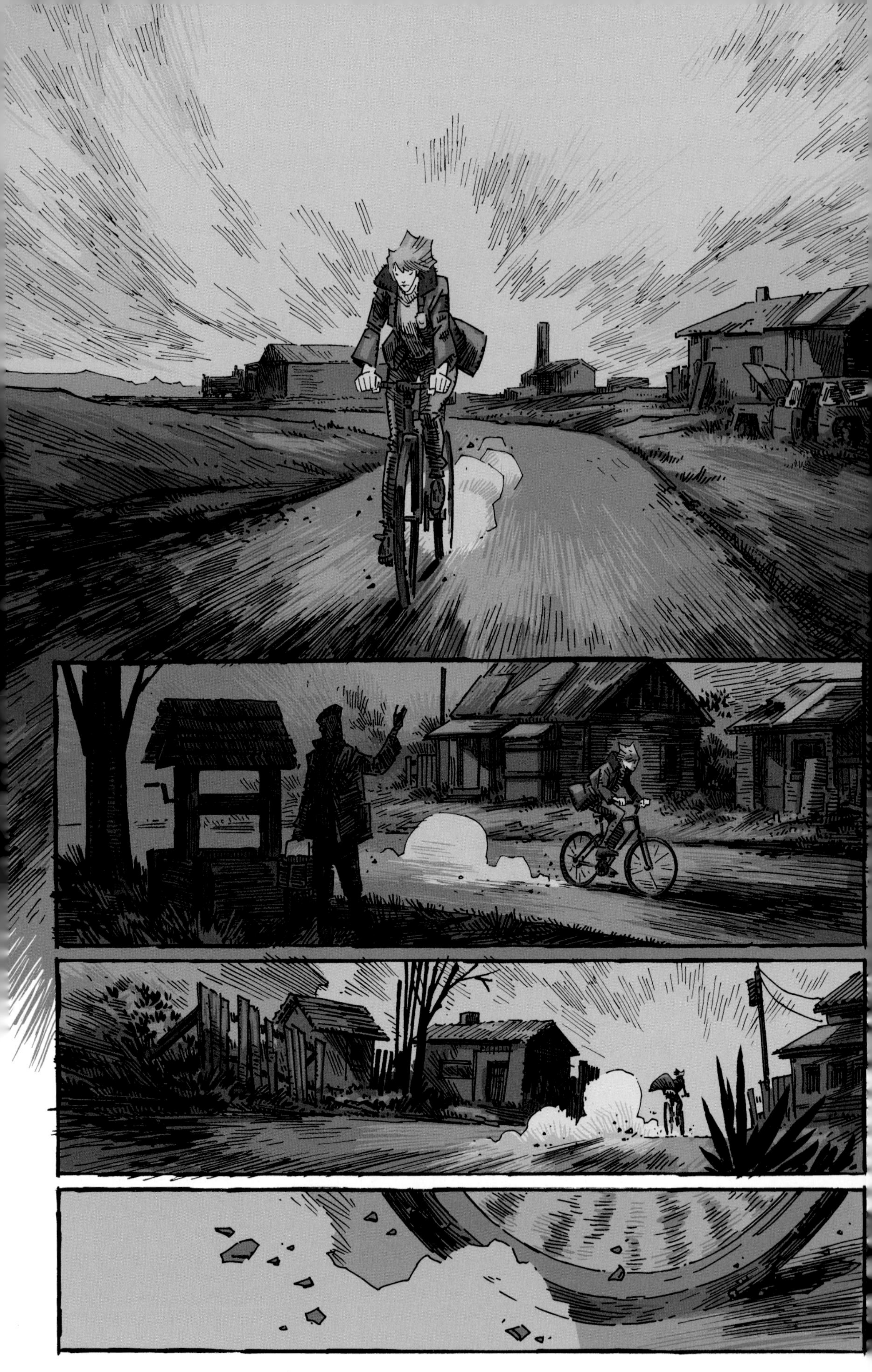

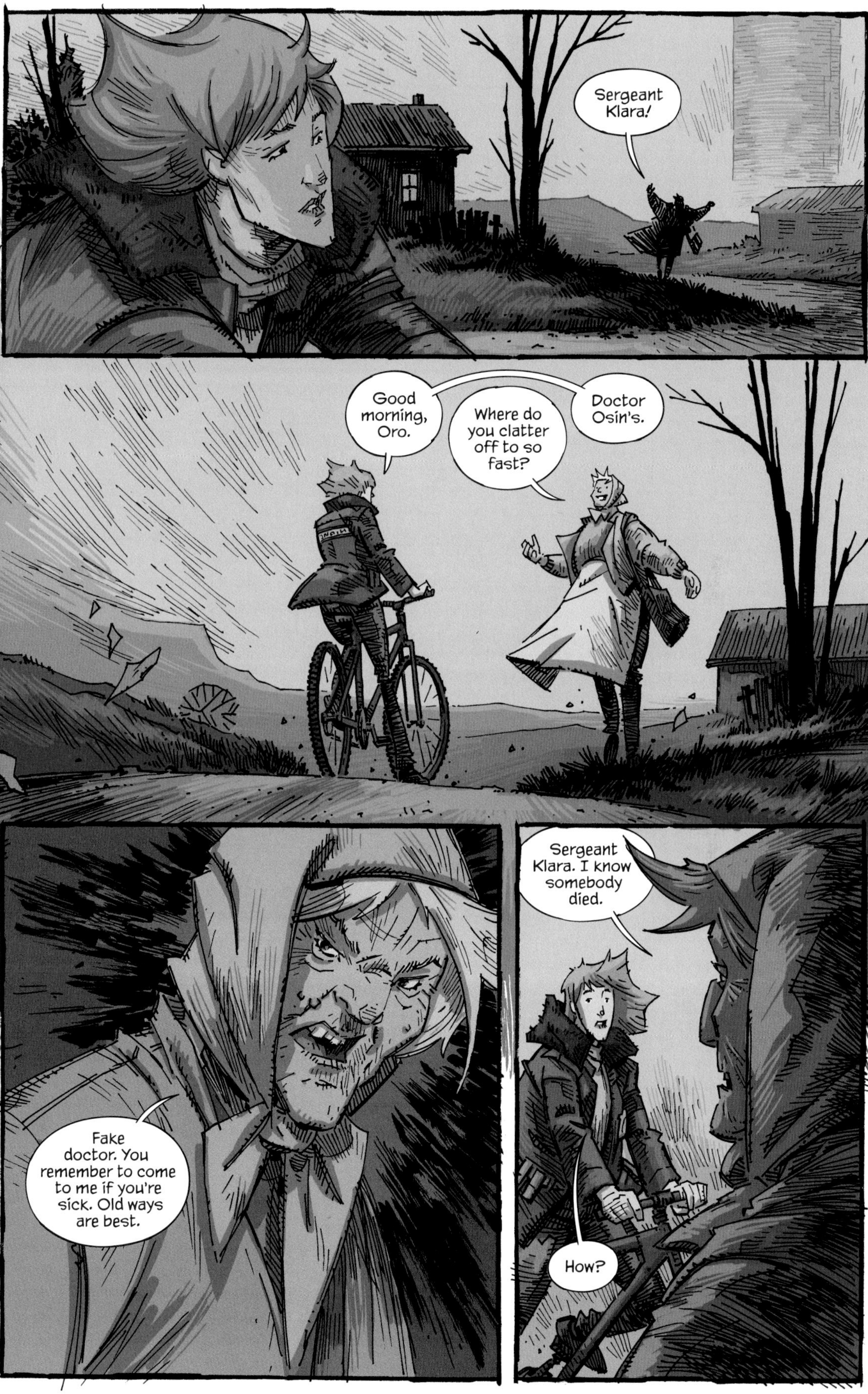
Sergeant Klara!
Good morning, Oro.
Where do you clatter off to so fast?
Doctor Osin's.
Fake doctor. You remember to come to me if you're sick. Old ways are best.
Sergeant Klara. I know somebody died.
How?

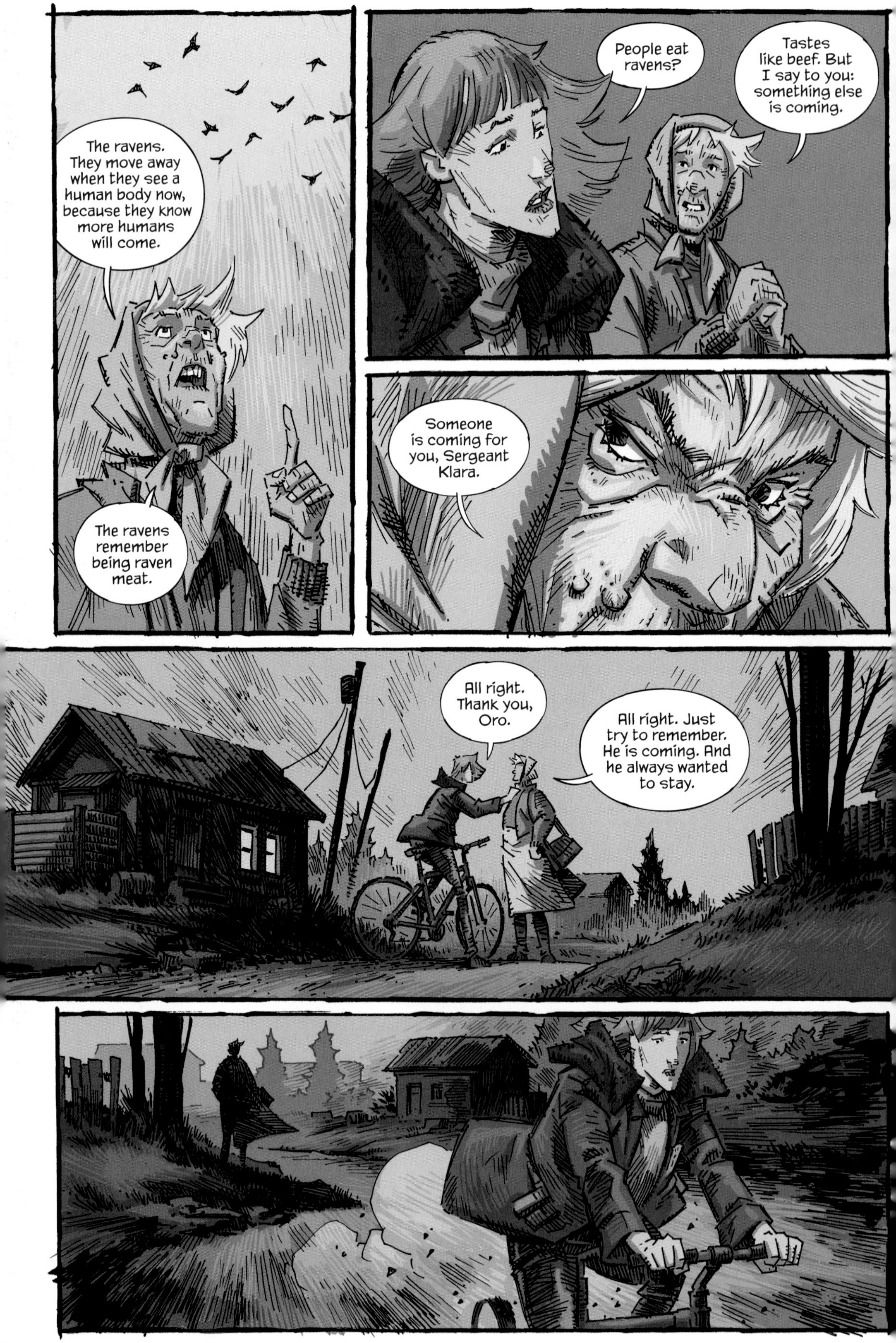
The ravens. They move away when they see a human body now, because they know more humans will come.
The ravens remember being raven meat.
People eat ravens?
Tastes like beef. But I say to you: something else is coming.
Someone is coming for you, Sergeant Klara.
All right. Thank you, Oro.
All right. Just try to remember. He is coming. And he always wanted to stay.

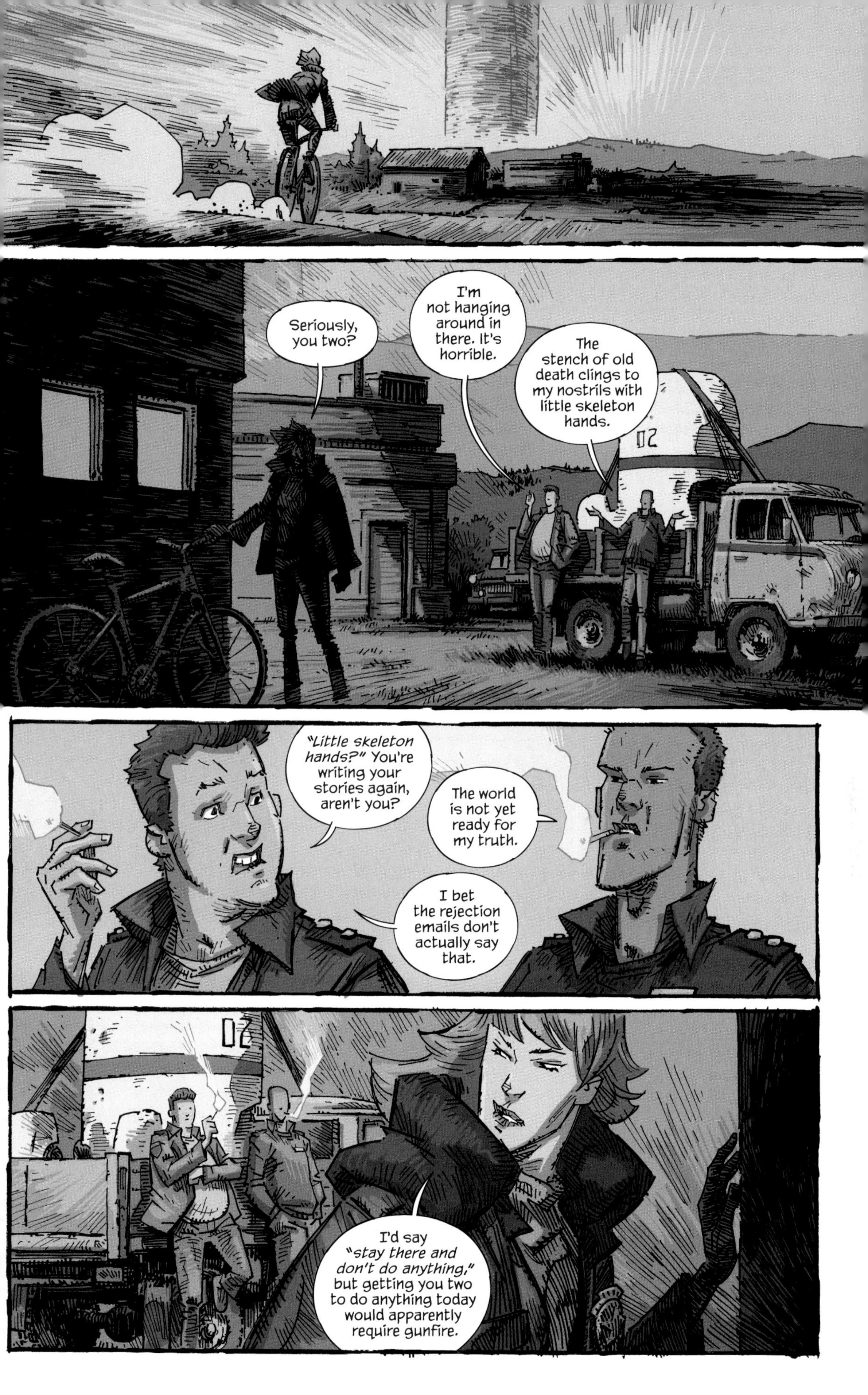
Seriously, you two?
I'm not hanging around in there. It's horrible.
The stench of old death clings to my nostrils with little skeleton hands.
02
"Little skeleton hands?" You're writing your stories again, aren't you?
The world is not yet ready for my truth.
I bet the rejection emails don't actually say that.
02
I'd say "stay there and don't do anything," but getting you two to do anything today would apparently require gunfire.

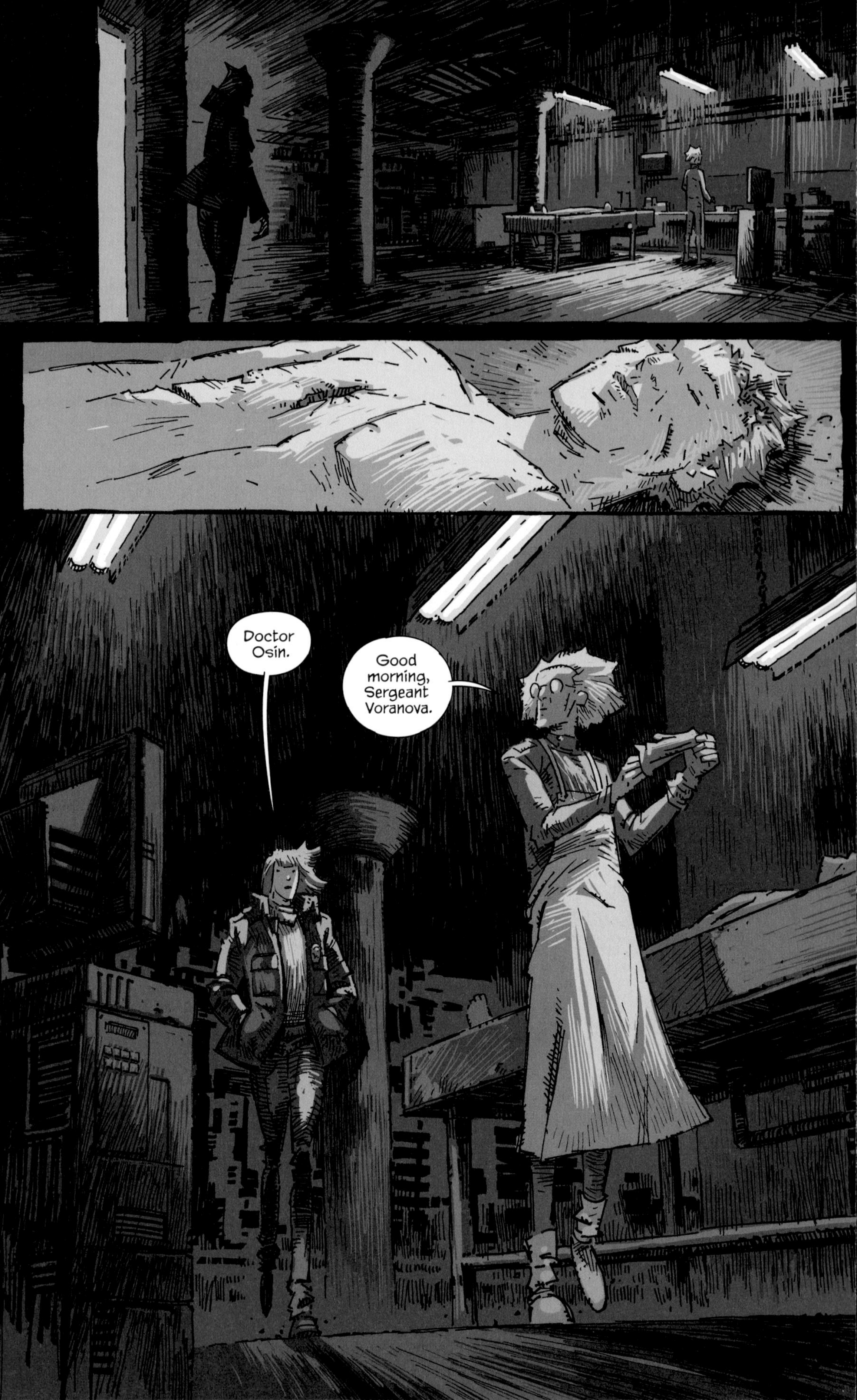
Doctor Osin.
Good morning, Sergeant Voranova.

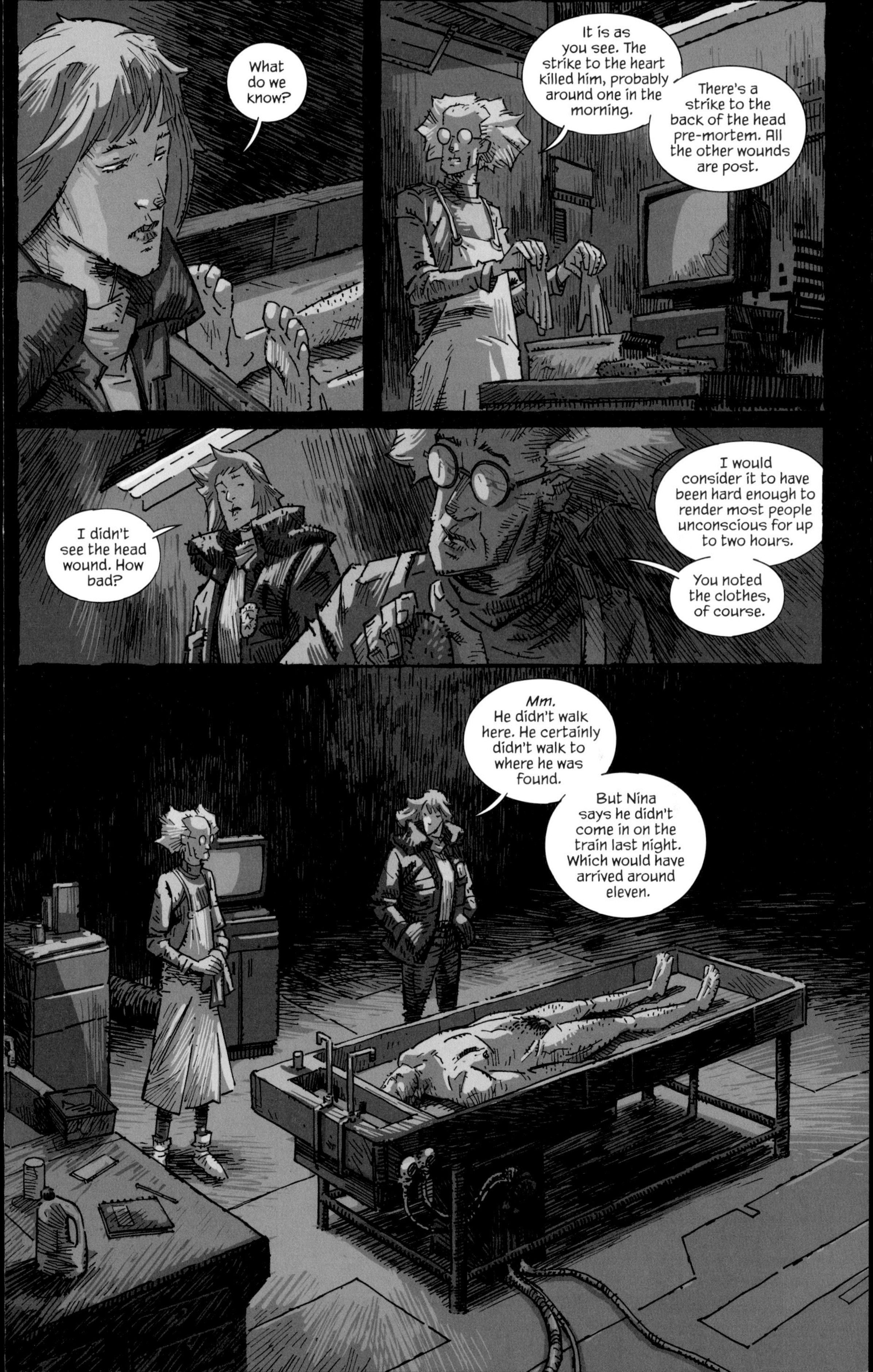
What do we know?
It is as you see. The strike to the heart killed him, probably around one in the morning.
There's a strike to the back of the head pre-mortem. All the other wounds are post.
I didn't see the head wound. How bad?
I would consider it to have been hard enough to render most people unconscious for up to two hours.
You noted the clothes, of course.
Mm. He didn't walk here. He certainly didn't walk to where he was found.
But Nina says he didn't come in on the train last night. Which would have arrived around eleven.

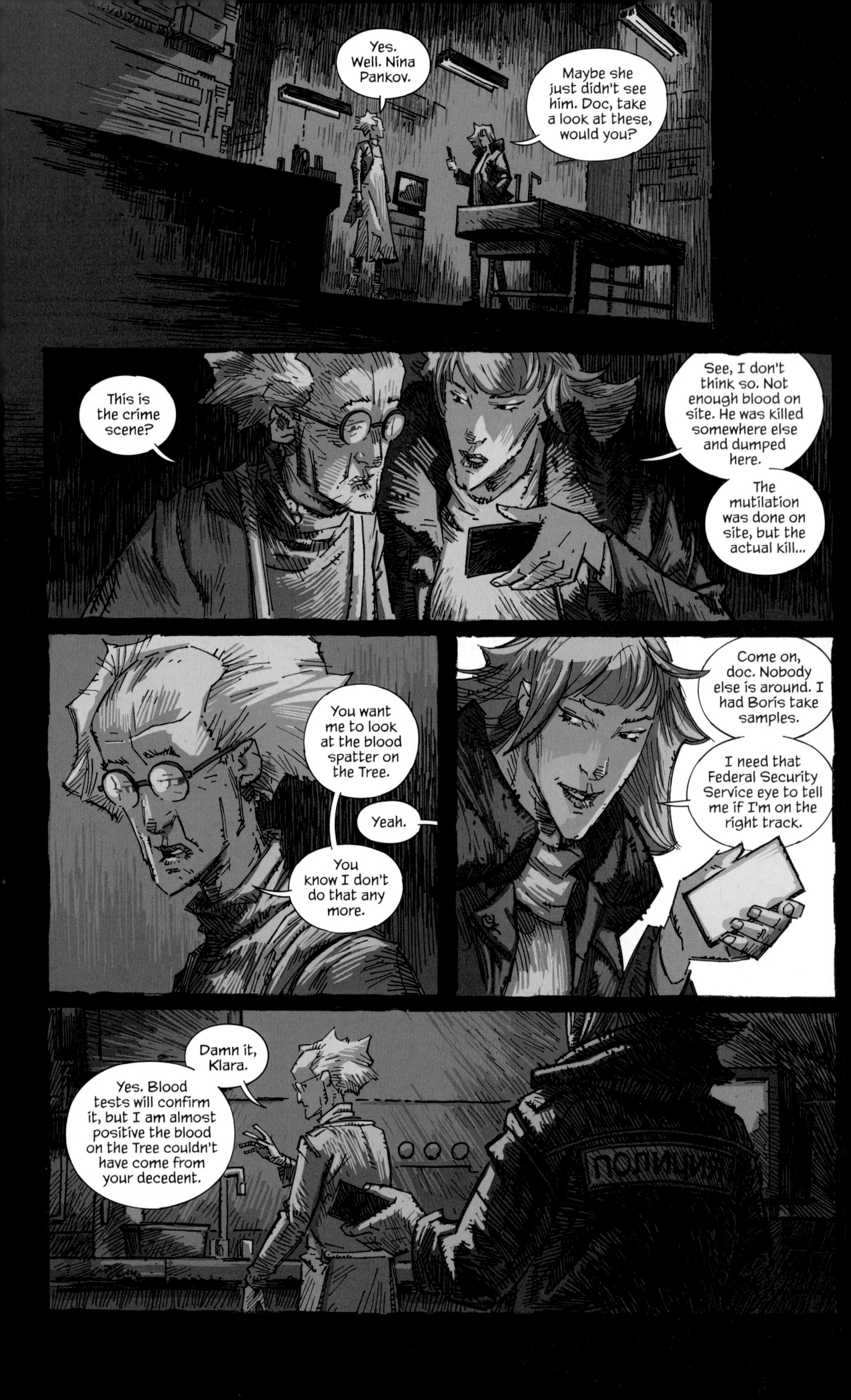
Yes. Well. Nina Pankov.
Maybe she just didn't see him. Doc, take a look at these, would you?
This is the crime scene?
See, I don't think so. Not enough blood on site. He was killed somewhere else and dumped here.
The mutilation was done on site, but the actual kill...
You want me to look at the blood spatter on the Tree.
Yeah.
You know I don't do that any more.
Come on, doc. Nobody else is around. I had Boris take samples.
I need that Federal Security Service eye to tell me if I'm on the right track.
Damn it, Klara.
Yes. Blood tests will confirm it, but I am almost positive the blood on the Tree couldn't have come from your decedent.
ПОЛИЦИЯ

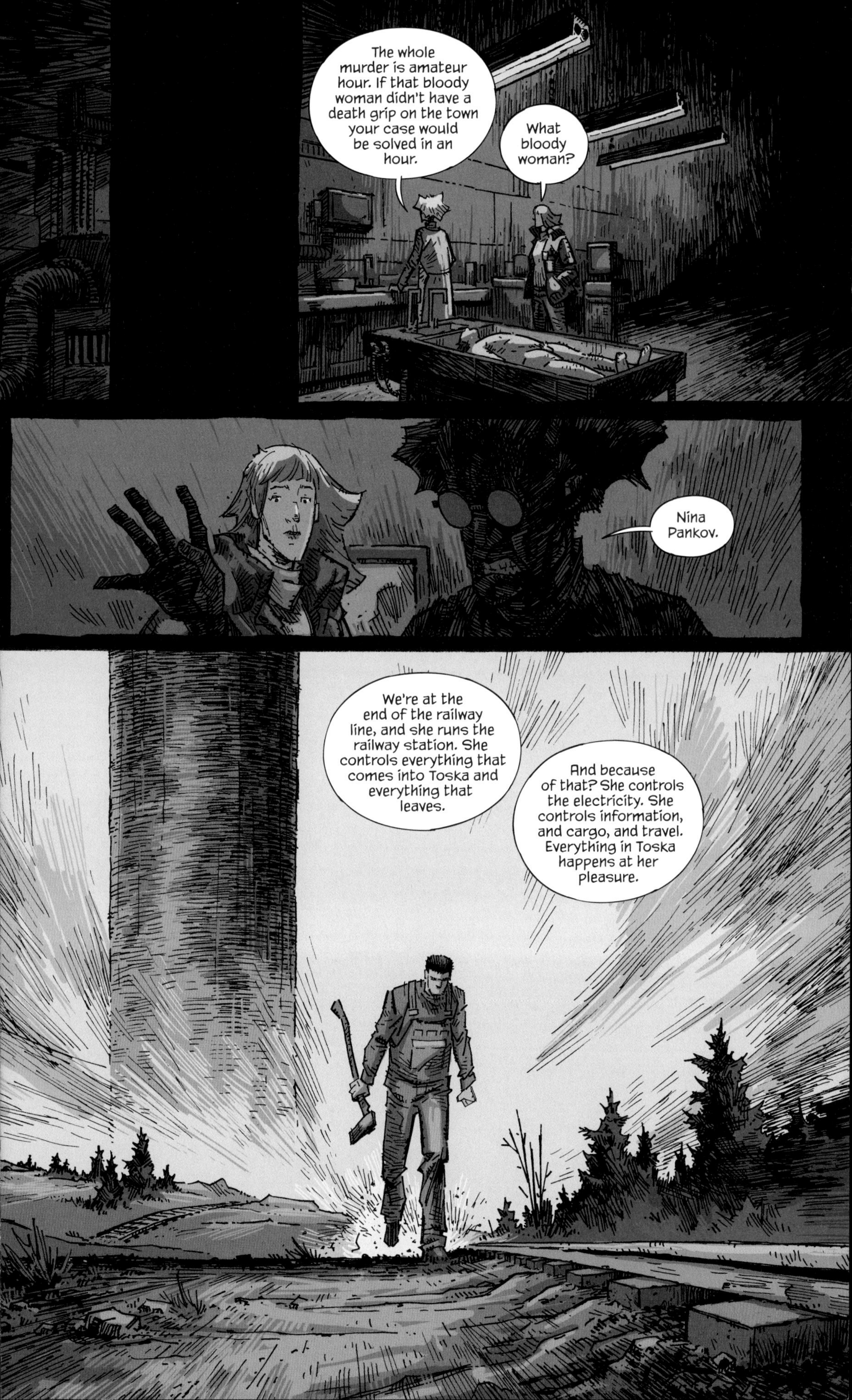
The whole murder is amateur hour. If that bloody woman didn't have a death grip on the town your case would be solved in an hour.
What bloody woman?
Nina Pankov.
We're at the end of the railway line, and she runs the railway station. She controls everything that comes into Toska and everything that leaves.
And because of that? She controls the electricity. She controls information, and cargo, and travel. Everything in Toska happens at her pleasure.

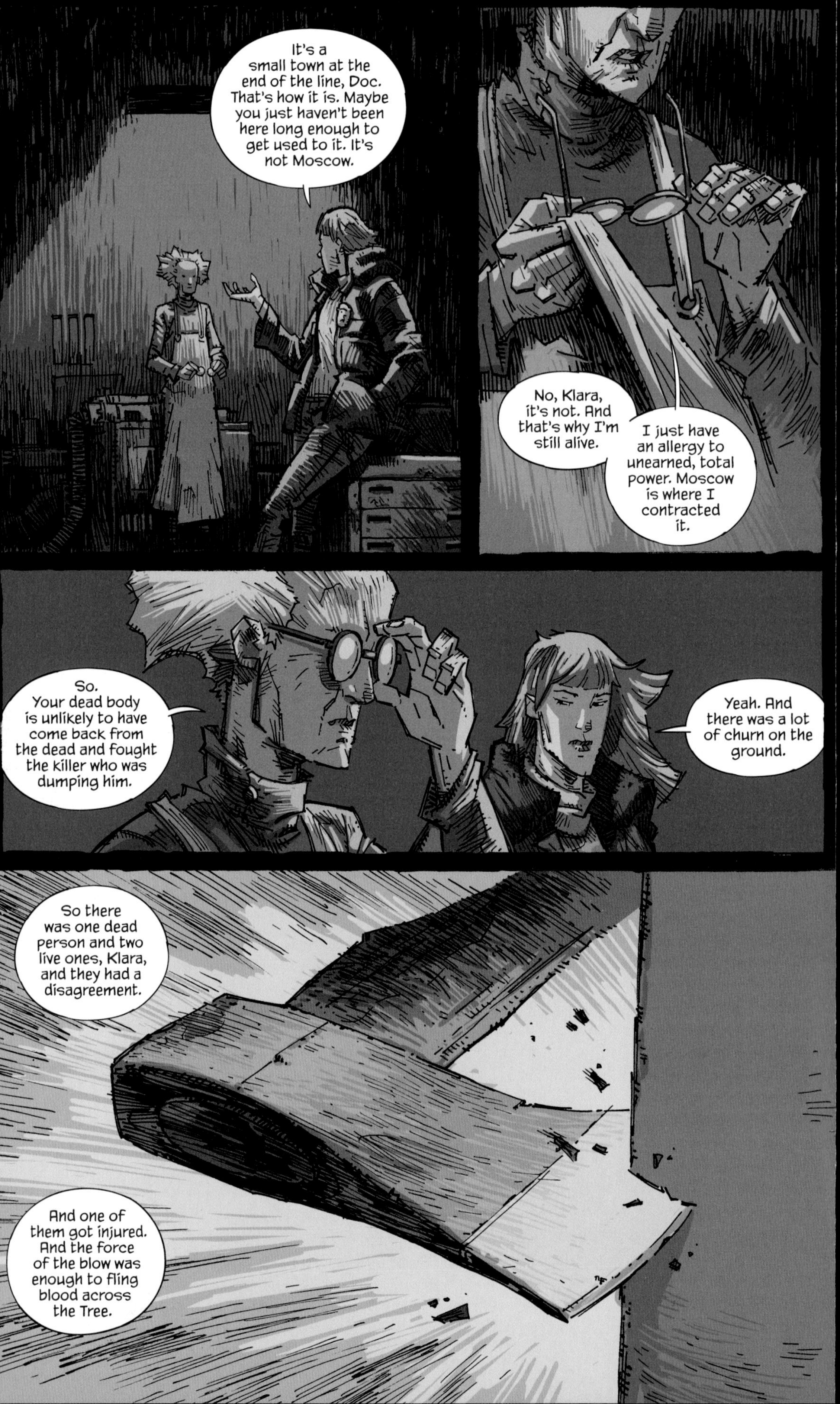
It's a small town at the end of the line, Doc. That's how it is. Maybe you just haven't been here long enough to get used to it. It's not Moscow.
No, Klara, it's not. And that's why I'm still alive.
I just have an allergy to unearned, total power. Moscow is where I contracted it.
So. Your dead body is unlikely to have come back from the dead and fought the killer who was dumping him.
Yeah. And there was a lot of churn on the ground.
So there was one dead person and two live ones, Klara, and they had a disagreement.
And one of them got injured. And the force of the blow was enough to fling blood across the Tree.

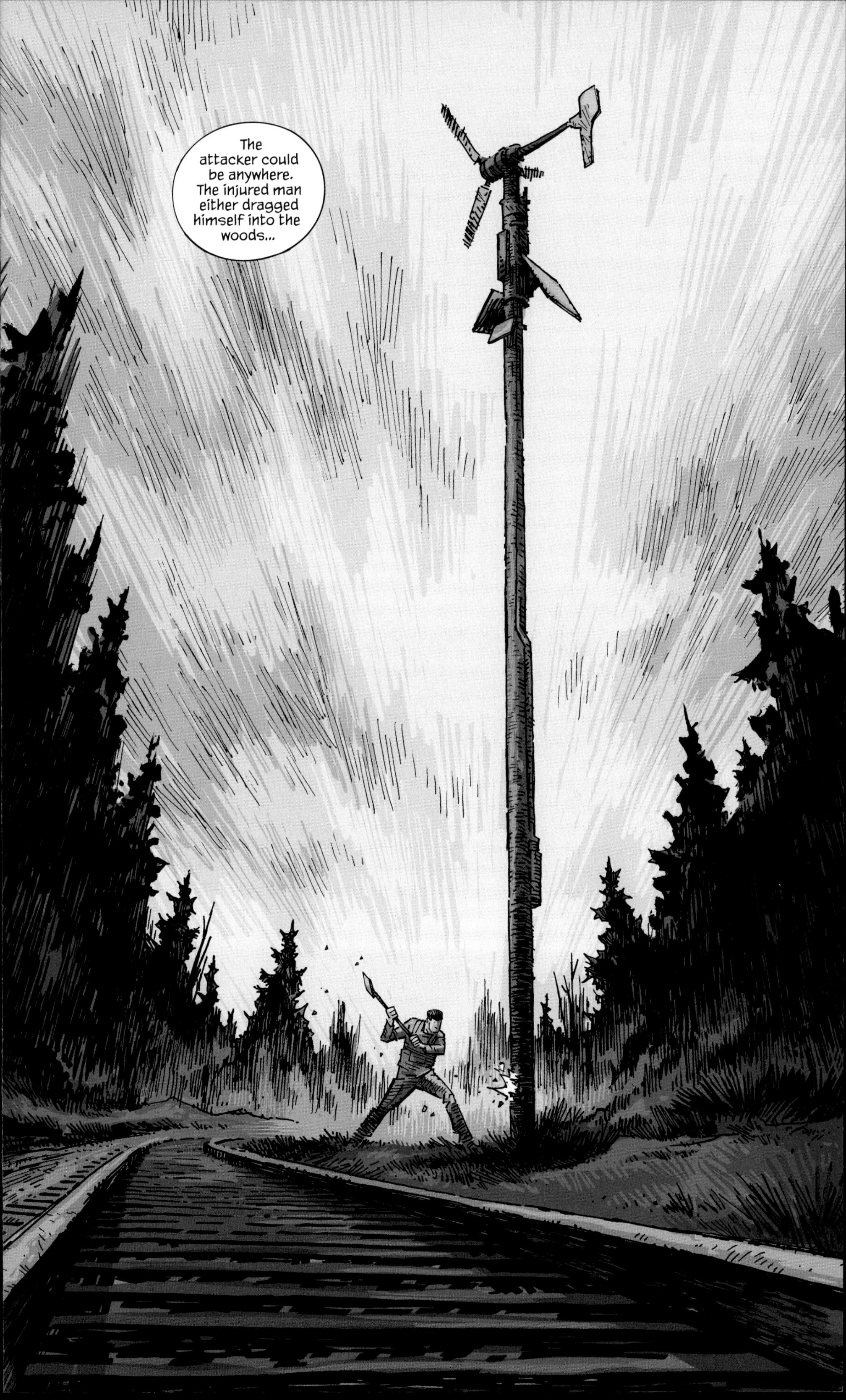
The attacker could be anywhere. The injured man either dragged himself into the woods...

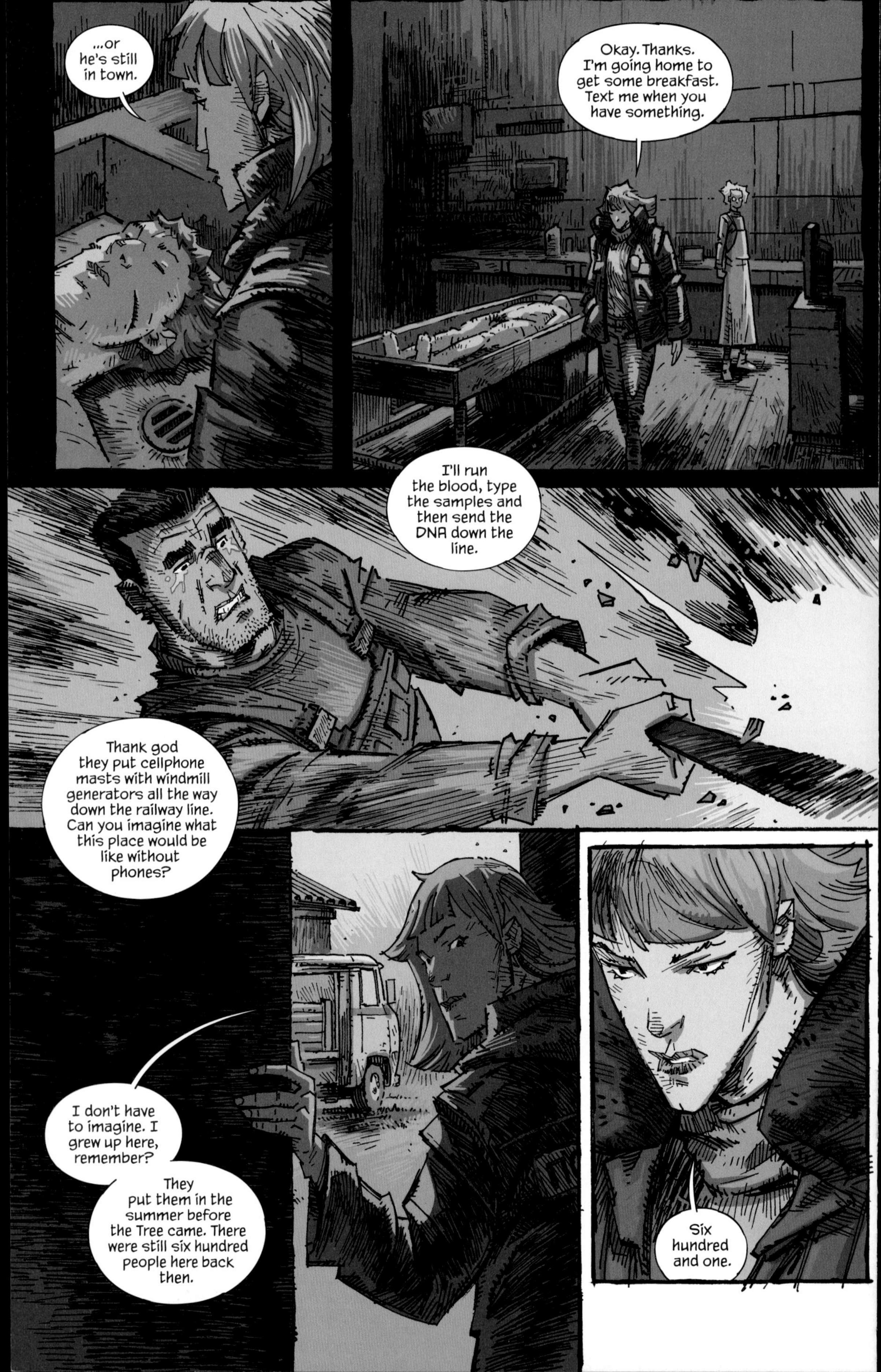
...or he's still in town.
Okay. Thanks. I'm going home to get some breakfast. Text me when you have something.
I'll run the blood, type the samples and then send the DNA down the line.
Thank god they put cellphone masts with windmill generators all the way down the railway line. Can you imagine what this place would be like without phones?
I don't have to imagine. I grew up here, remember?
They put them in the summer before the Tree came. There were still six hundred people here back then.
Six hundred and one.

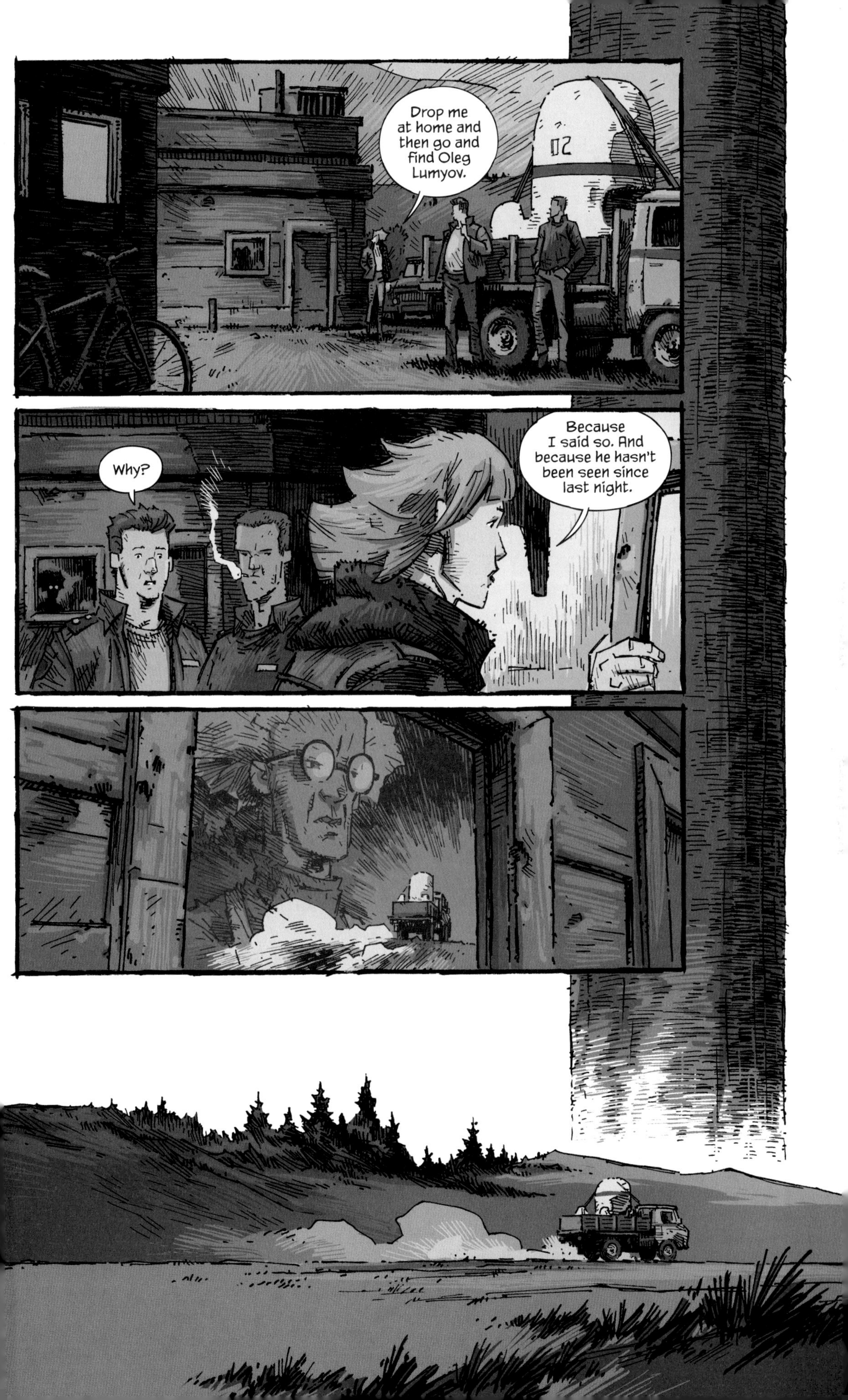

Drop me at home and then go and find Oleg Lumyov.
02
Why?
Because I said so. And because he hasn't been seen since last night.

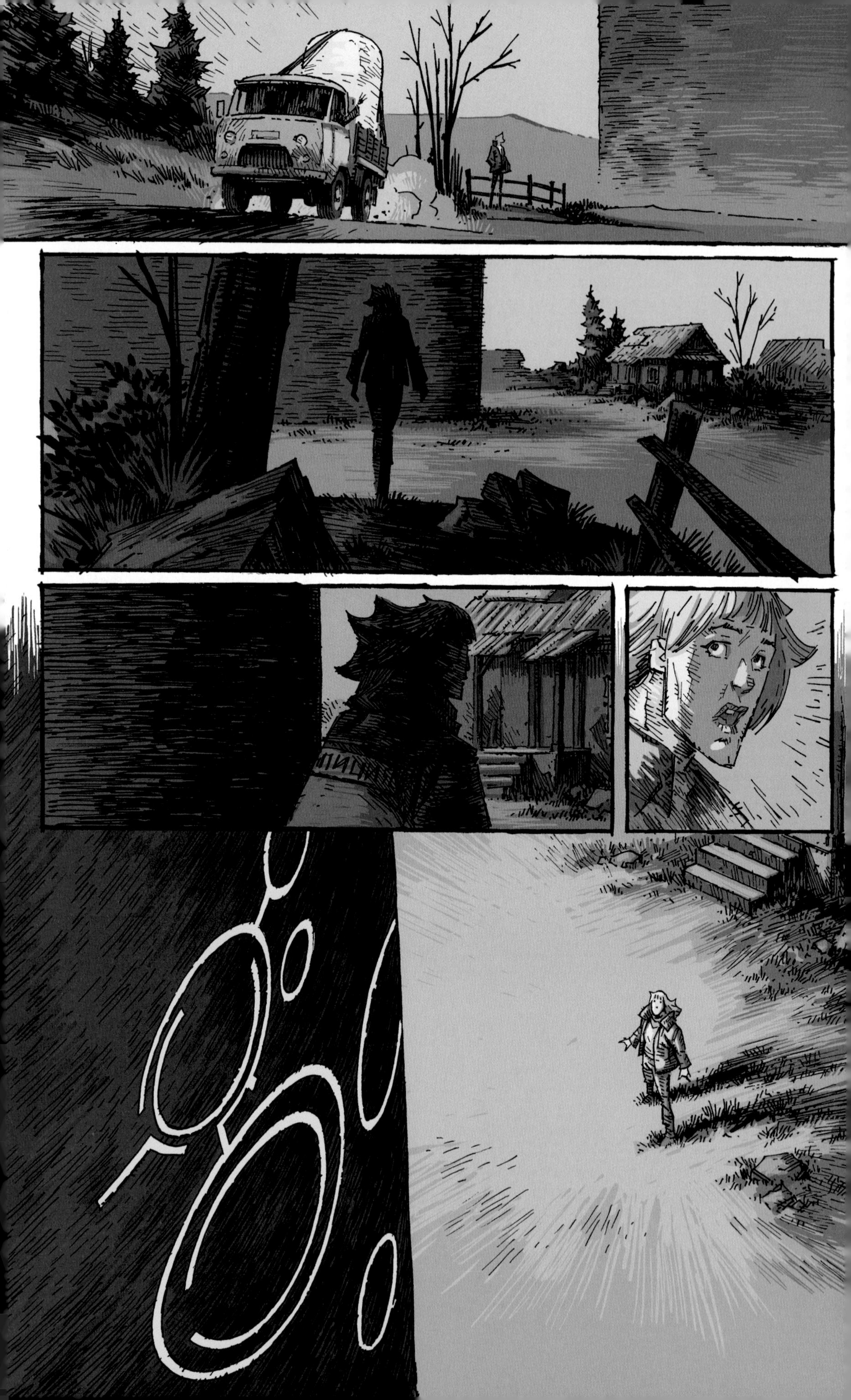

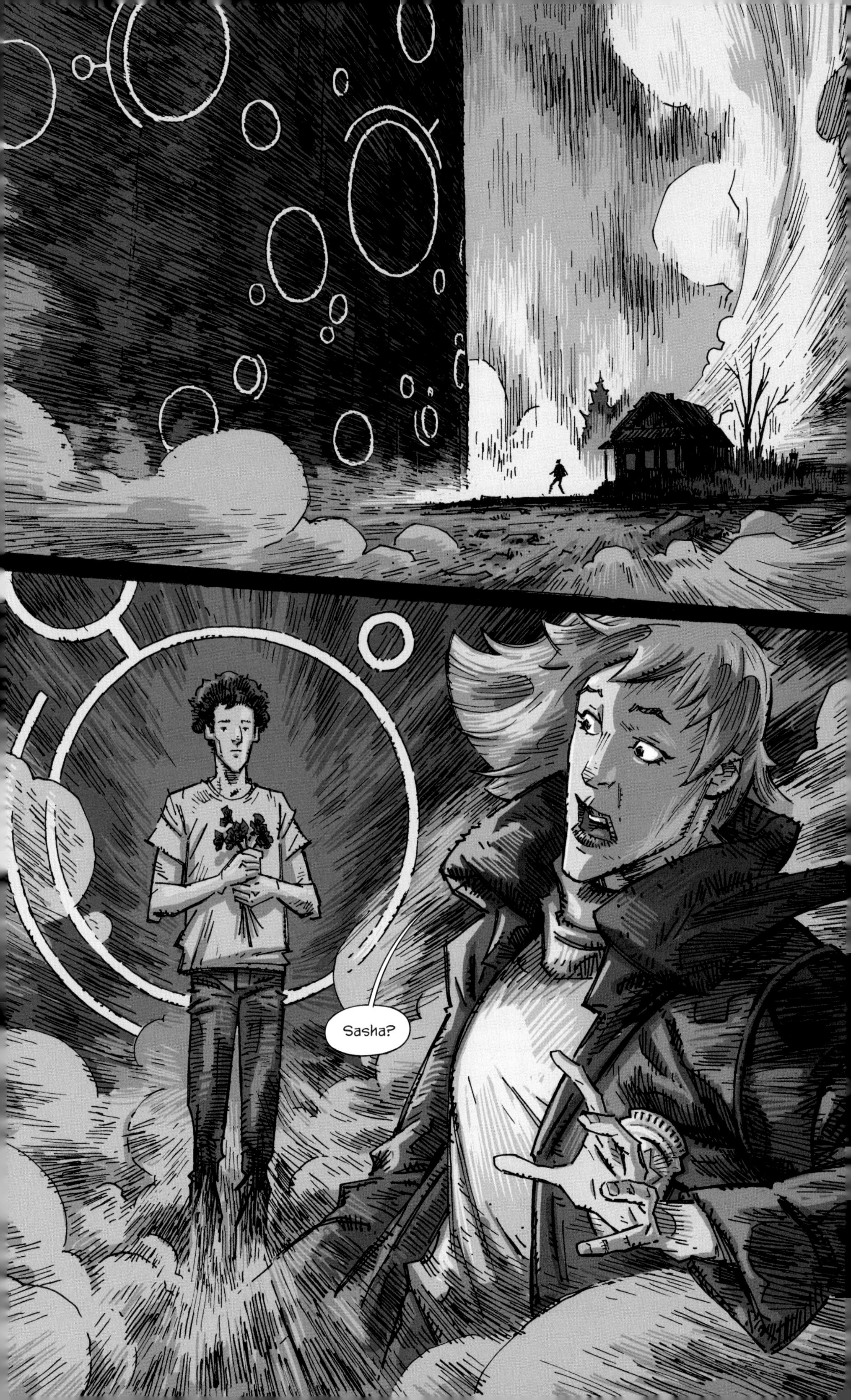
Sasha?

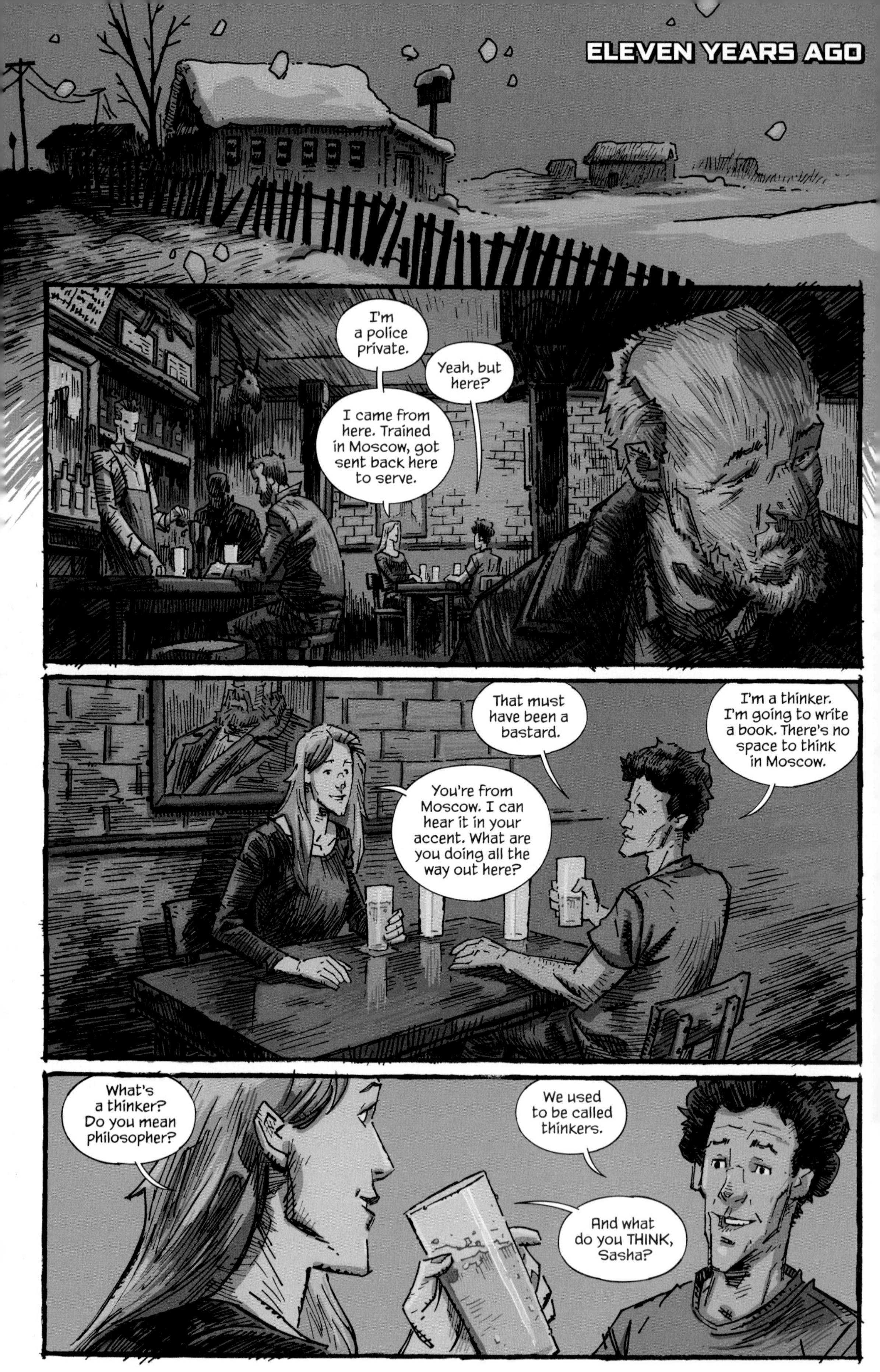
ELEVEN YEARS AGO
I'm a police private.
I came from here. Trained in Moscow, got sent back here to serve.
Yeah, but here?
You're from Moscow. I can hear it in your accent. What are you doing all the way out here?
That must have been a bastard.
I'm a thinker. I'm going to write a book. There's no space to think in Moscow.
What's a thinker? Do you mean philosopher?
We used to be called thinkers.
And what do you THINK, Sasha?

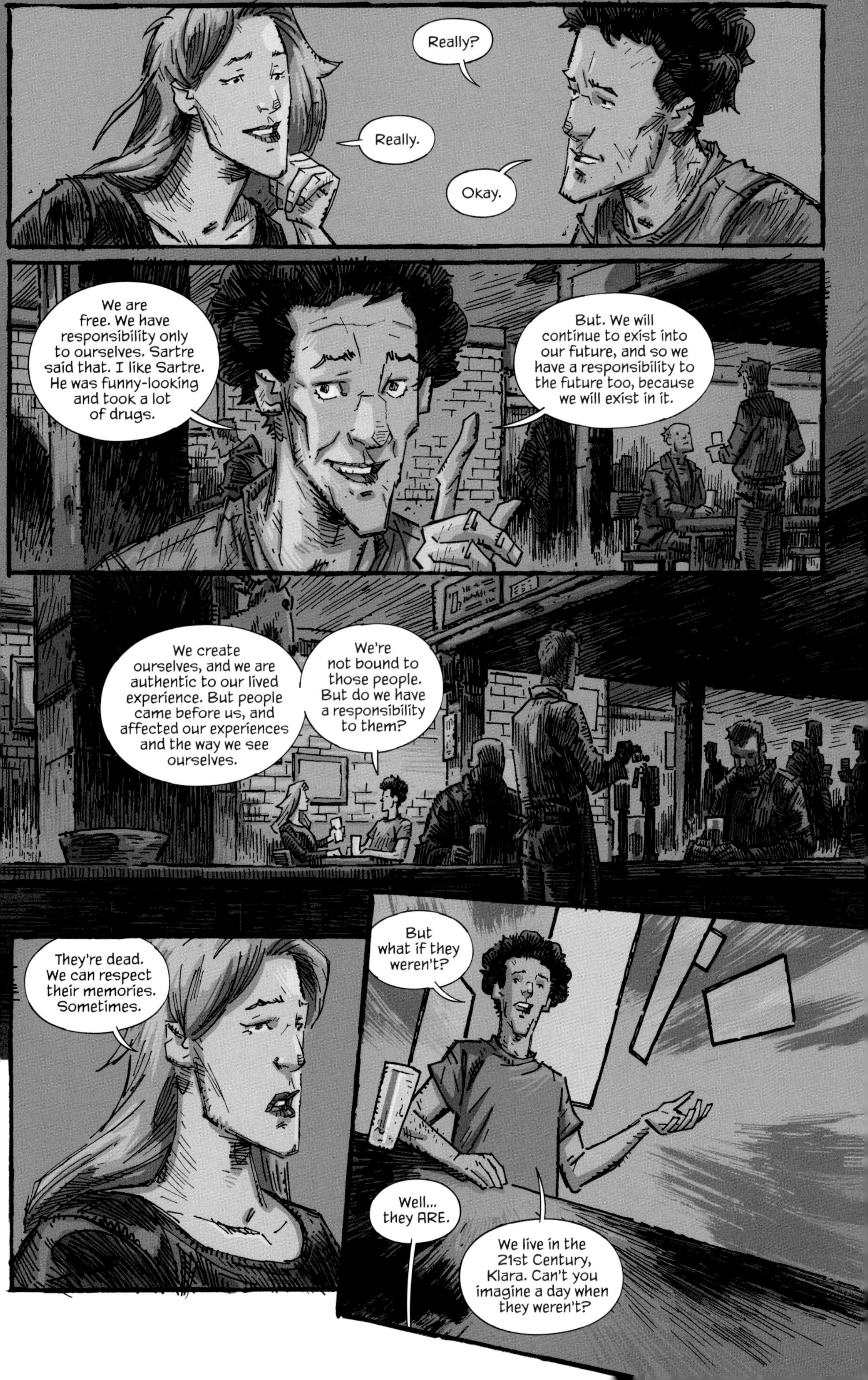
Really?
Really.
Okay.
We are free. We have responsibility only to ourselves. Sartre said that. I like Sartre. He was funny-looking and took a lot of drugs.
But. We will continue to exist into our future, and so we have a responsibility to the future too, because we will exist in it.
We create ourselves, and we are authentic to our lived experience. But people came before us, and affected our experiences and the way we see ourselves.
We're not bound to those people. But do we have a responsibility to them?
They're dead. We can respect their memories. Sometimes.
But what if they weren't?
Well... they ARE.
We live in the 21st Century, Klara. Can't you imagine a day when they weren't?

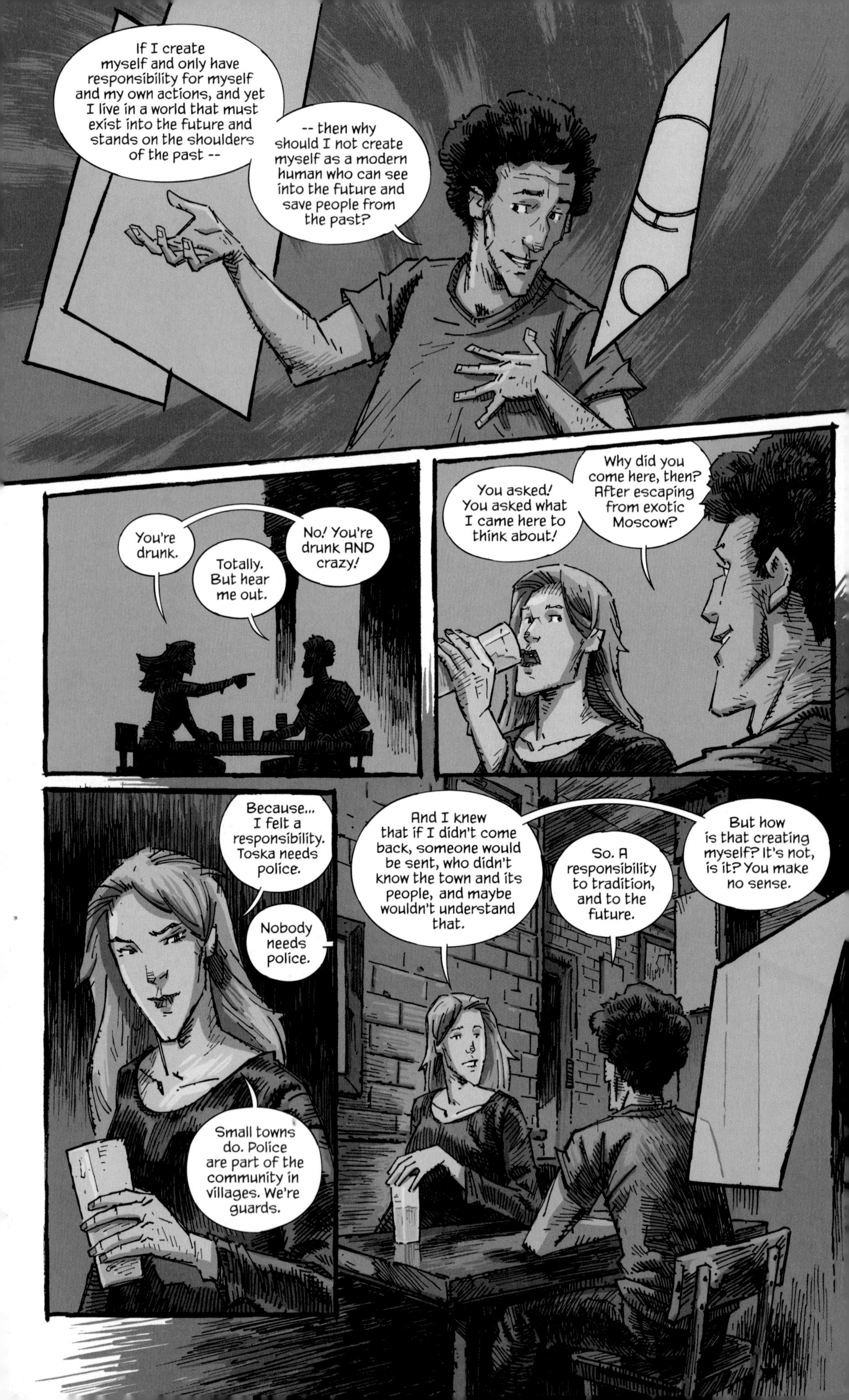
If I create myself and only have responsibility for myself and my own actions, and yet I live in a world that must exist into the future and stands on the shoulders of the past --
-- then why should I not create myself as a modern human who can see into the future and save people from the past?
You're drunk.
No! You're drunk AND crazy!
Totally. But hear me out.
You asked! You asked what I came here to think about!
Why did you come here, then? After escaping from exotic Moscow?
Because... I felt a responsibility. Toska needs police.
Nobody needs police.
Small towns do. Police are part of the community in villages. We're guards.
And I knew that if I didn't come back, someone would be sent, who didn't know the town and its people, and maybe wouldn't understand that.
So. A responsibility to tradition, and to the future.
But how is that creating myself? It's not, is it? You make no sense.

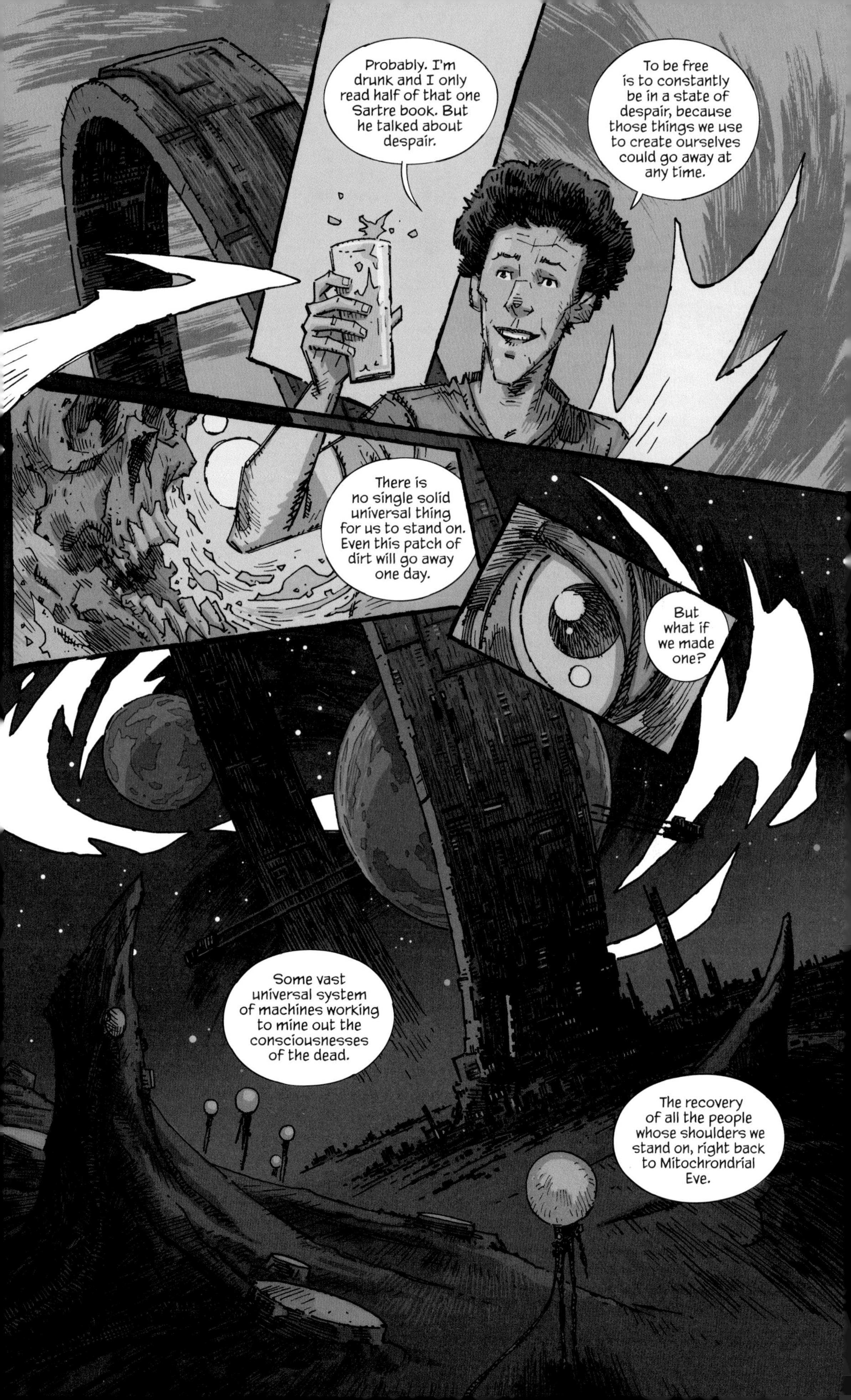
Probably. I'm drunk and I only read half of that one Sartre book. But he talked about despair.
To be free is to constantly be in a state of despair, because those things we use to create ourselves could go away at any time.
There is no single solid universal thing for us to stand on. Even this patch of dirt will go away one day.
But what if we made one?
Some vast universal system of machines working to mine out the consciousnesses of the dead.
The recovery of all the people whose shoulders we stand on, right back to Mitochrondrial Eve.

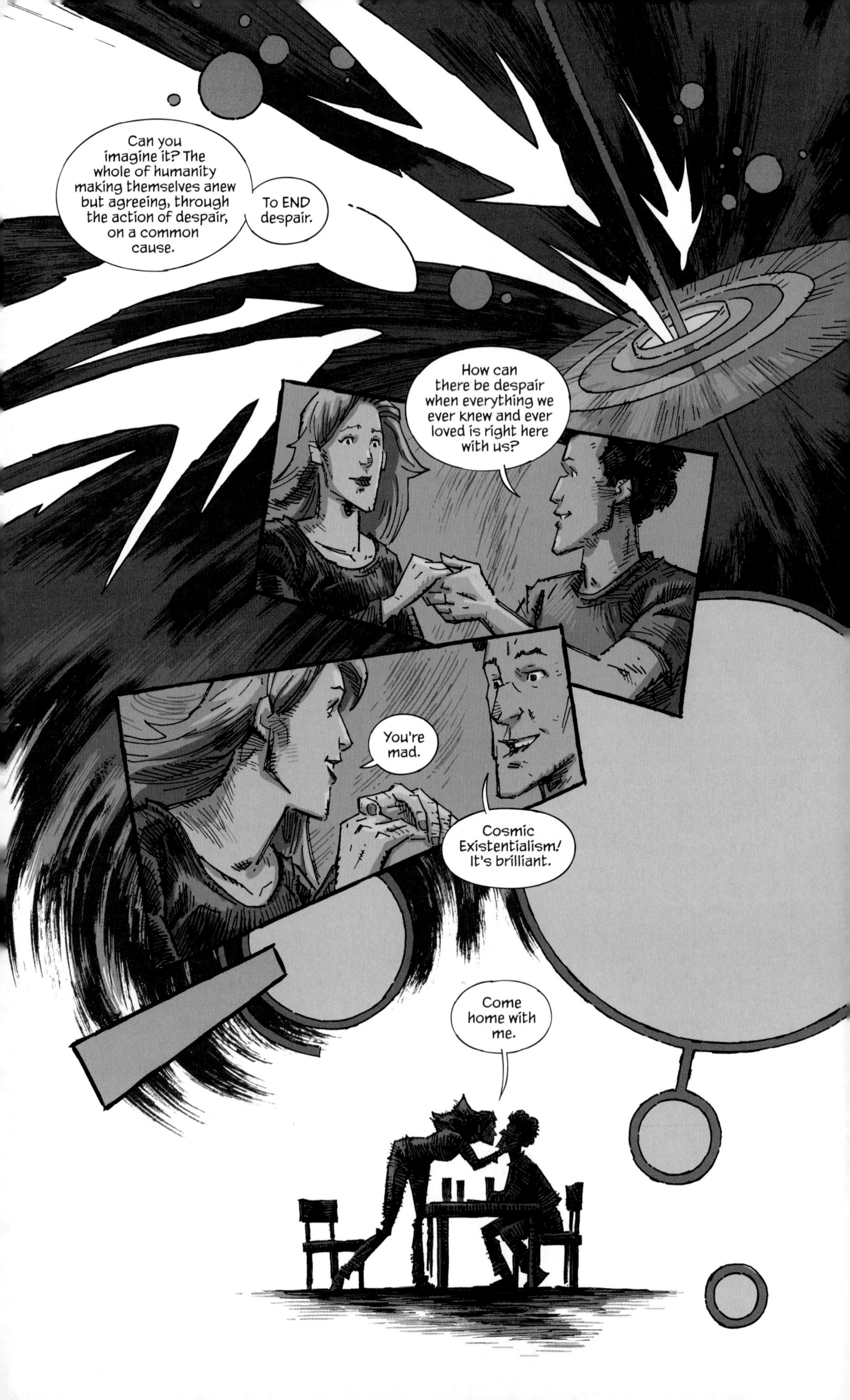
Can you imagine it? The whole of humanity making themselves anew but agreeing, through the action of despair, on a common cause.
To END despair.
How can there be despair when everything we ever knew and ever loved is right here with us?
You're mad.
Cosmic Existentialism! It's brilliant.
Come home with me.

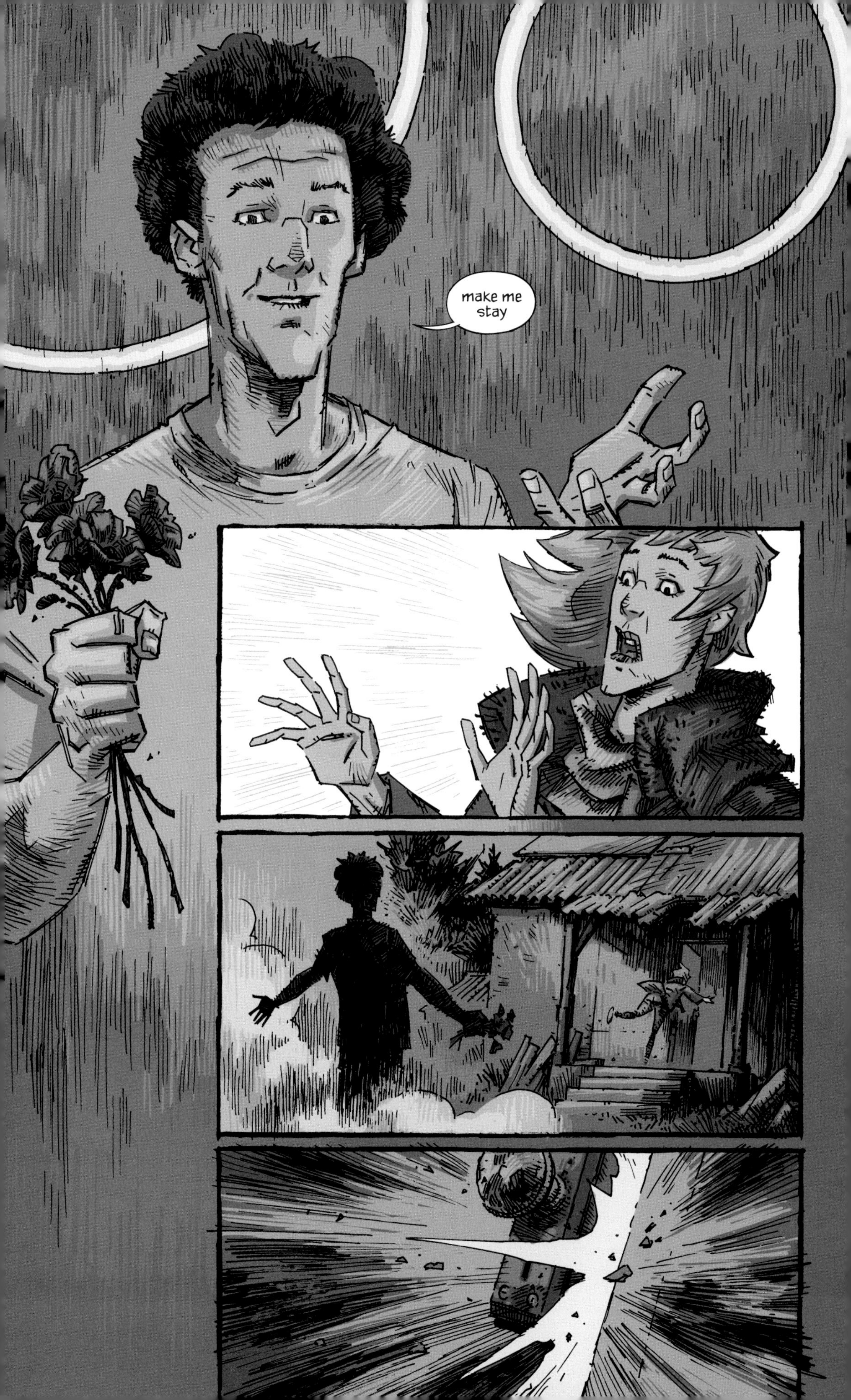
make me stay

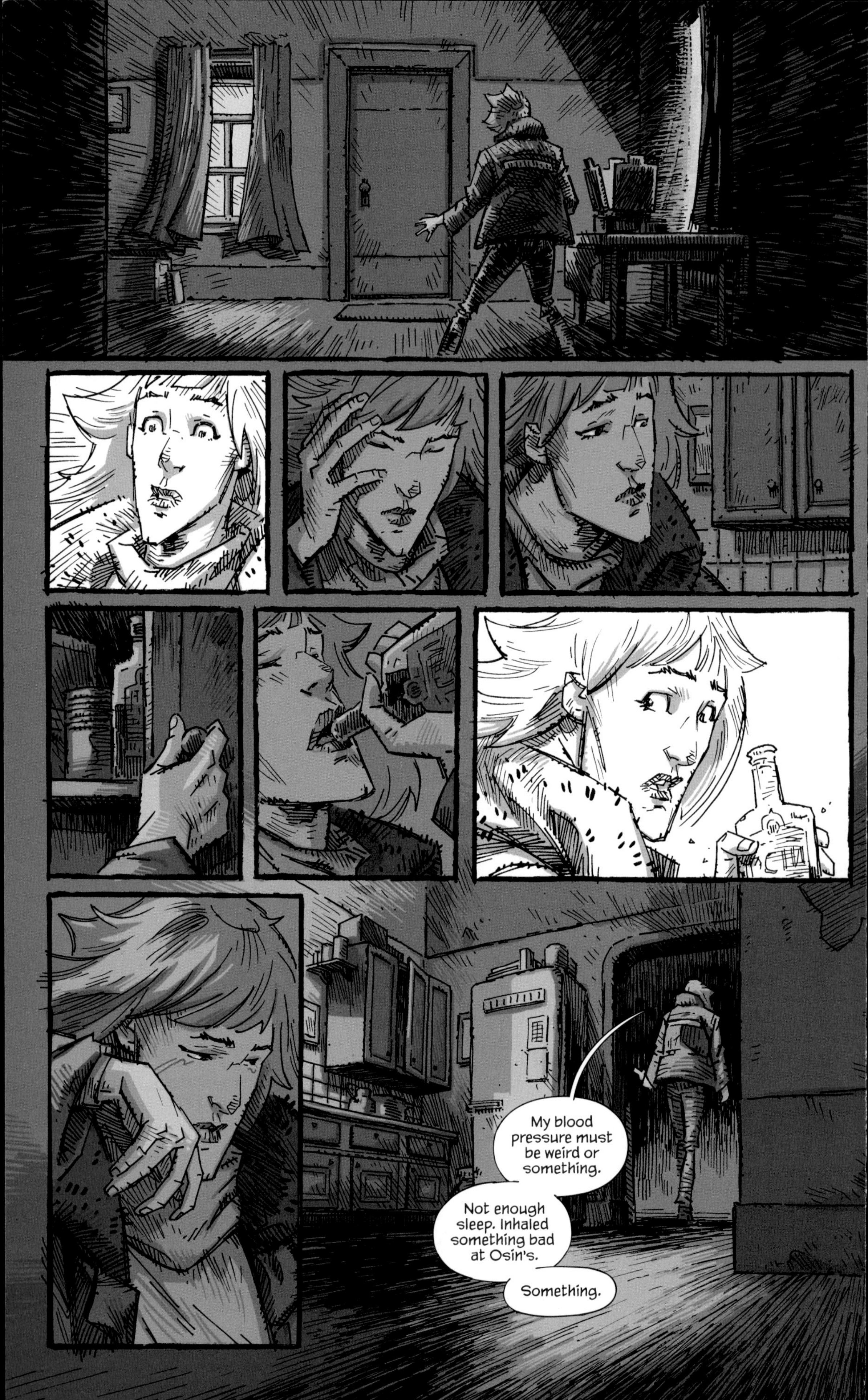
My blood pressure must be weird or something.
Not enough sleep. Inhaled something bad at Osin's.
Something.

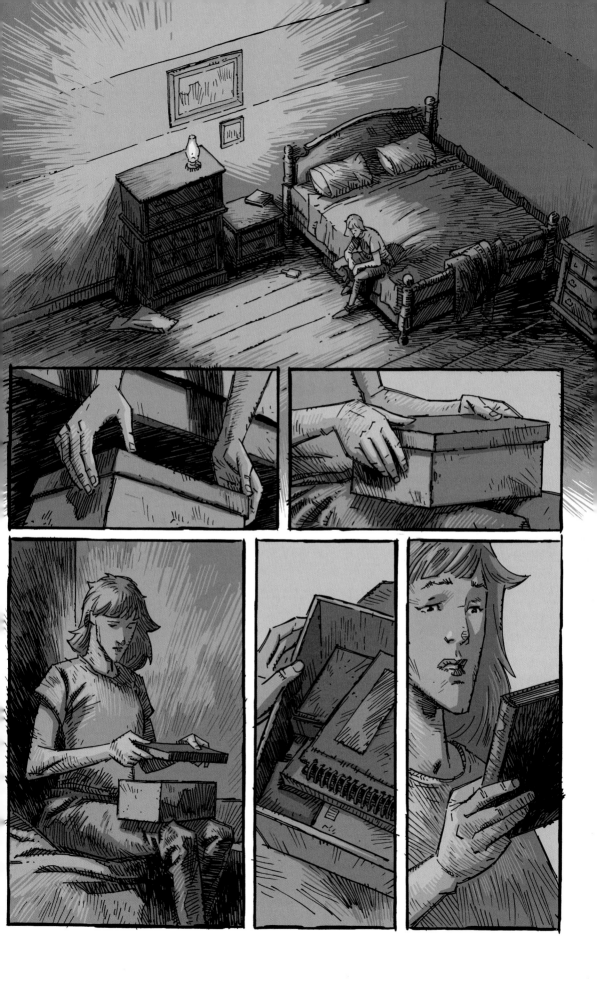

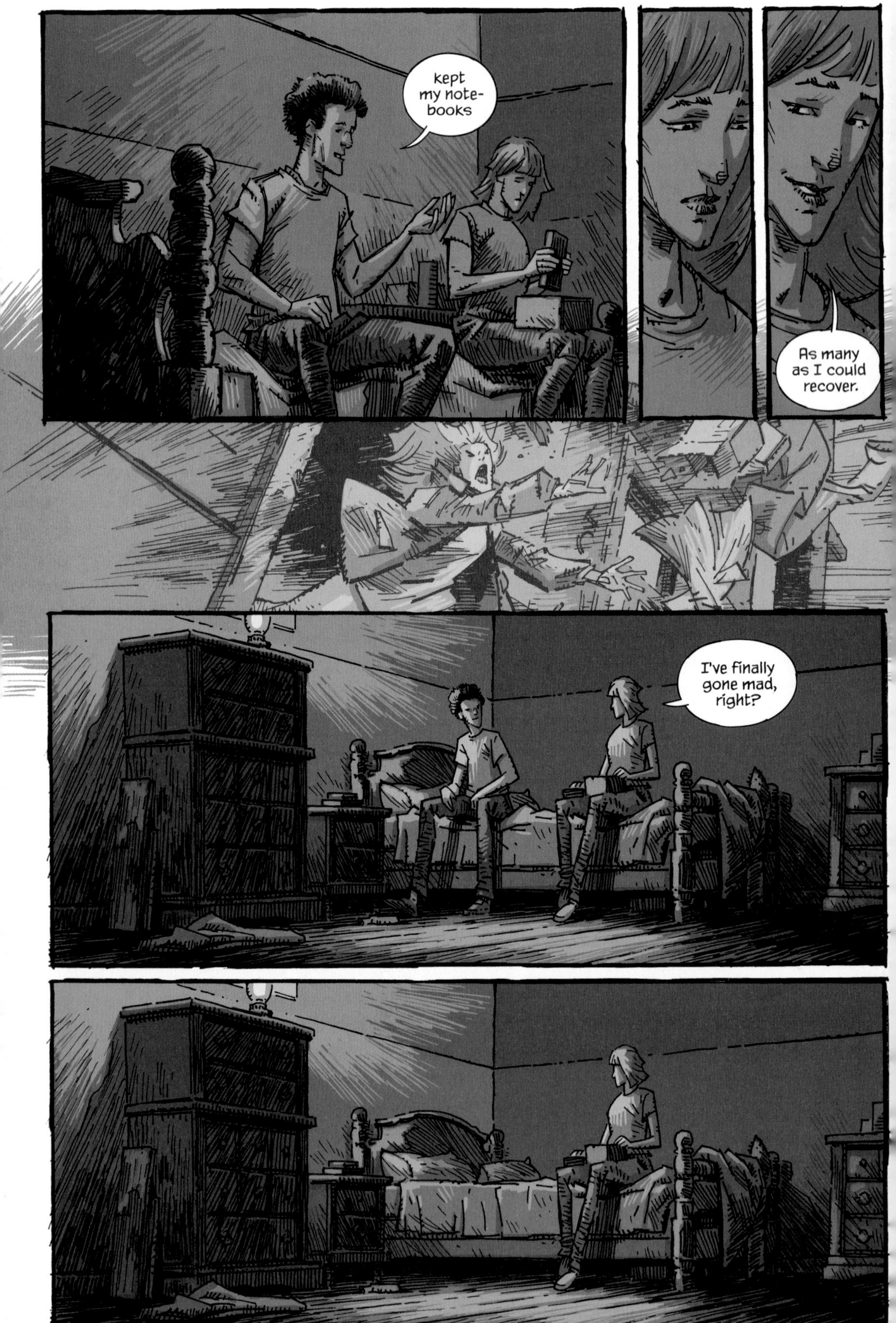
kept my note-books
As many as I could recover.
I've finally gone mad, right?

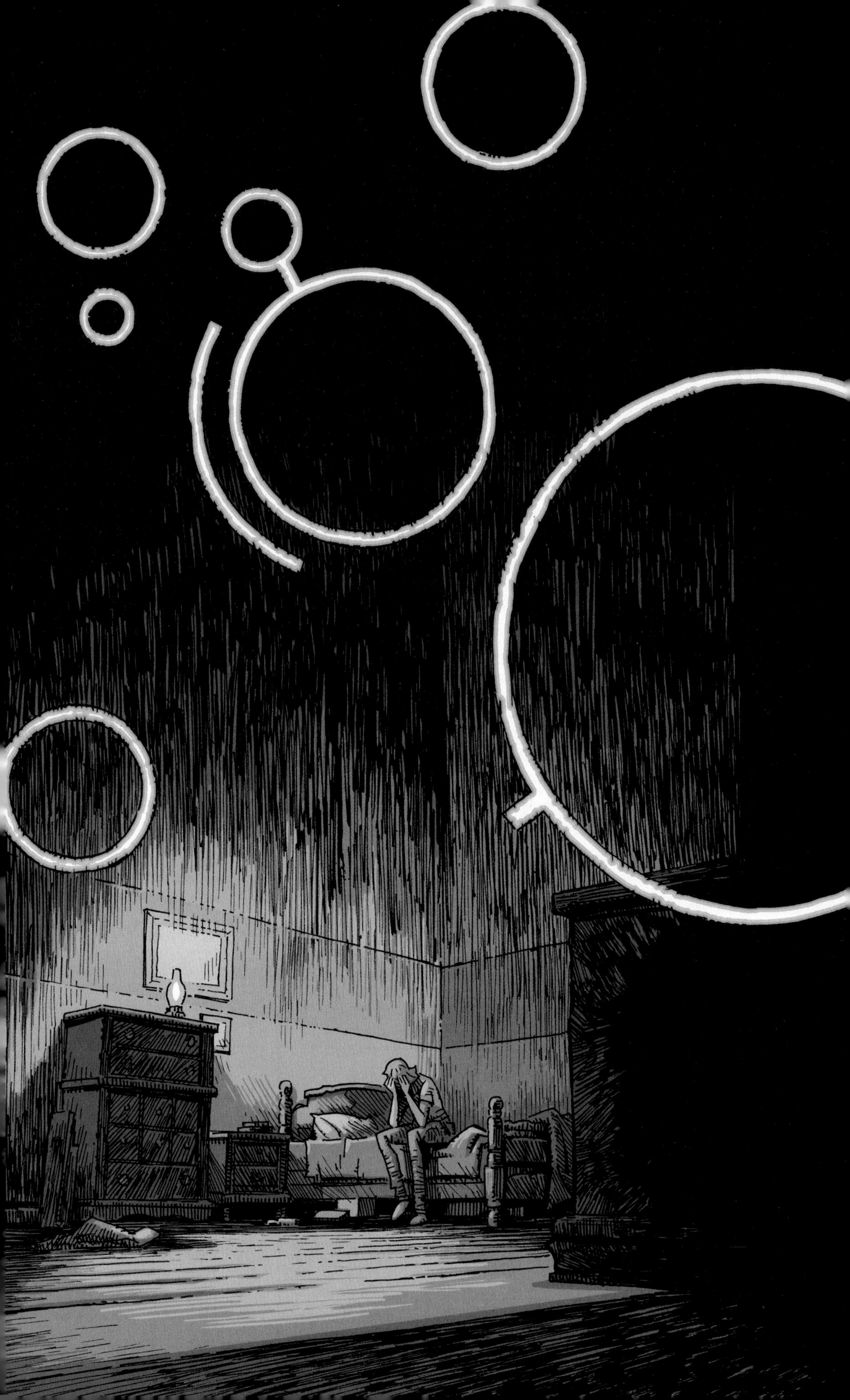

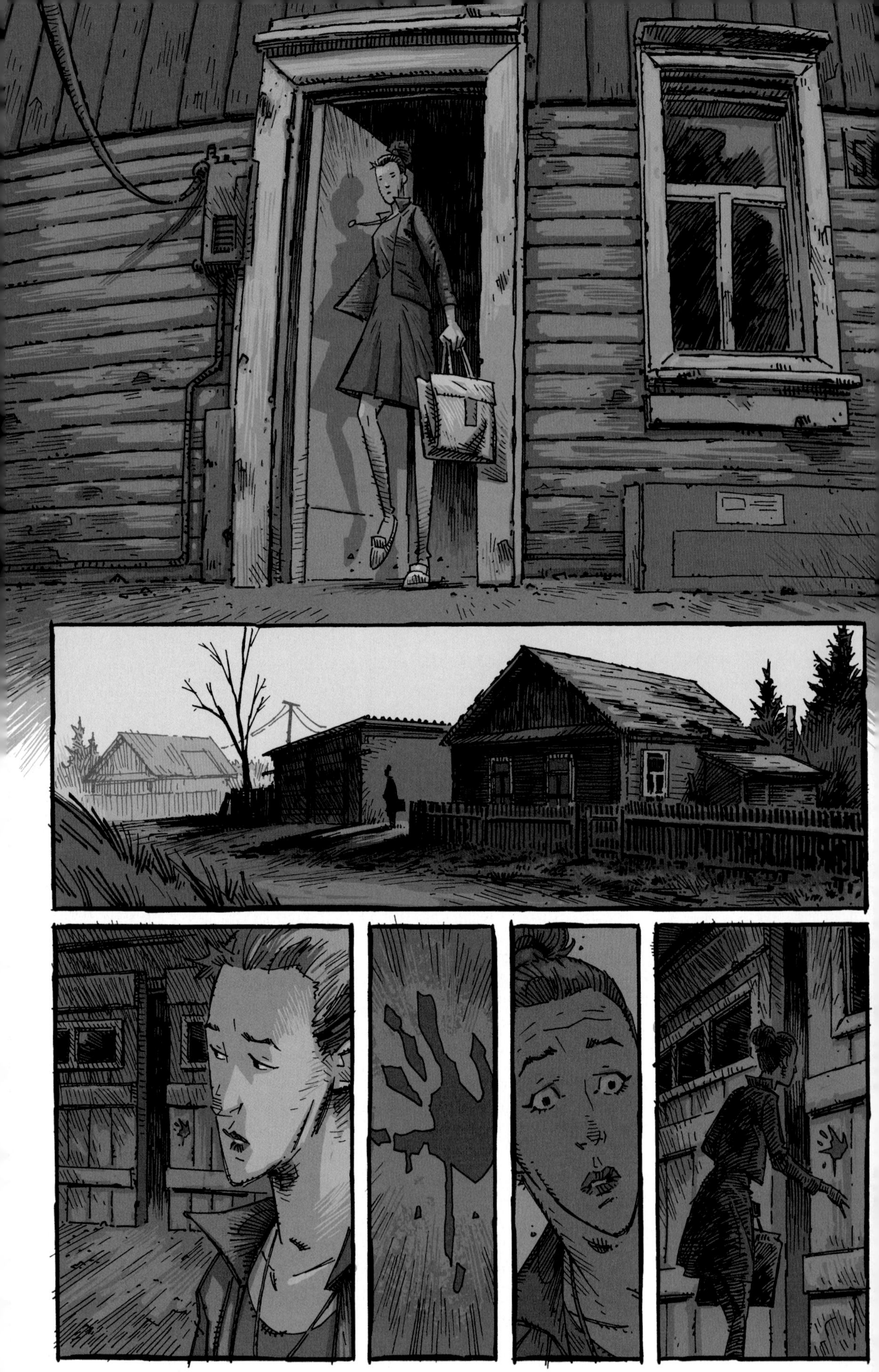

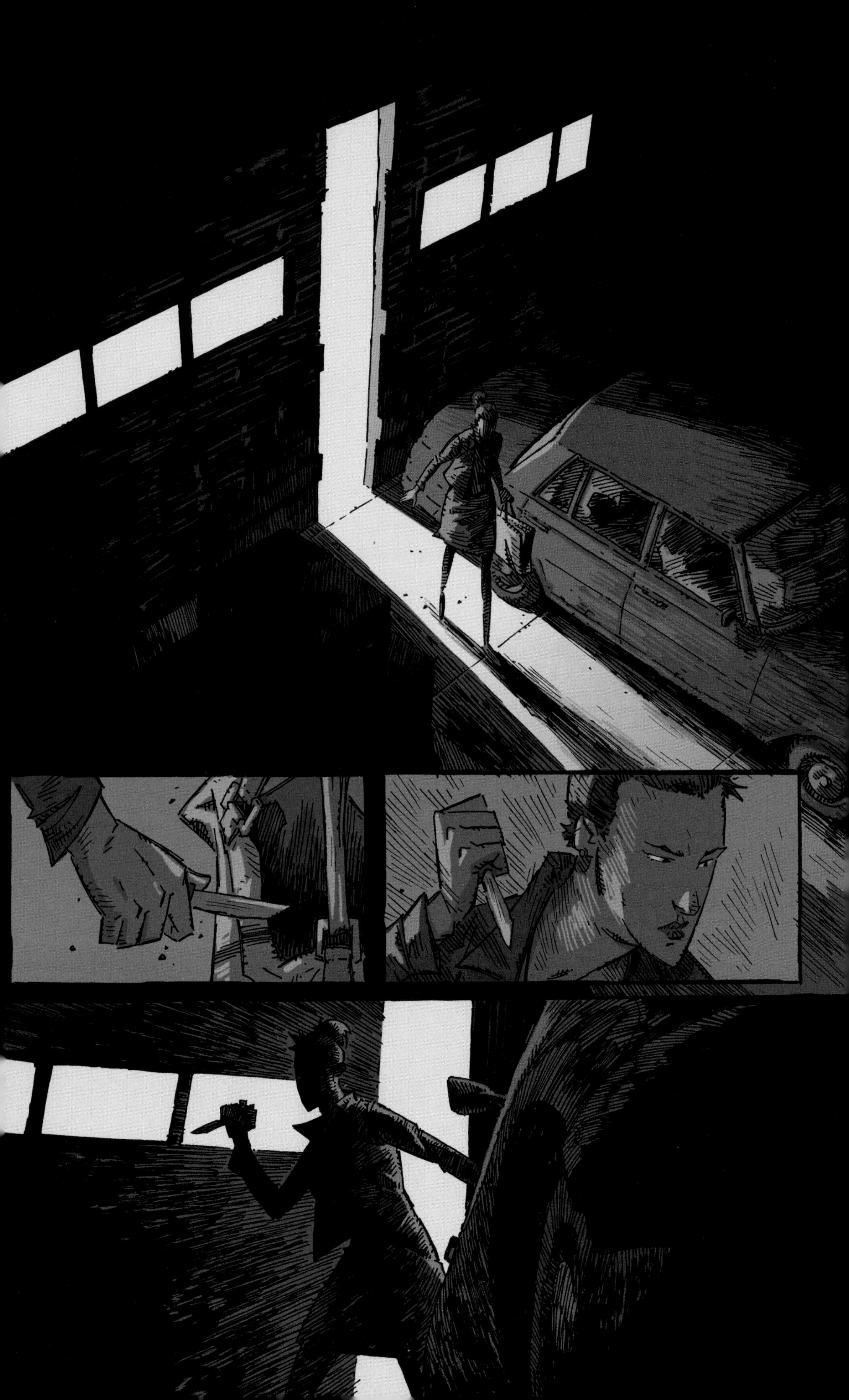

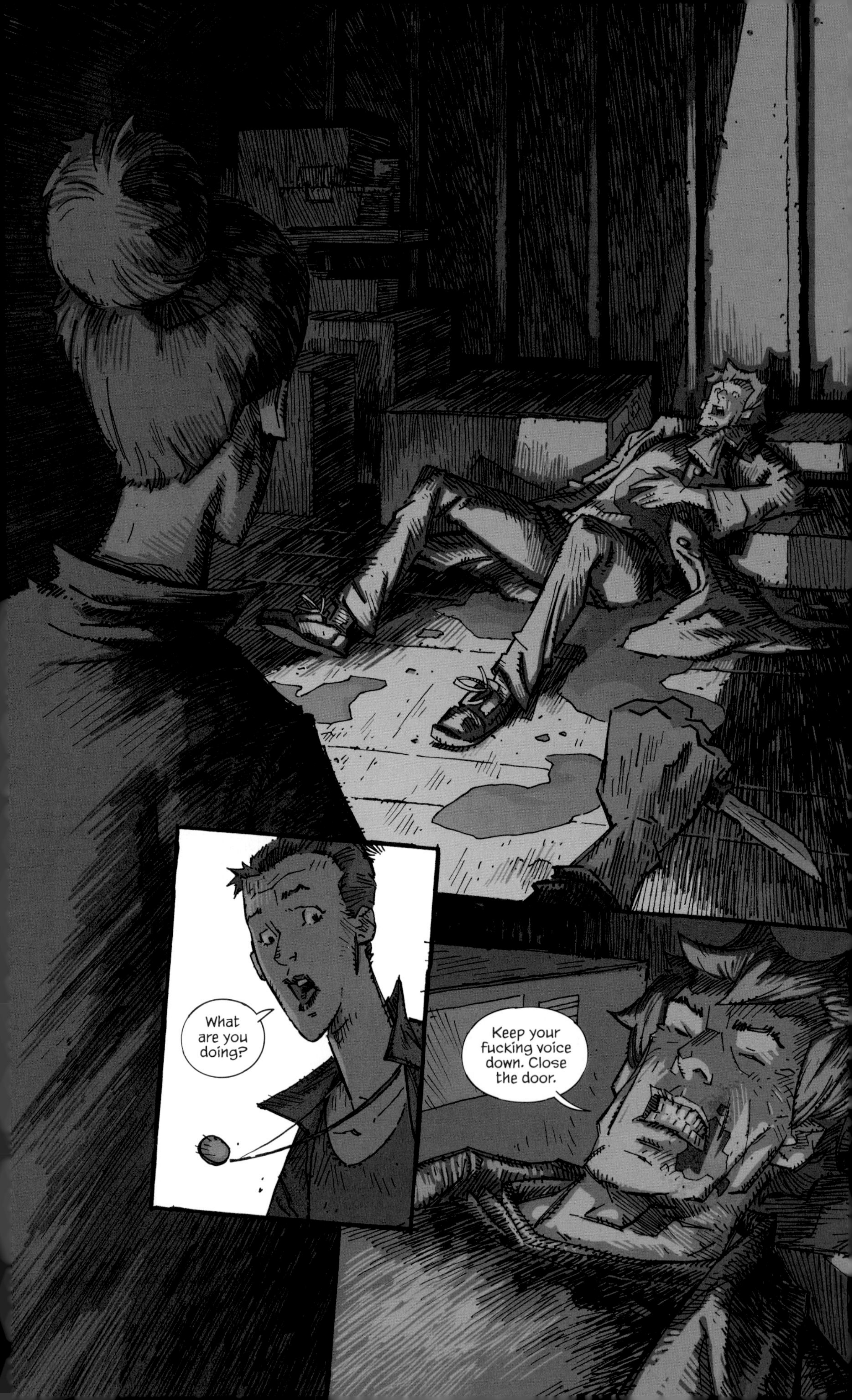
What are you doing?
Keep your fucking voice down. Close the door.

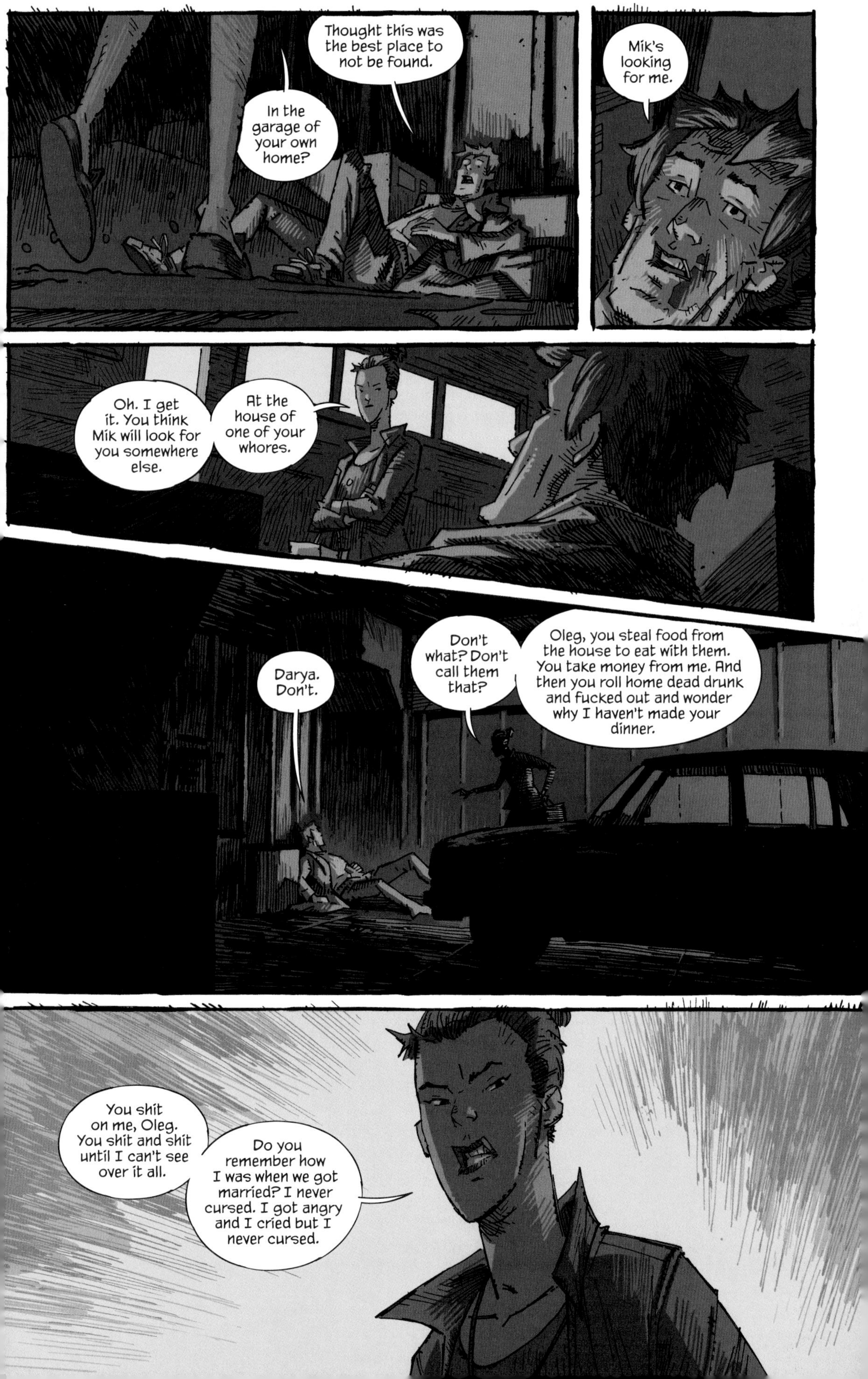
Thought this was the best place to not be found.
In the garage of your own home?
Mik's looking for me.
Oh. I get it. You think Mik will look for you somewhere else.
At the house of one of your whores.
Darya. Don't.
Don't what? Don't call them that?
Oleg, you steal food from the house to eat with them. You take money from me. And then you roll home dead drunk and fucked out and wonder why I haven't made your dinner.
You shit on me, Oleg. You shit and shit until I can't see over it all.
Do you remember how I was when we got married? I never cursed. I got angry and I cried but I never cursed.

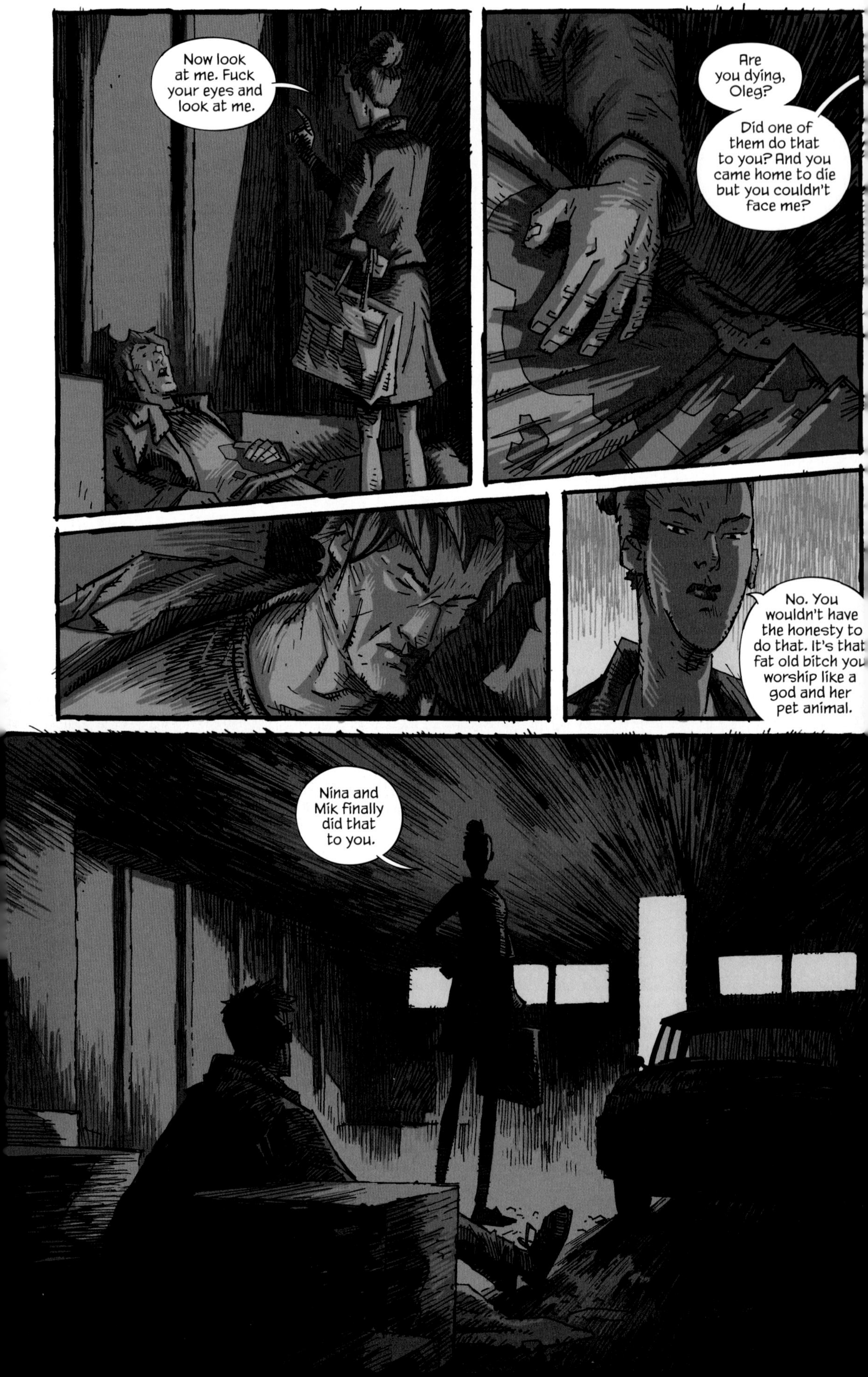
Now look at me. Fuck your eyes and look at me.
Are you dying, Oleg?
Did one of them do that to you? And you came home to die but you couldn't face me?
No. You wouldn't have the honesty to do that. It's that fat old bitch you worship like a god and her pet animal.
Nina and Mik finally did that to you.

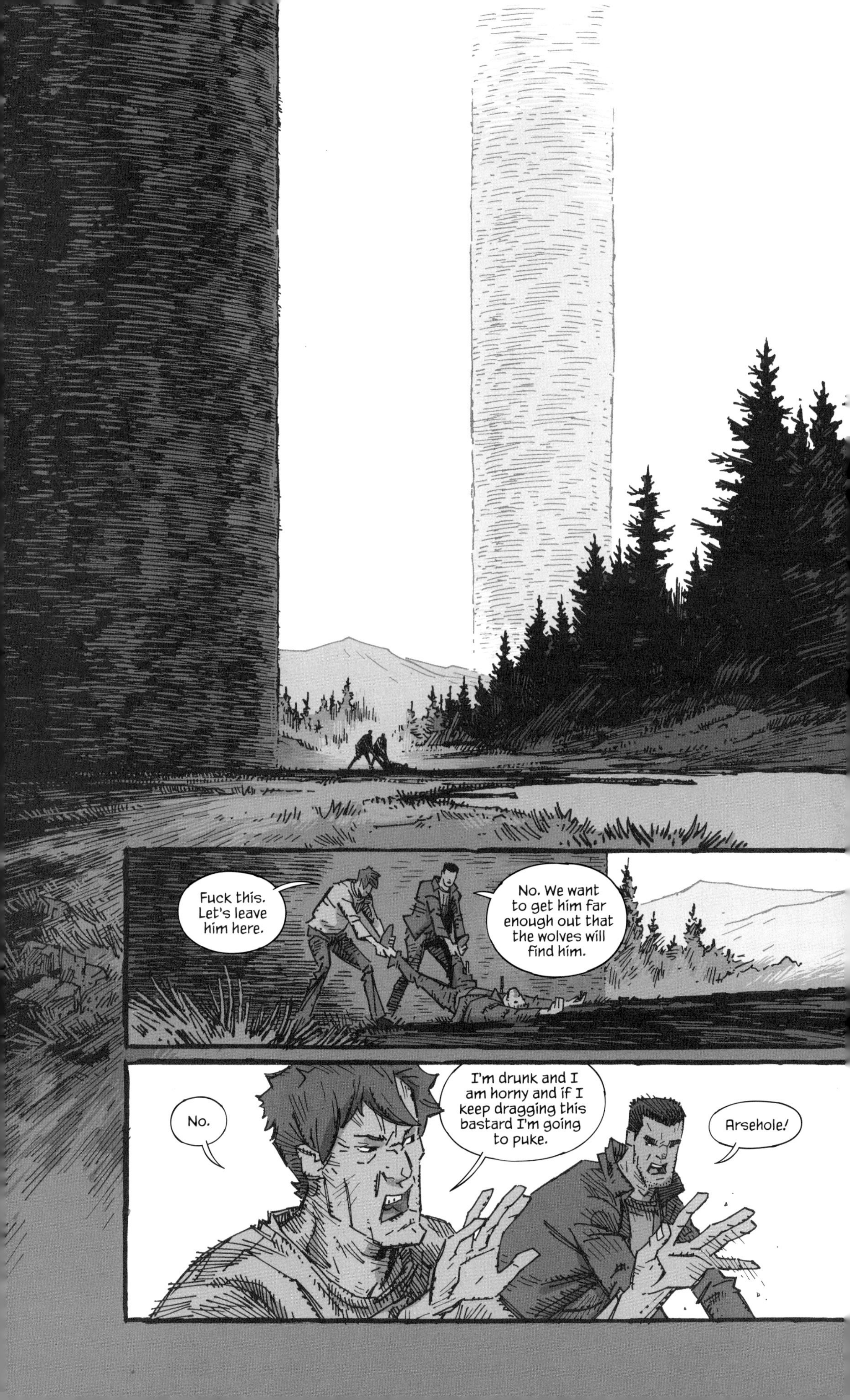
Fuck this. Let's leave him here.
No. We want to get him far enough out that the wolves will find him.
No.
I'm drunk and I am horny and if I keep dragging this bastard I'm going to puke.
Arsehole!

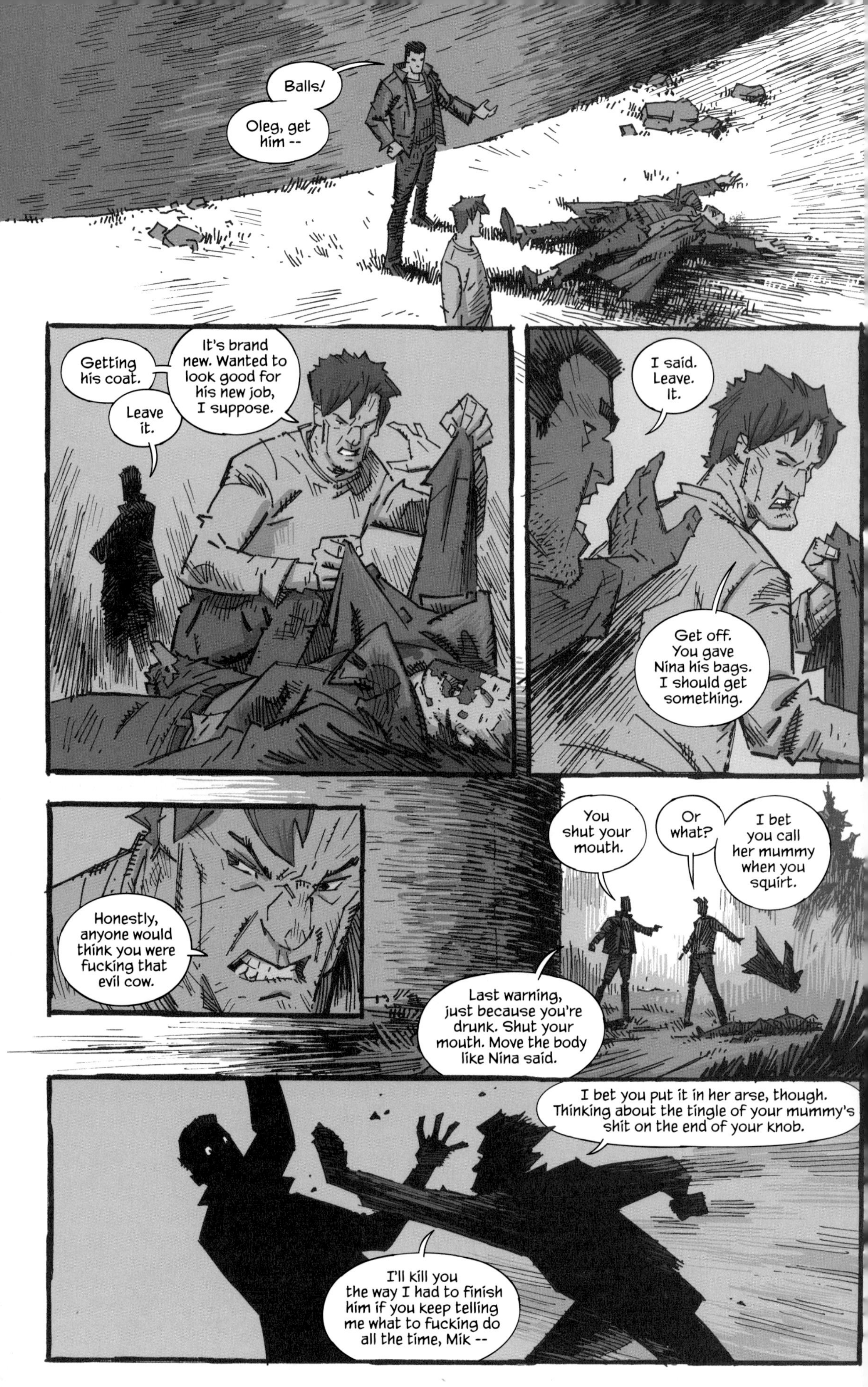

Balls!
Oleg, get him --
Getting his coat.
It's brand new. Wanted to look good for his new job, I suppose.
Leave it.
I said. Leave. It.
Get off. You gave Nina his bags. I should get something.
Honestly, anyone would think you were fucking that evil cow.
You shut your mouth.
Or what?
I bet you call her mummy when you squirt.
Last warning, just because you're drunk. Shut your mouth. Move the body like Nina said.
I bet you put it in her arse, though. Thinking about the tingle of your mummy's shit on the end of your knob.
I'll kill you the way I had to finish him if you keep telling me what to fucking do all the time, Mik --

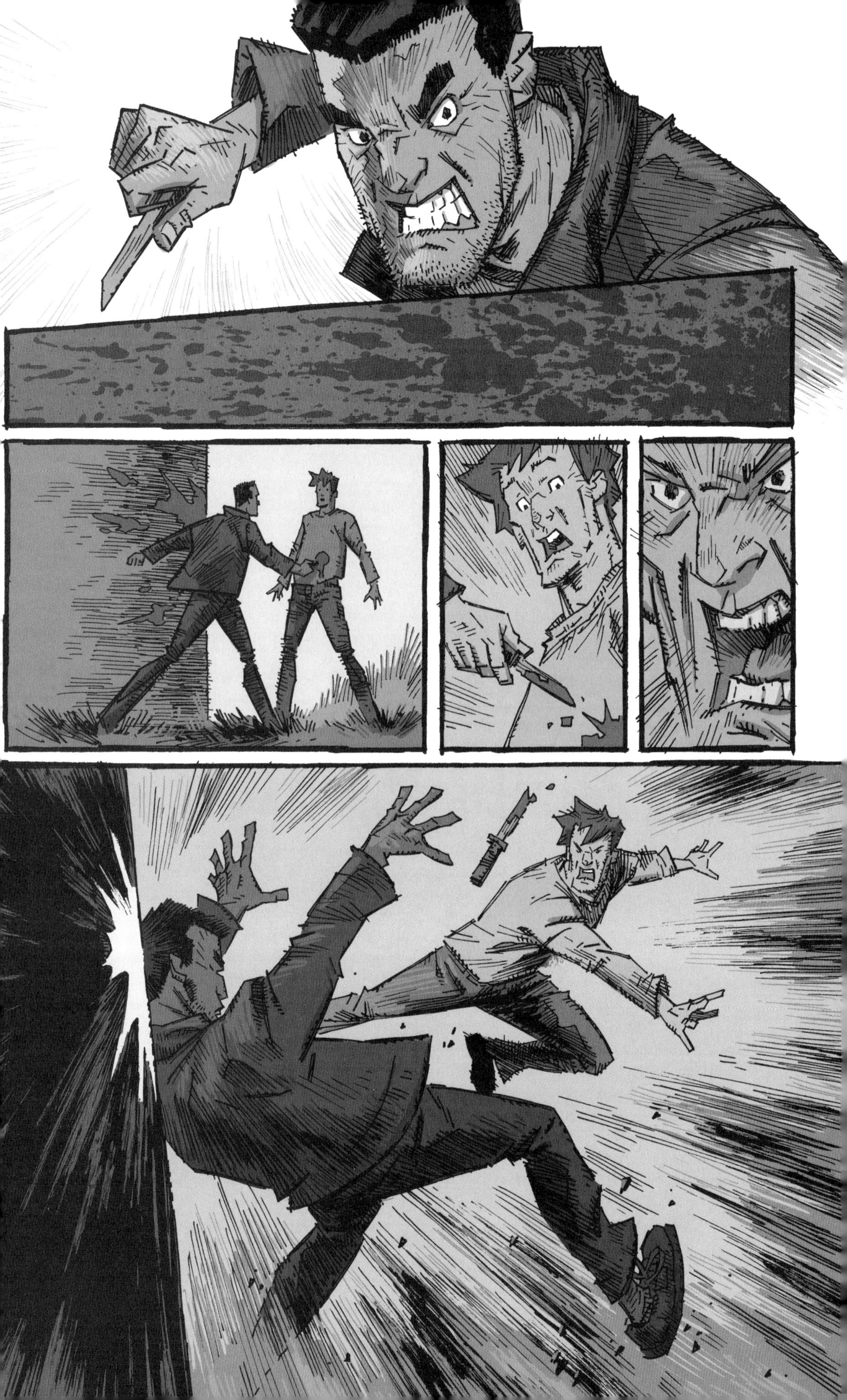

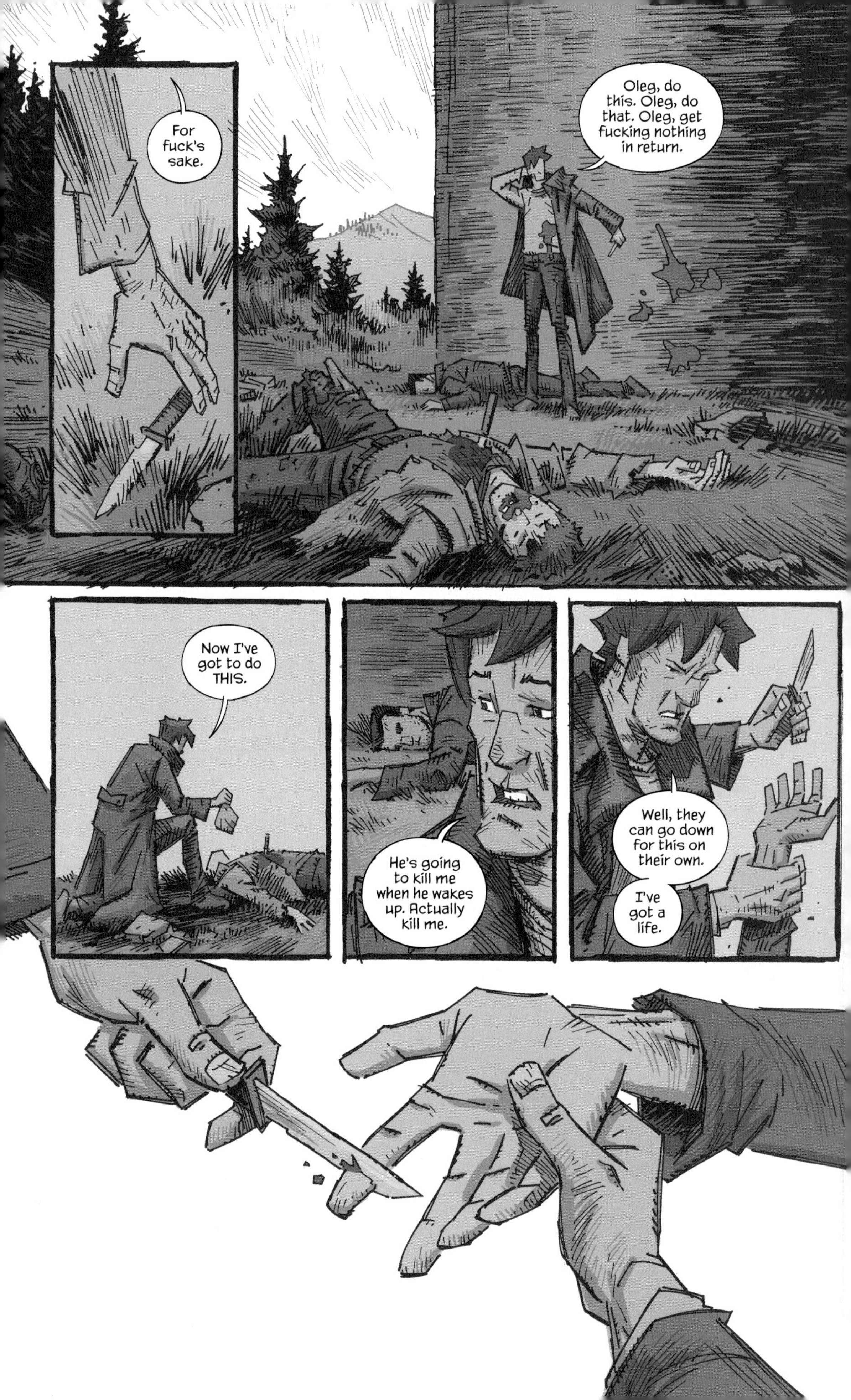
For fuck's sake.
Oleg, do this. Oleg, do that. Oleg, get fucking nothing in return.
Now I've got to do THIS.
He's going to kill me when he wakes up. Actually kill me.
Well, they can go down for this on their own.
I've got a life.

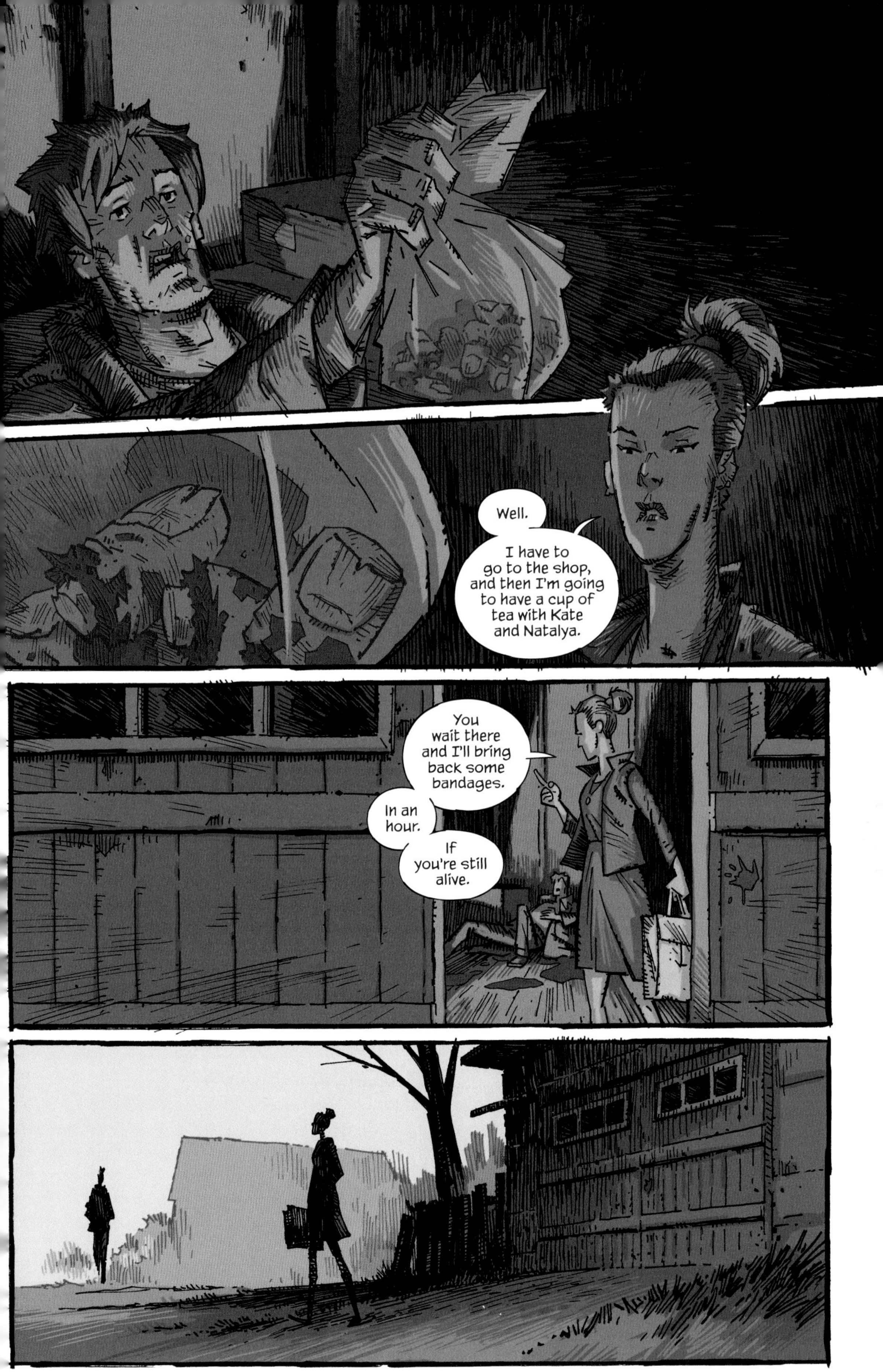
Well.
I have to go to the shop, and then I'm going to have a cup of tea with Kate and Natalya.
You wait there and I'll bring back some bandages.
In an hour.
If you're still alive.

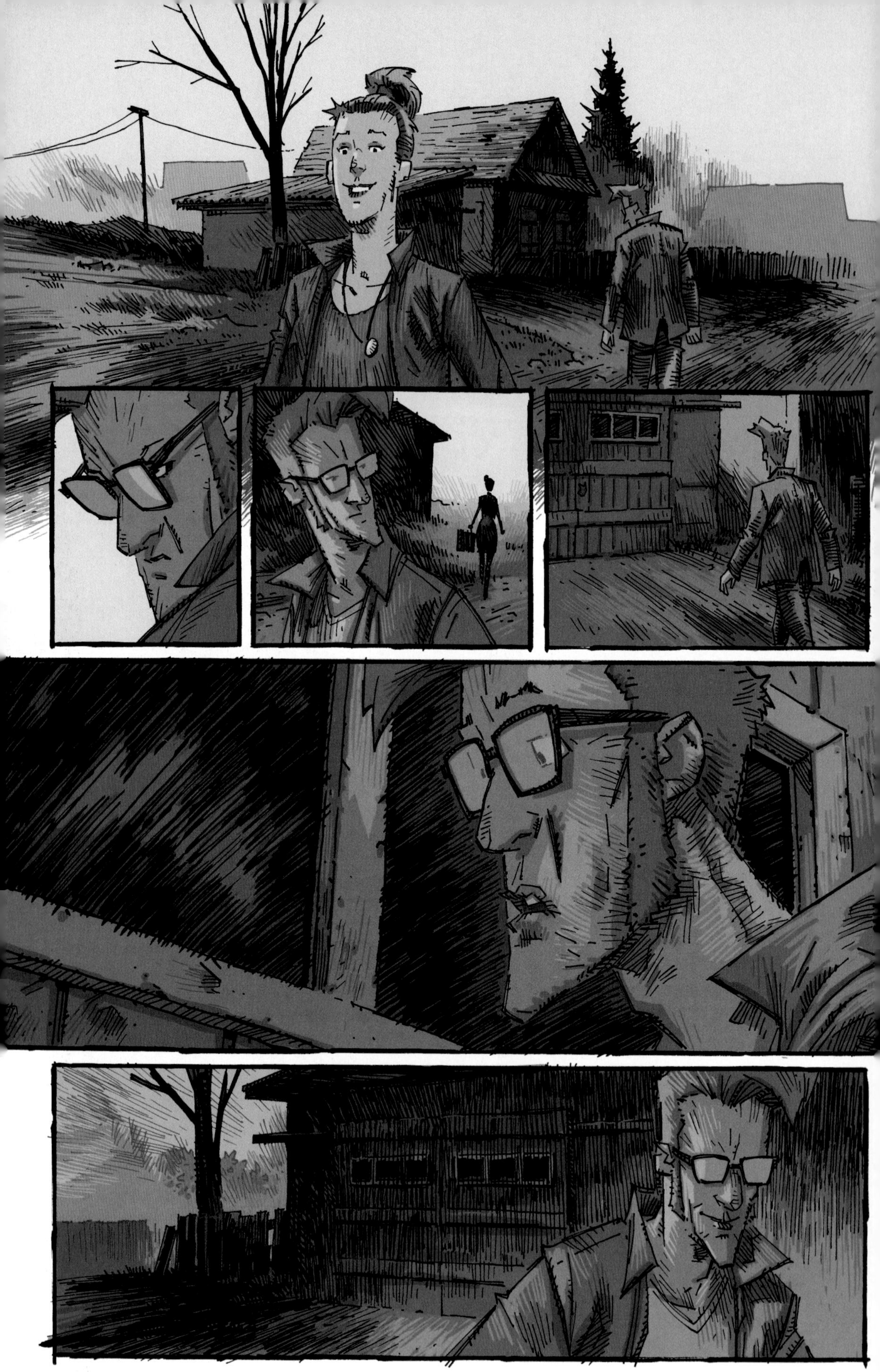

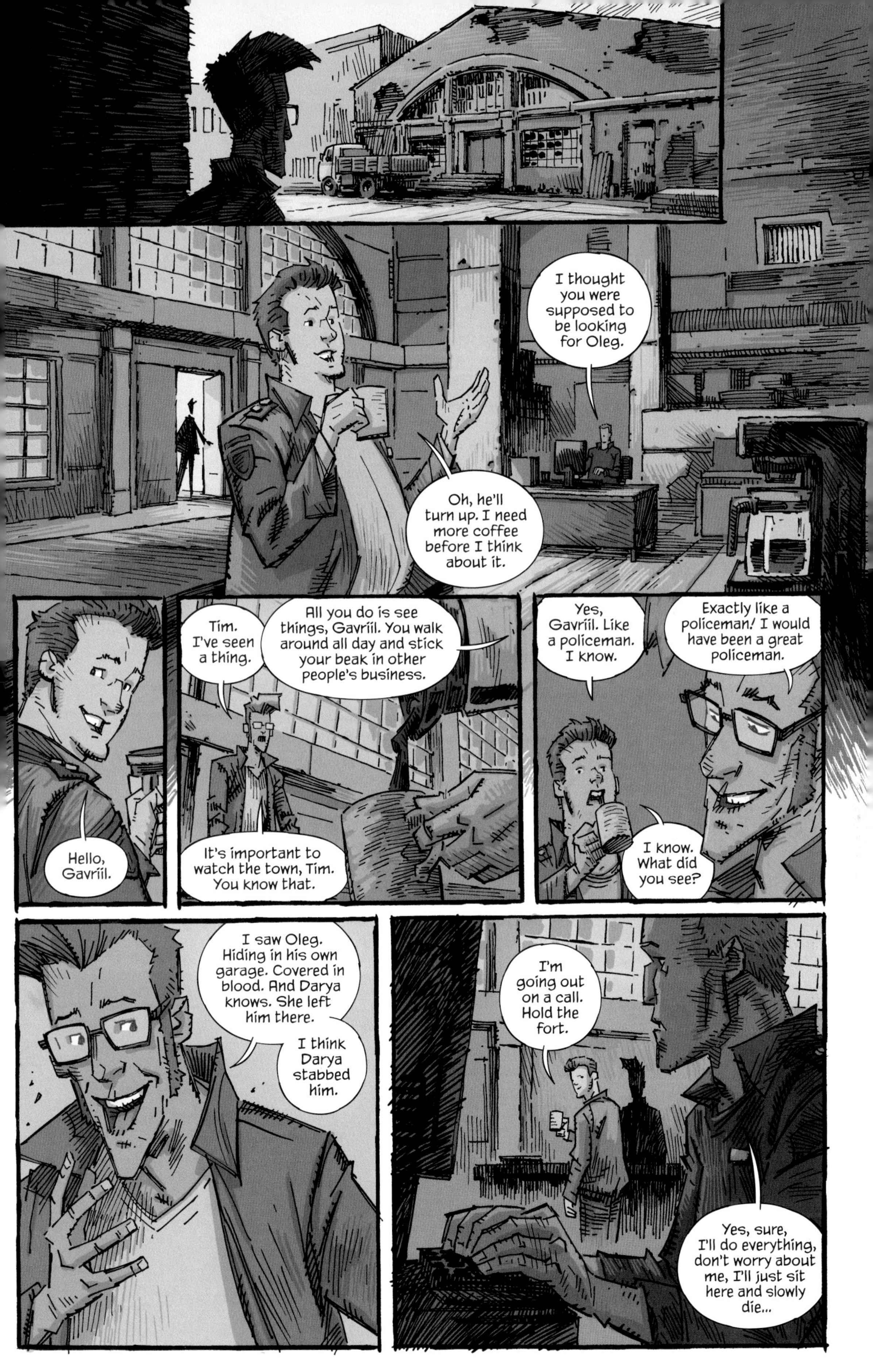
I thought you were supposed to be looking for Oleg.
Oh, he'll turn up. I need more coffee before I think about it.
Hello, Gavriil.
Tim. I've seen a thing.
All you do is see things, Gavriil. You walk around all day and stick your beak in other people's business.
It's important to watch the town, Tim. You know that.
Yes, Gavriil. Like a policeman. I know.
Exactly like a policeman! I would have been a great policeman.
I know. What did you see?
I saw Oleg. Hiding in his own garage. Covered in blood. And Darya knows. She left him there.
I think Darya stabbed him.
I'm going out on a call. Hold the fort.
Yes, sure, I'll do everything, don't worry about me, I'll just sit here and slowly die...

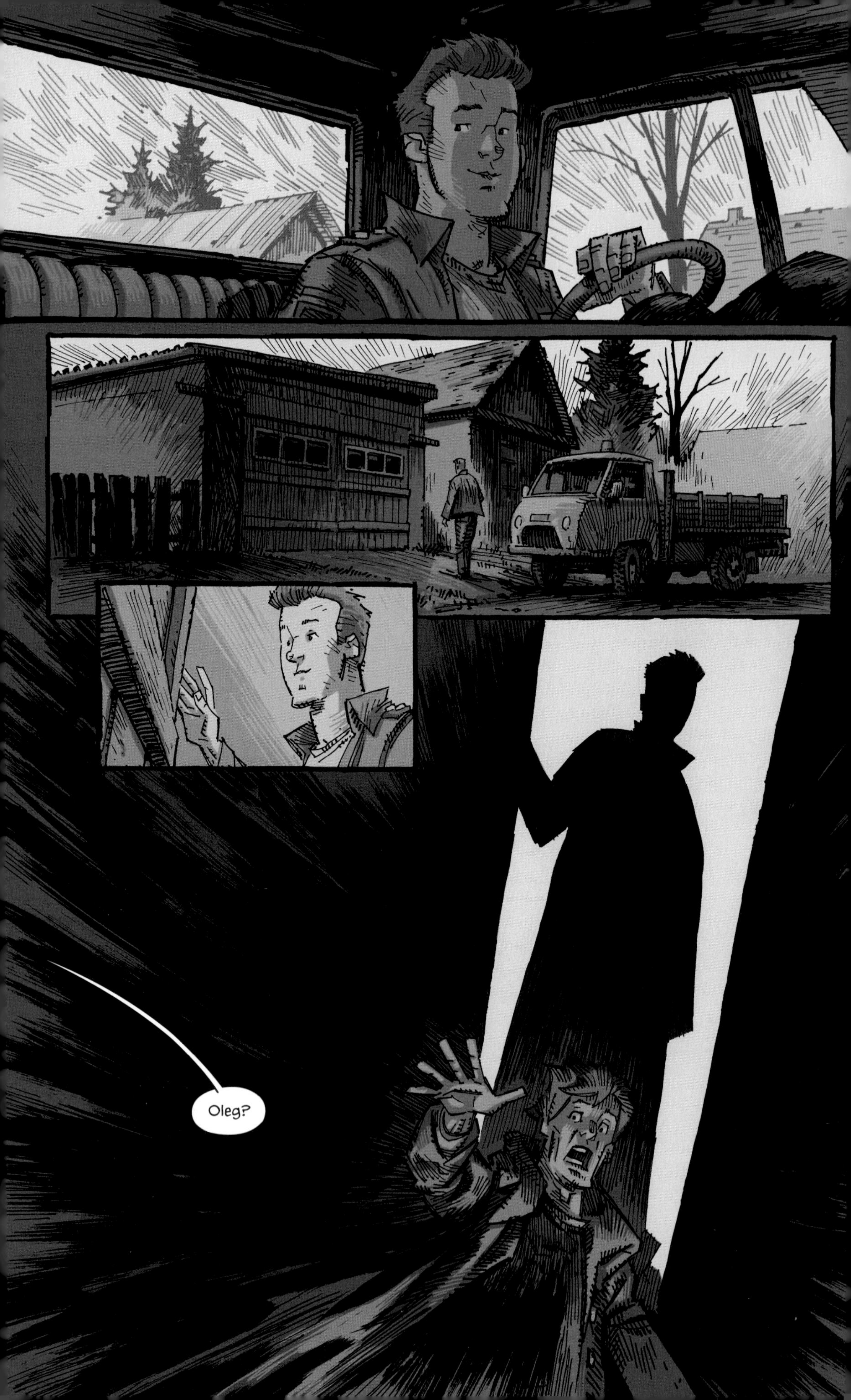
Oleg?

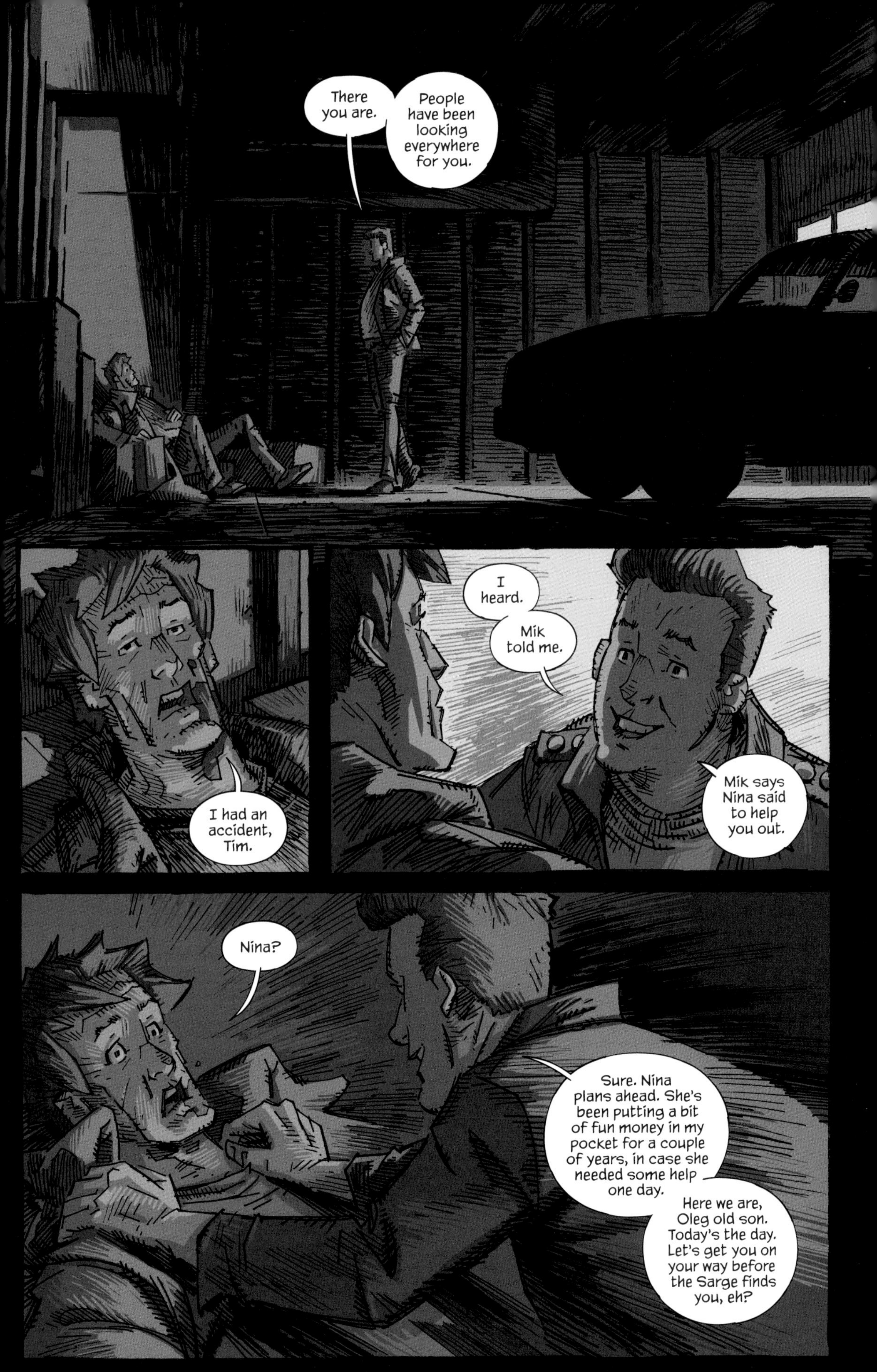
There you are.
People have been looking everywhere for you.
I had an accident, Tim.
I heard.
Mik told me.
Mik says Nina said to help you out.
Nina?
Sure. Nina plans ahead. She's been putting a bit of fun money in my pocket for a couple of years, in case she needed some help one day.
Here we are, Oleg old son. Today's the day. Let's get you on your way before the Sarge finds you, eh?

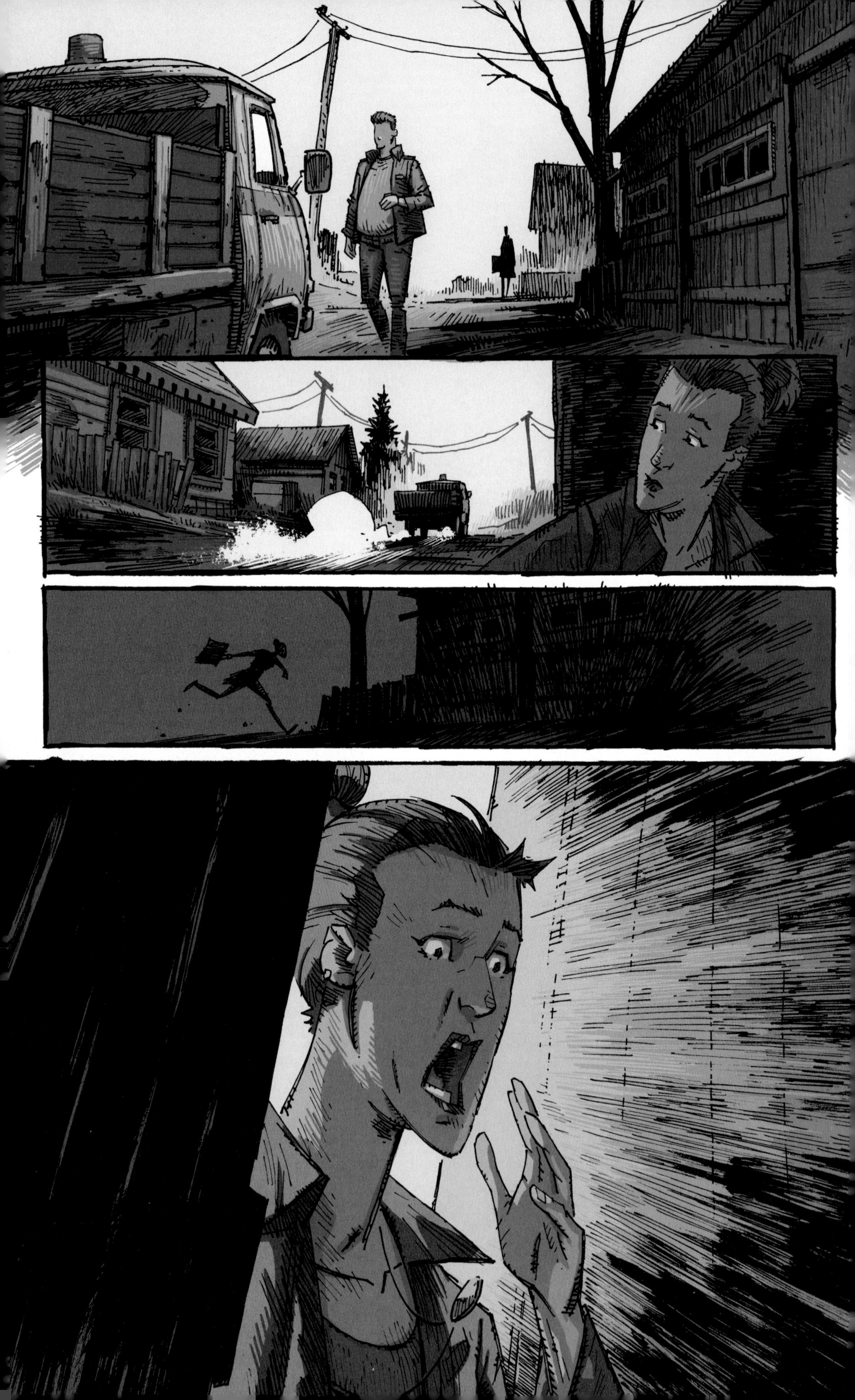

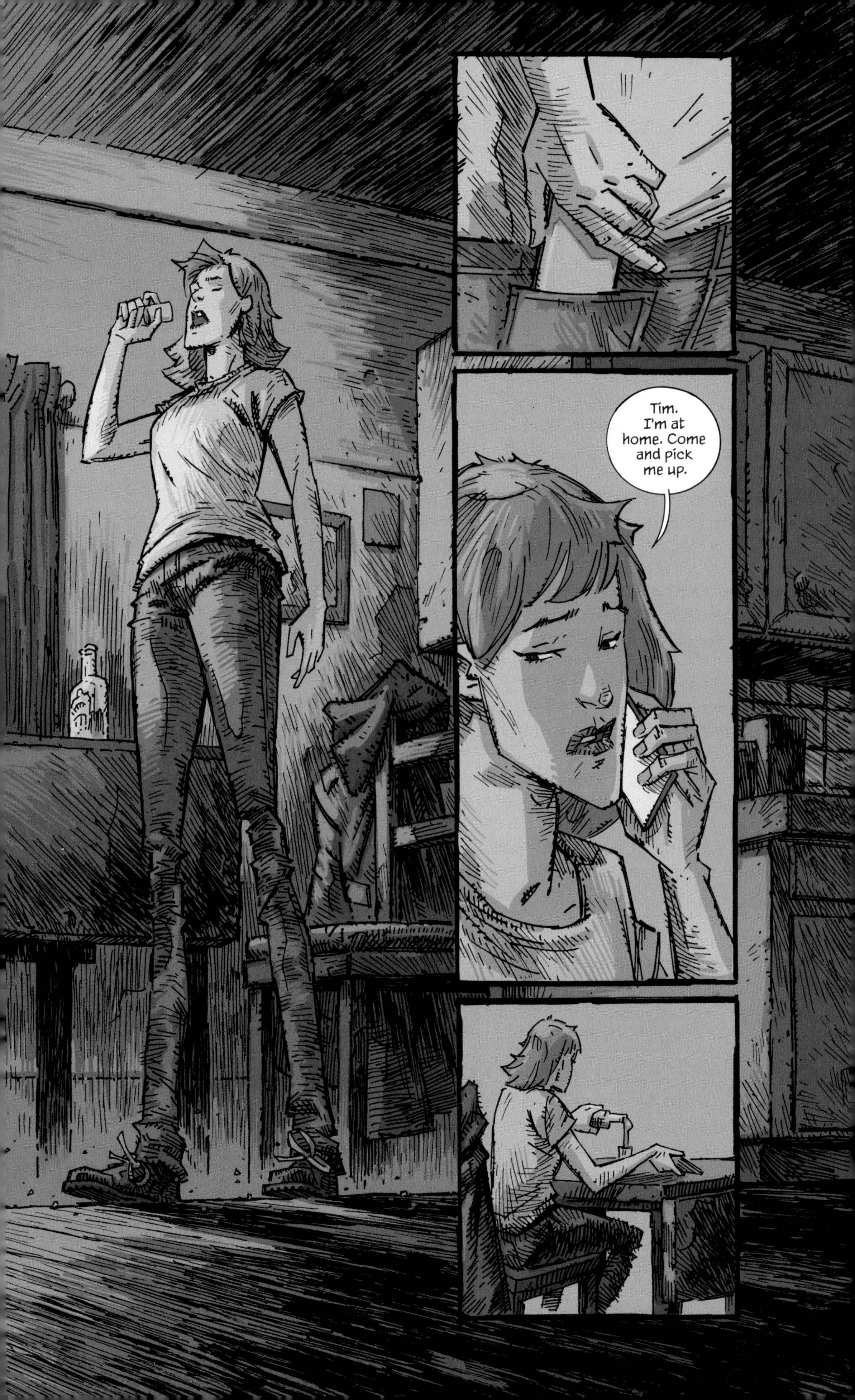
Tim. I'm at home. Come and pick me up.

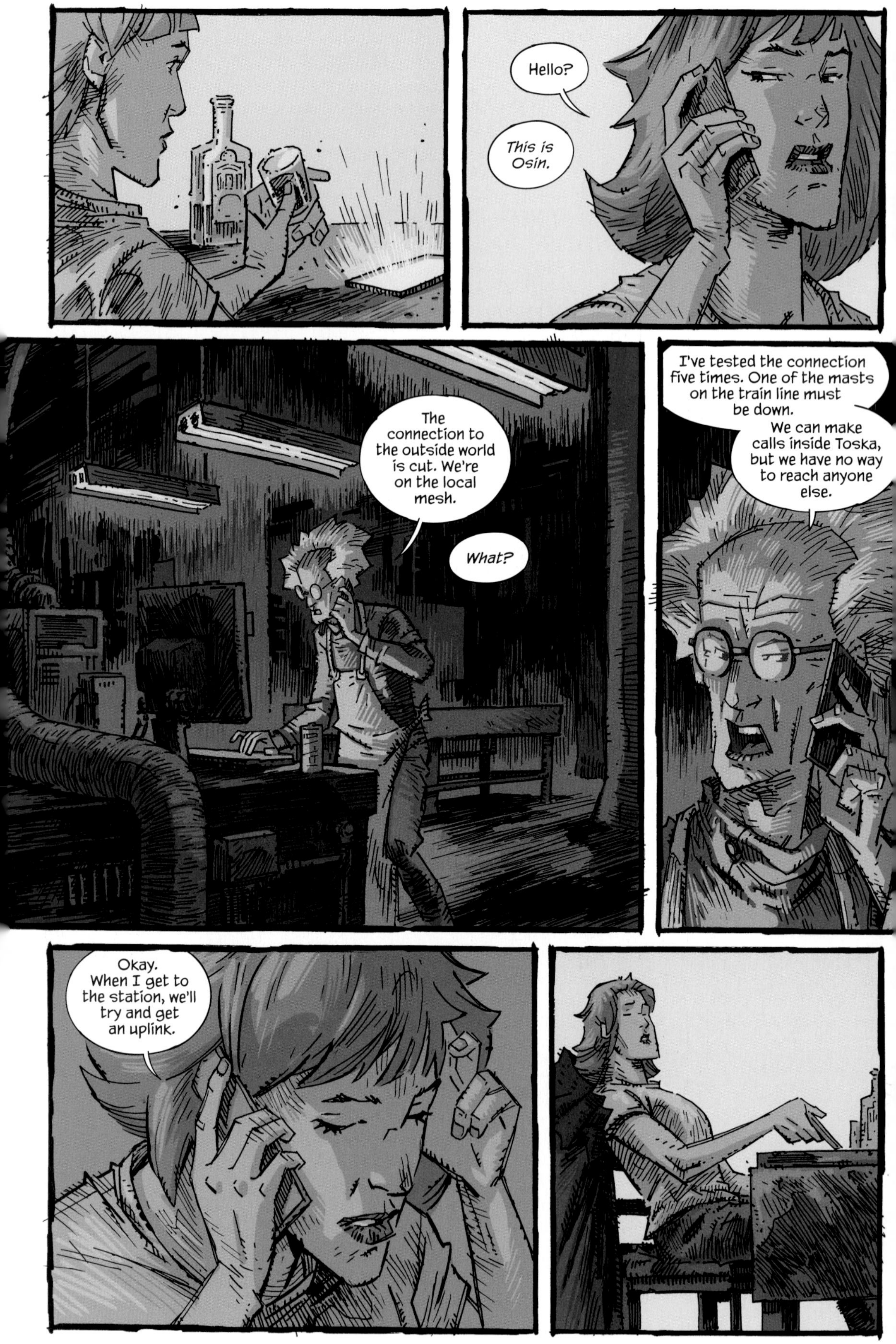
Hello?
This is Osin.
The connection to the outside world is cut. We're on the local mesh.
What?
I've tested the connection five times. One of the masts on the train line must be down.
We can make calls inside Toska, but we have no way to reach anyone else.
Okay. When I get to the station, we'll try and get an uplink.

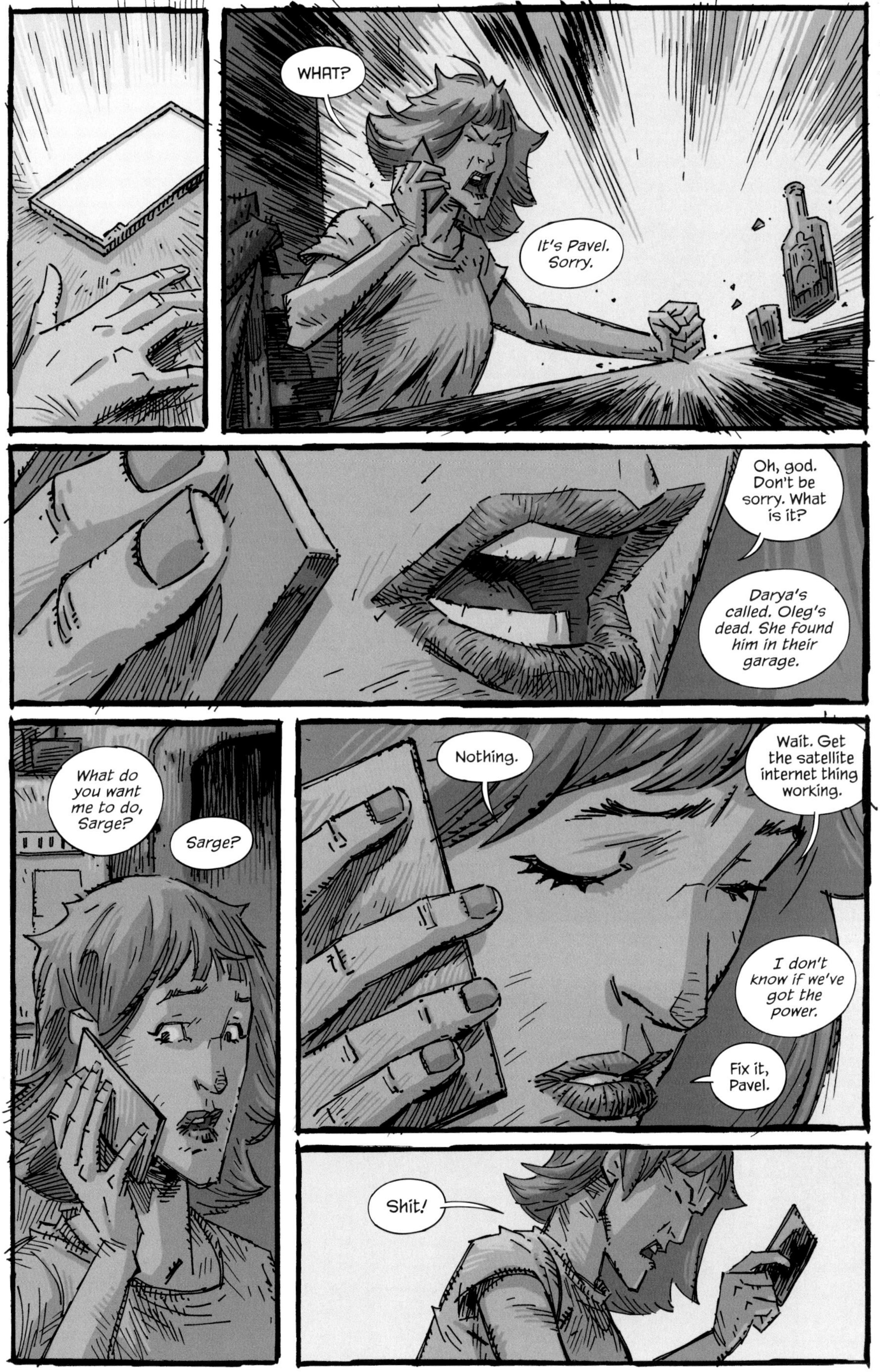
WHAT?
It's Pavel. Sorry.
Oh, god. Don't be sorry. What is it?
Darya's called. Oleg's dead. She found him in their garage.
What do you want me to do, Sarge?
Sarge?
Nothing.
Wait. Get the satellite internet thing working.
I don't know if we've got the power.
Fix it, Pavel.
Shit!

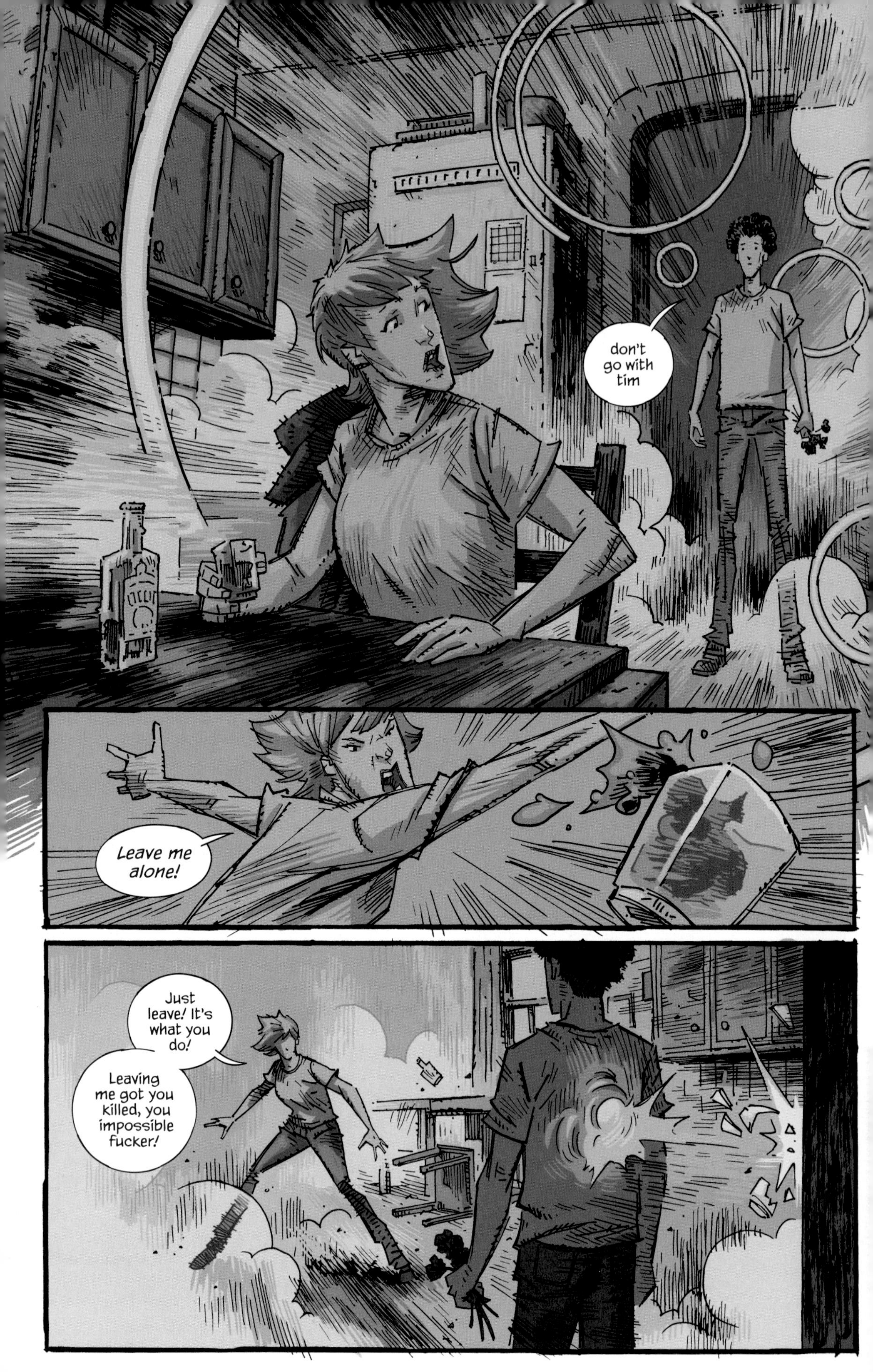
don't go with tim
Leave me alone!
Just leave! It's what you do!
Leaving me got you killed, you impossible fucker!

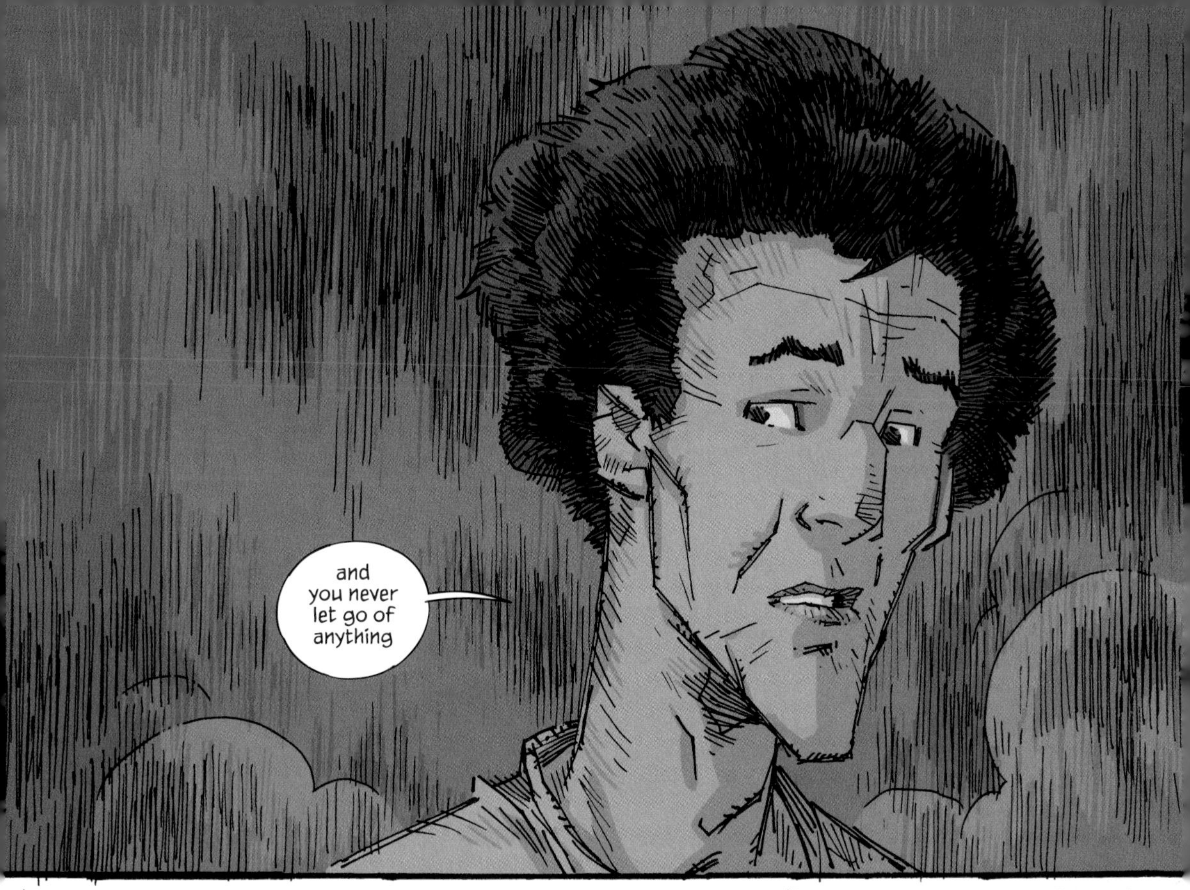
and you never let go of anything

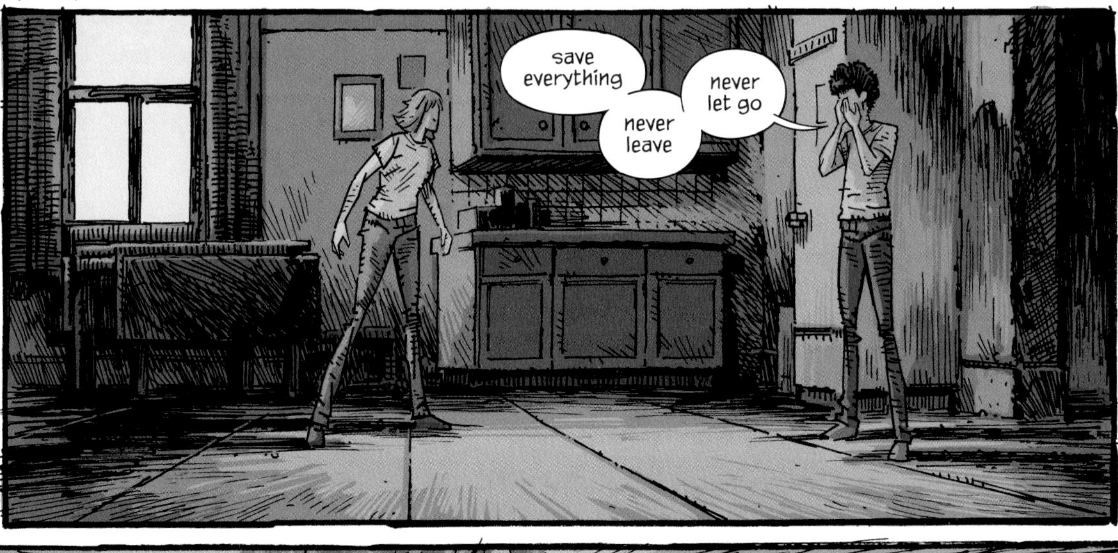
save everything
never leave
never let go

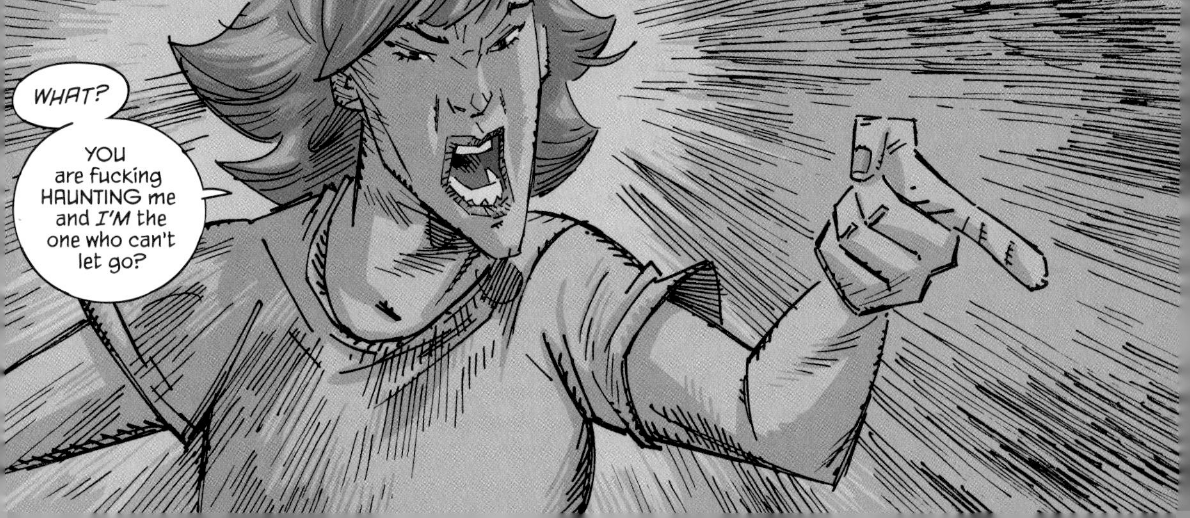
WHAT?
YOU are fucking HAUNTING me and I'M the one who can't let go?

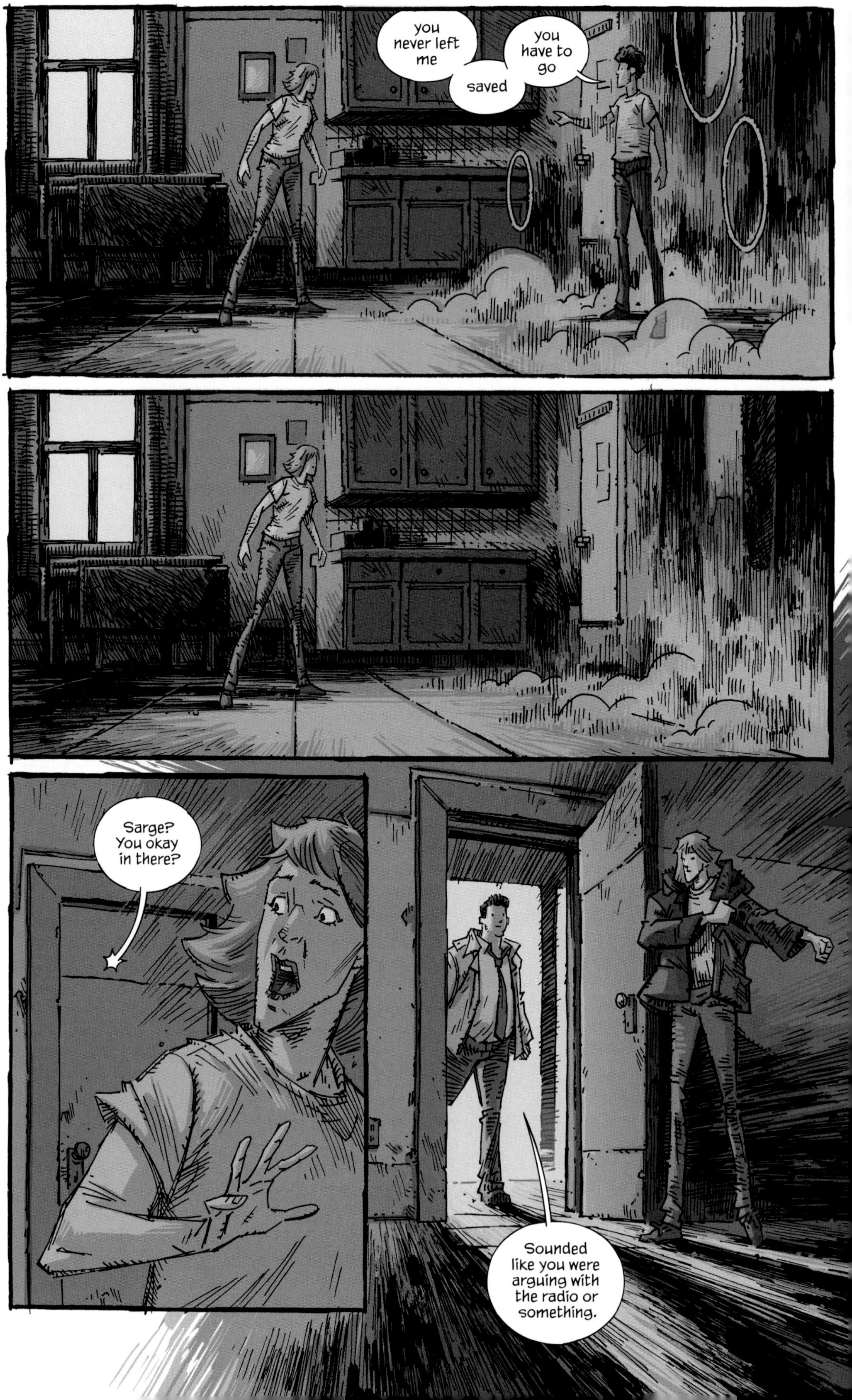
you never left me
saved
you have to go
Sarge? You okay in there?
Sounded like you were arguing with the radio or something.

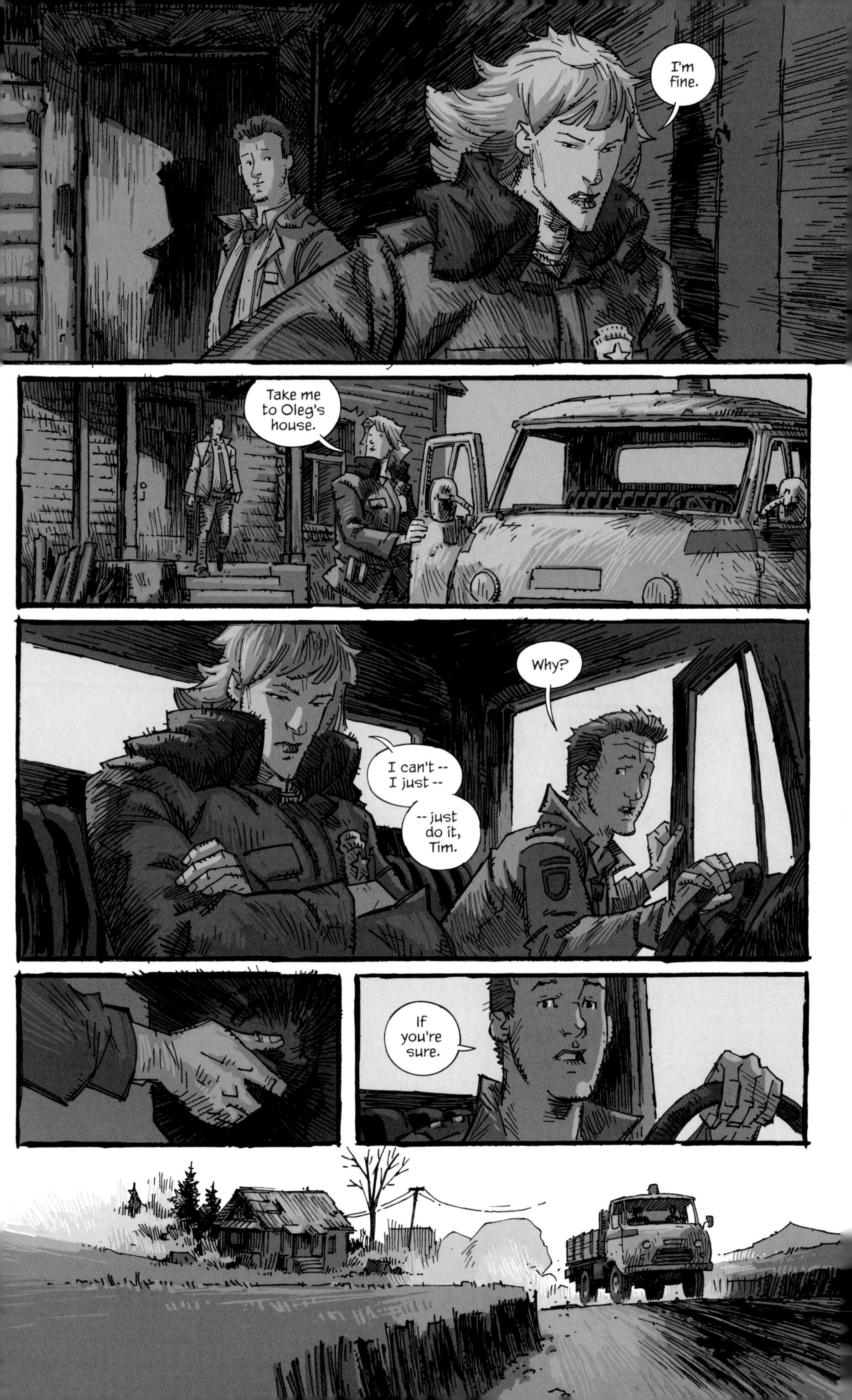
I'm fine.
Take me to Oleg's house.
Why?
I can't -- I just --
-- just do it, Tim.
If you're sure.

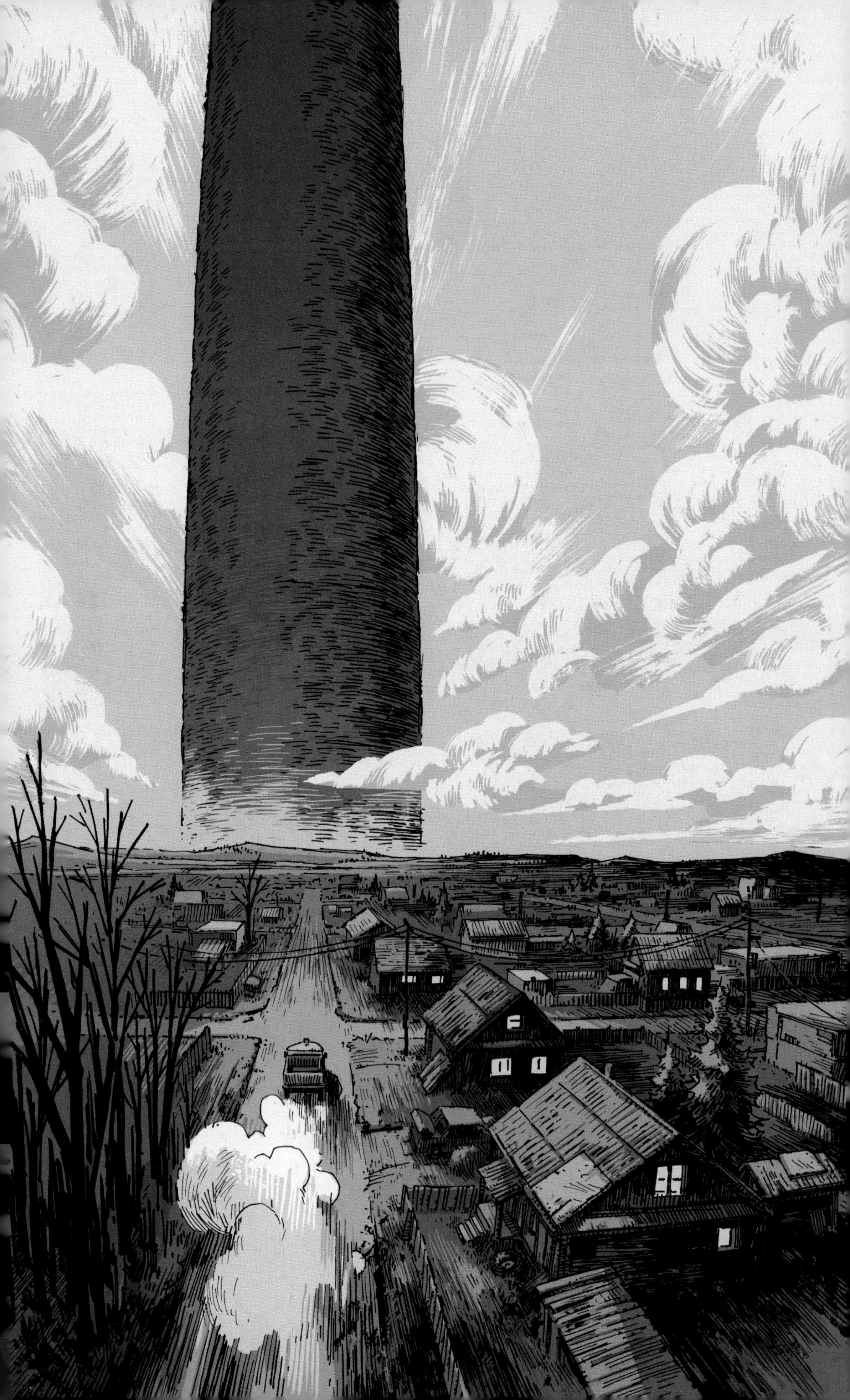

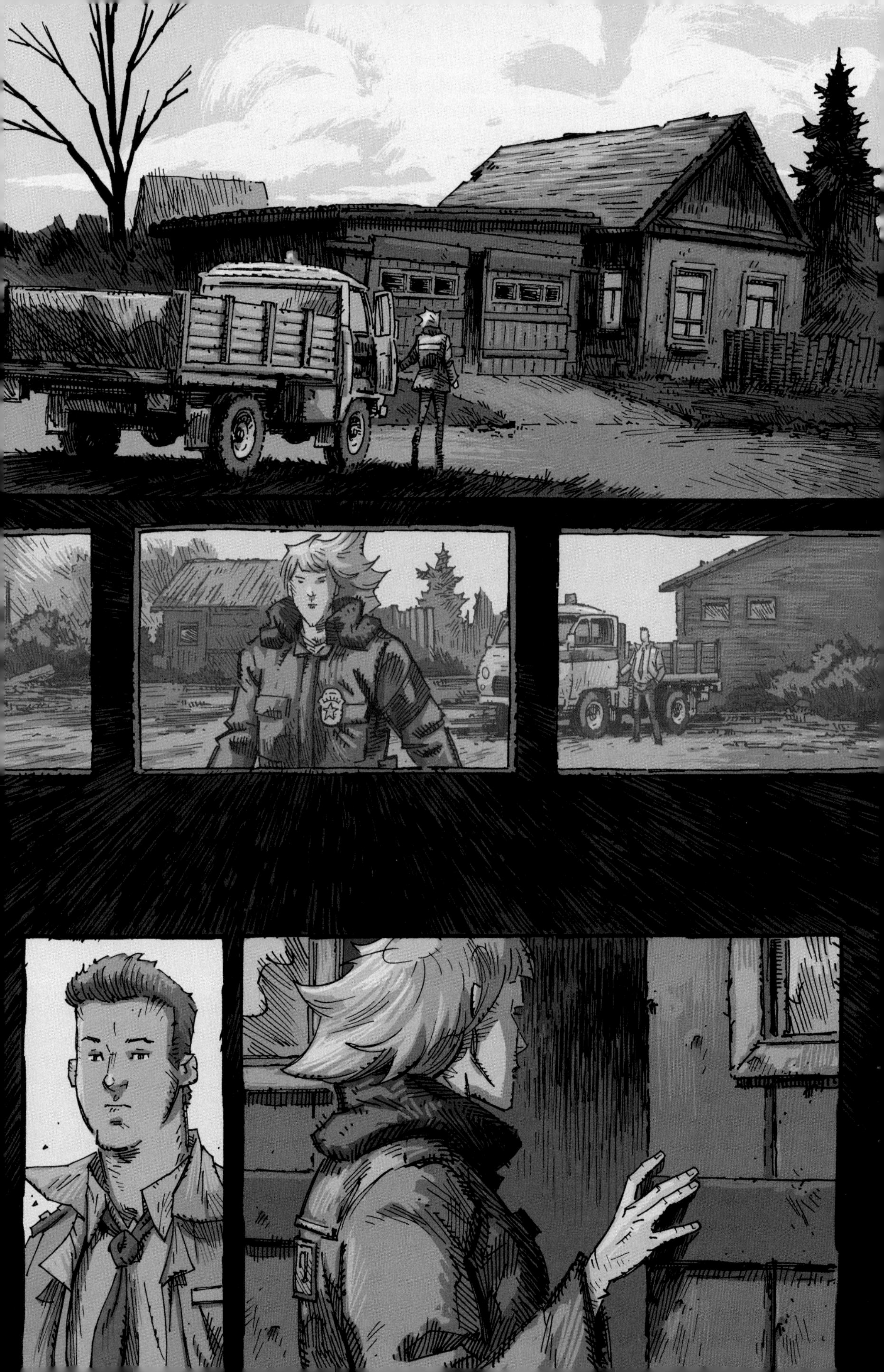

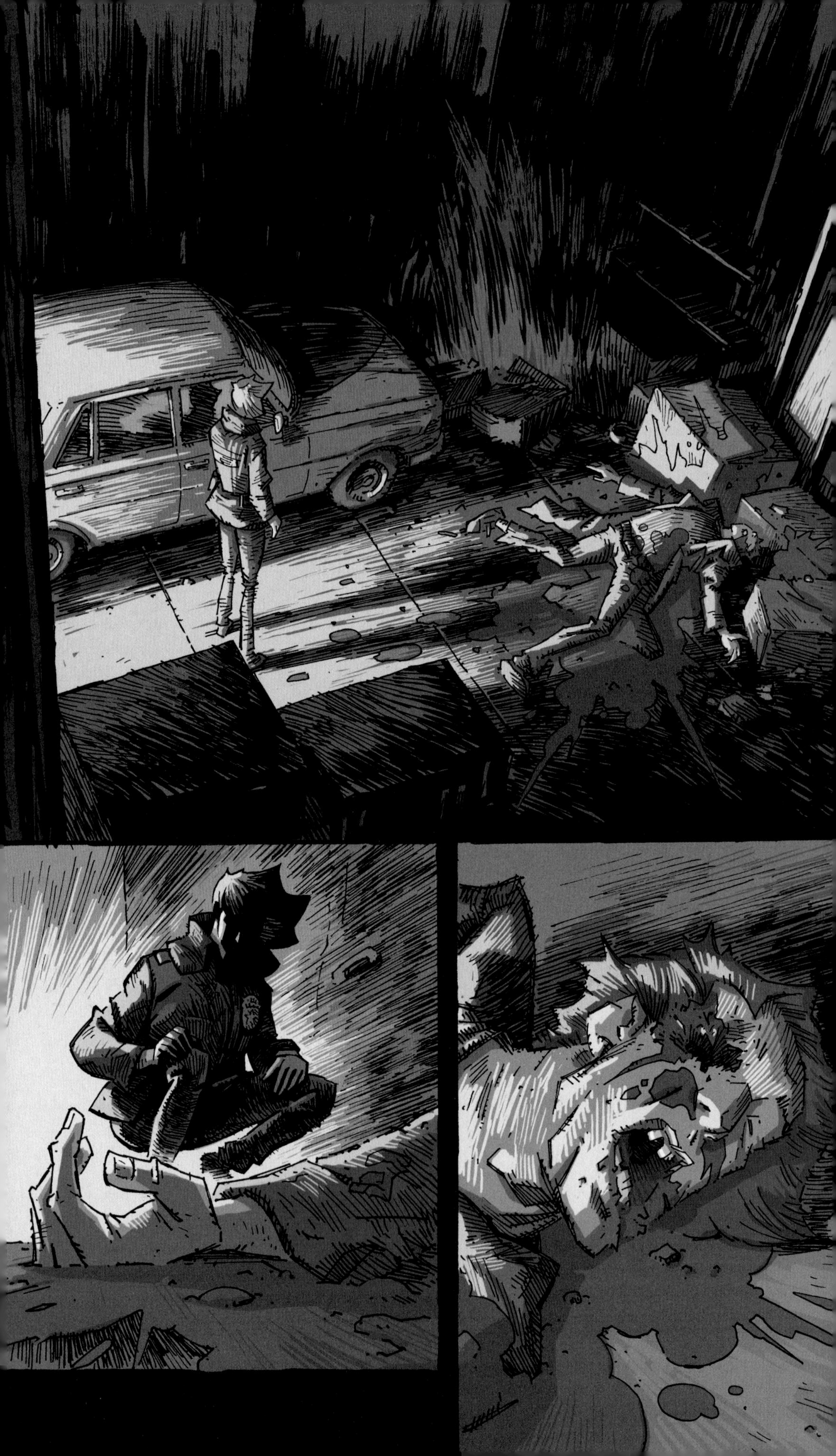

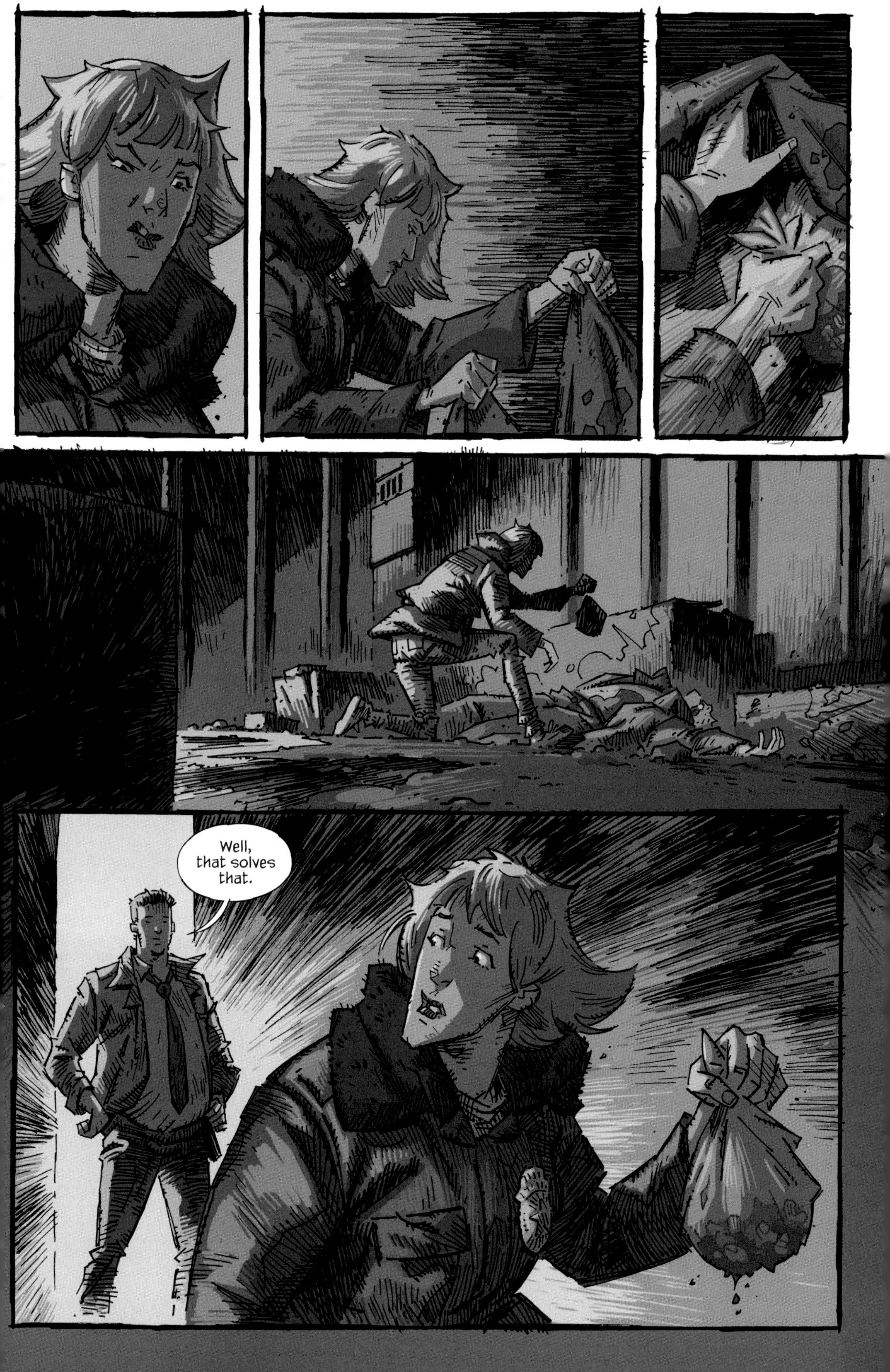
Well, that solves that.

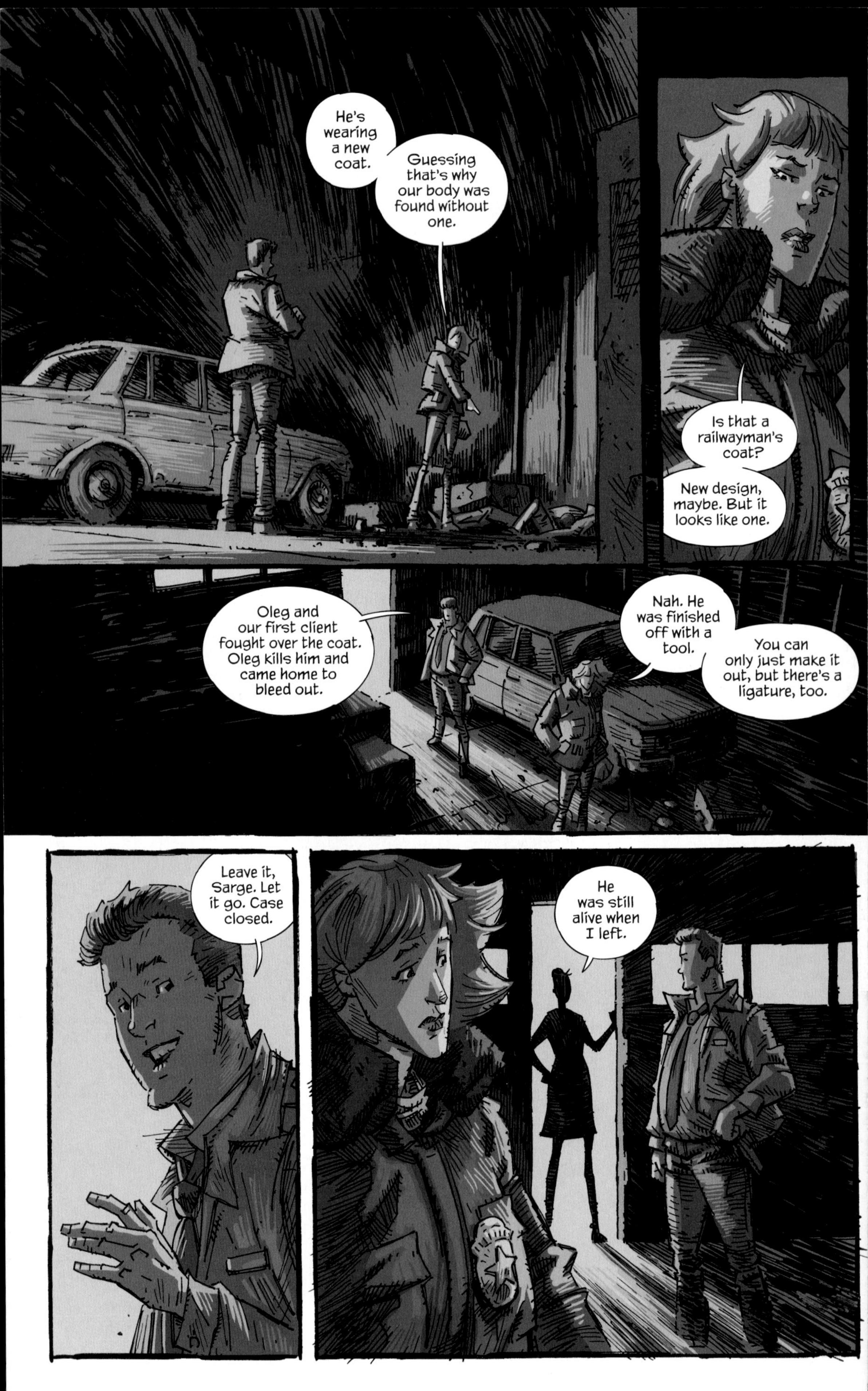
He's wearing a new coat.
Guessing that's why our body was found without one.
Is that a railwayman's coat?
New design, maybe. But it looks like one.
Oleg and our first client fought over the coat. Oleg kills him and came home to bleed out.
Nah. He was finished off with a tool.
You can only just make it out, but there's a ligature, too.
Leave it, Sarge. Let it go. Case closed.
He was still alive when I left.

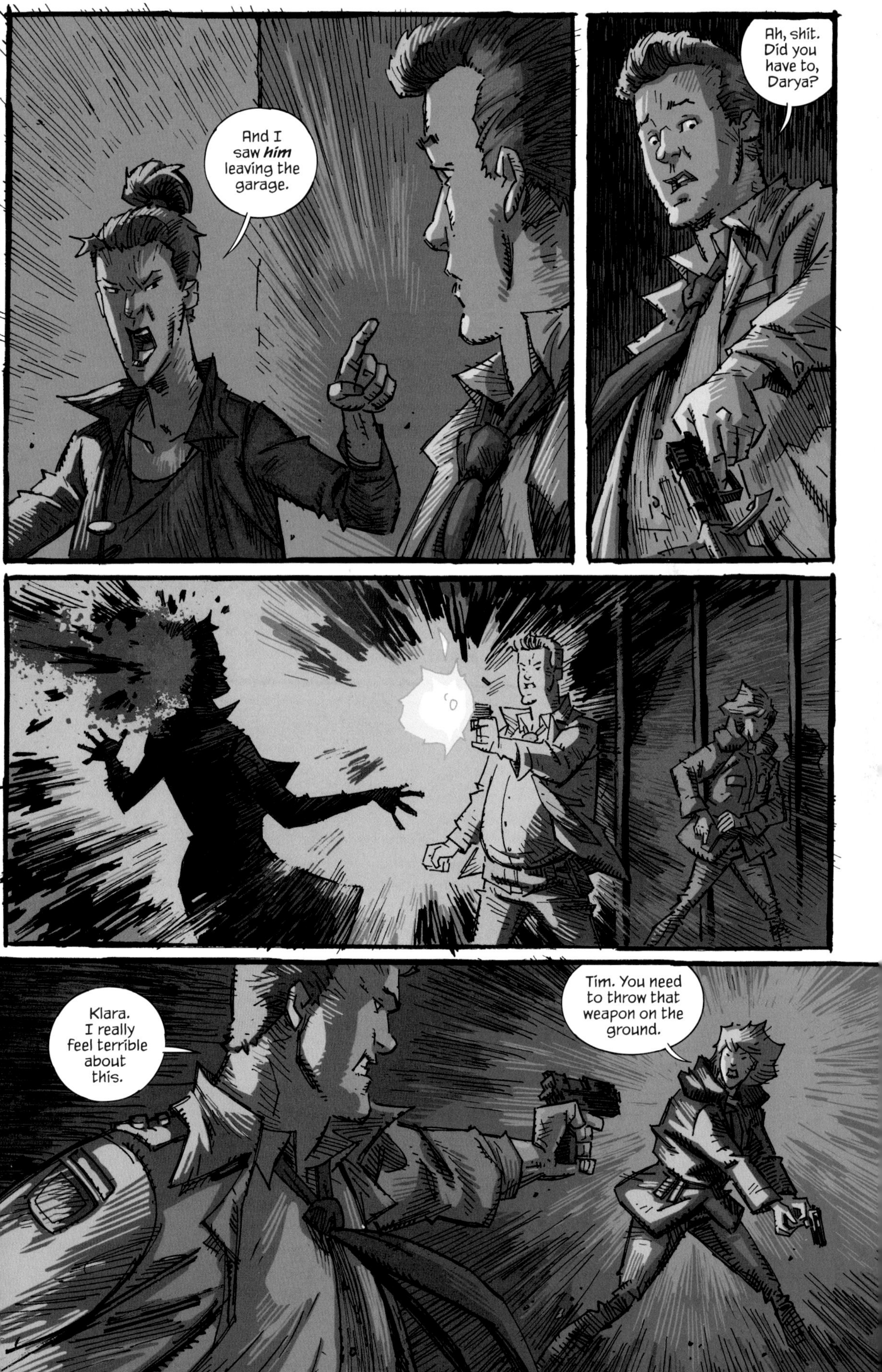
And I saw *him* leaving the garage.
Ah, shit. Did you have to, Darya?
Klara. I really feel terrible about this.
Tim. You need to throw that weapon on the ground.

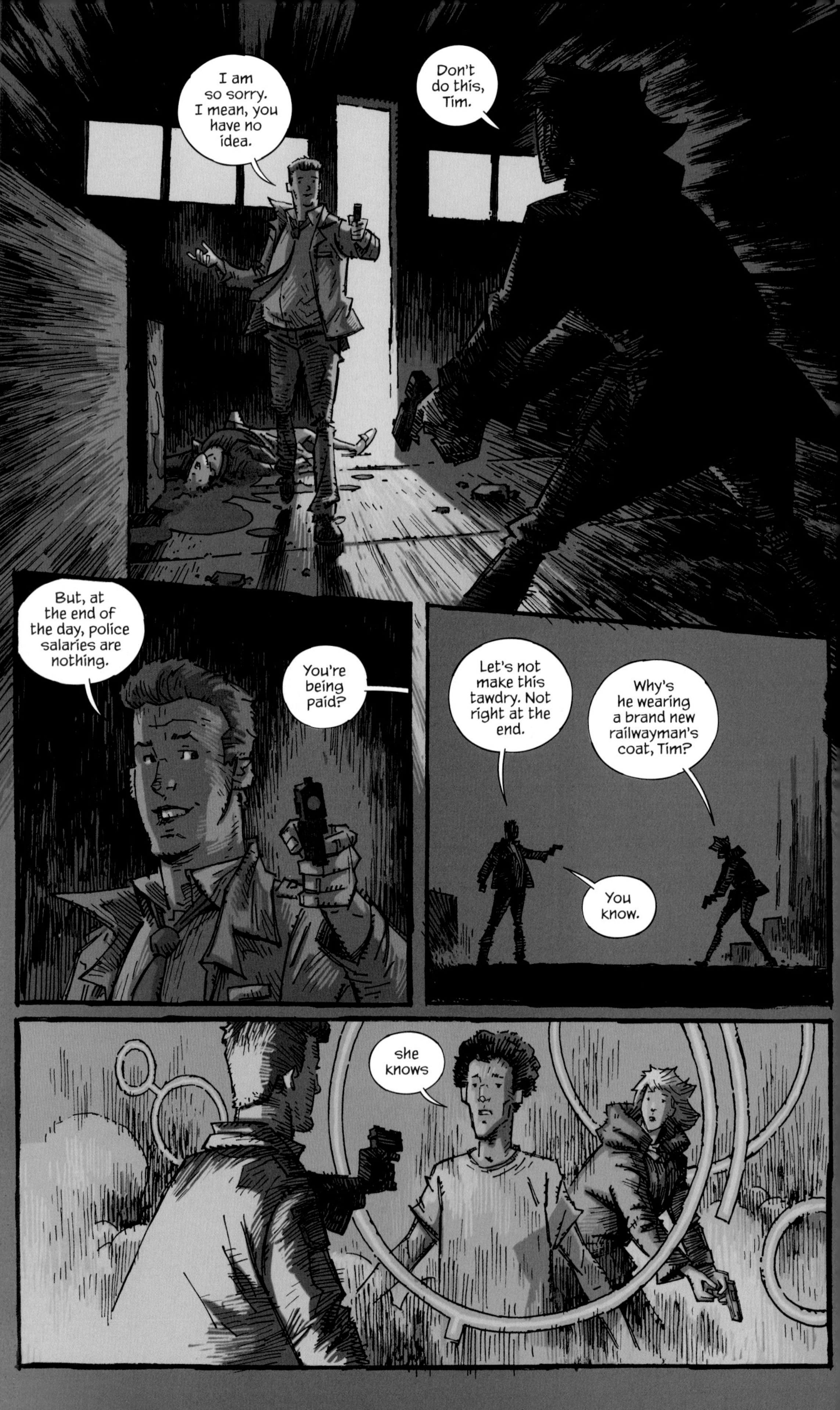
I am so sorry. I mean, you have no idea.
Don't do this, Tim.
But, at the end of the day, police salaries are nothing.
You're being paid?
Let's not make this tawdry. Not right at the end.
Why's he wearing a brand new railwayman's coat, Tim?
You know.
she knows

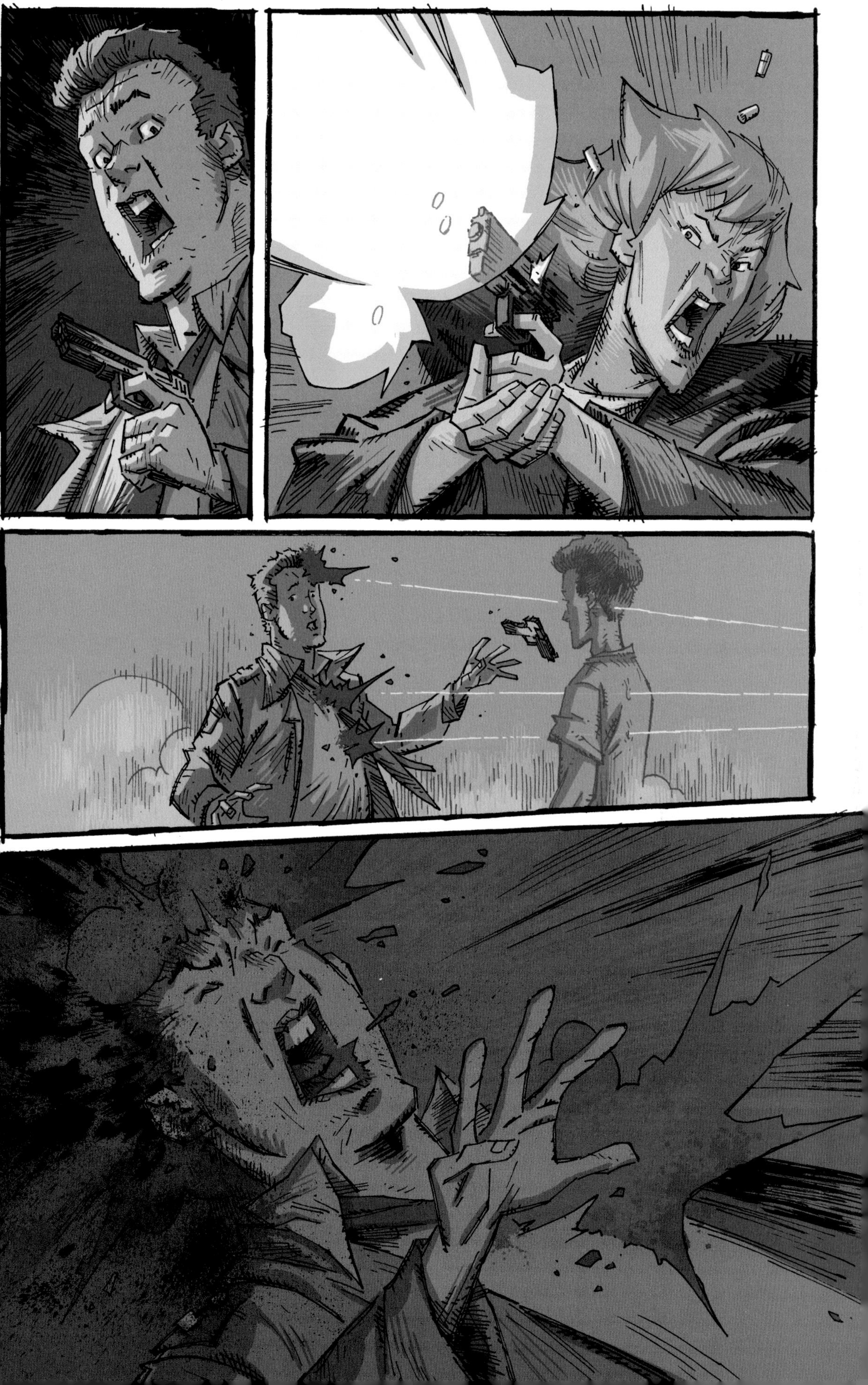

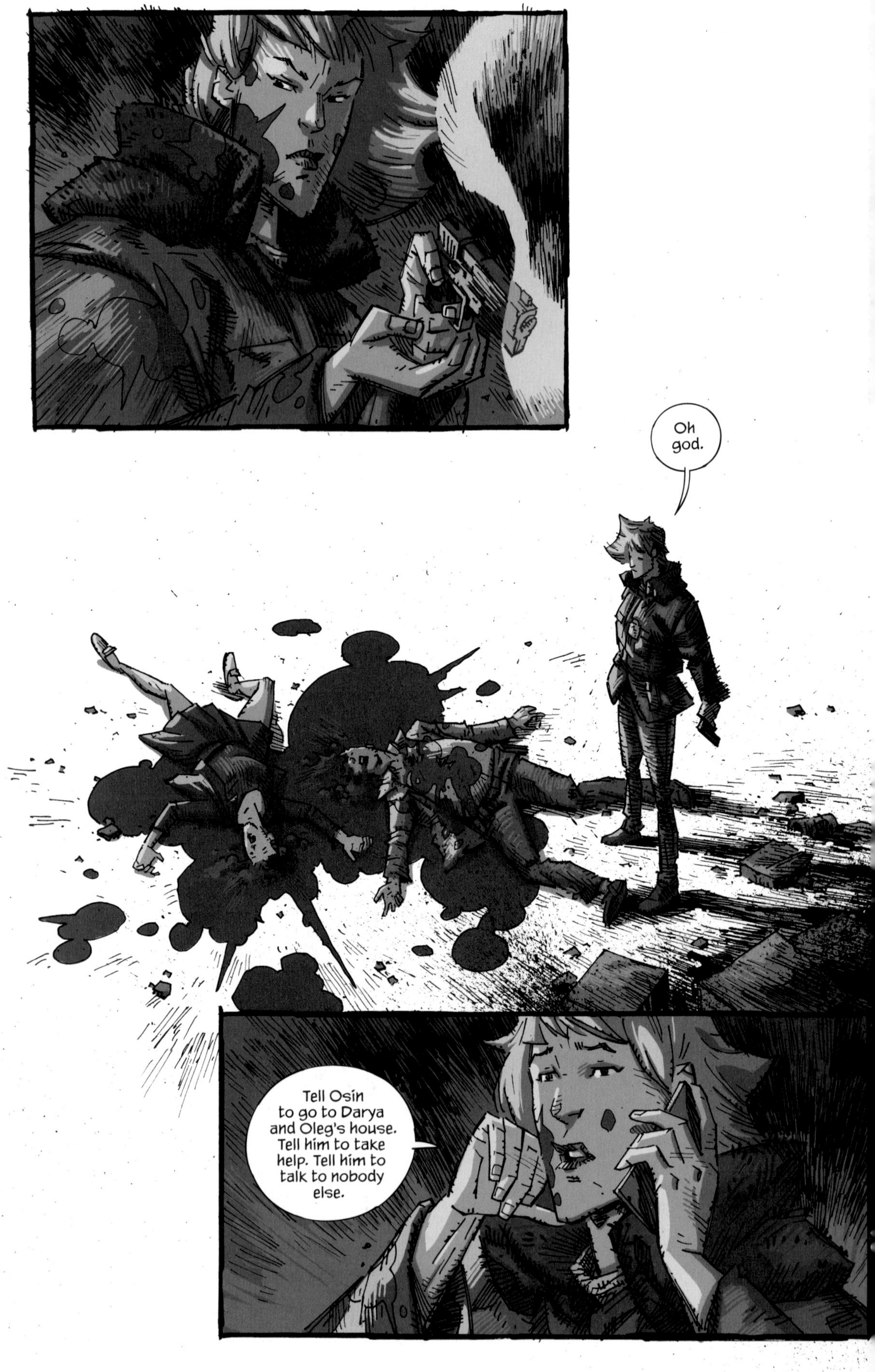
Oh god.
Tell Osín to go to Darya and Oleg's house. Tell him to take help. Tell him to talk to nobody else.

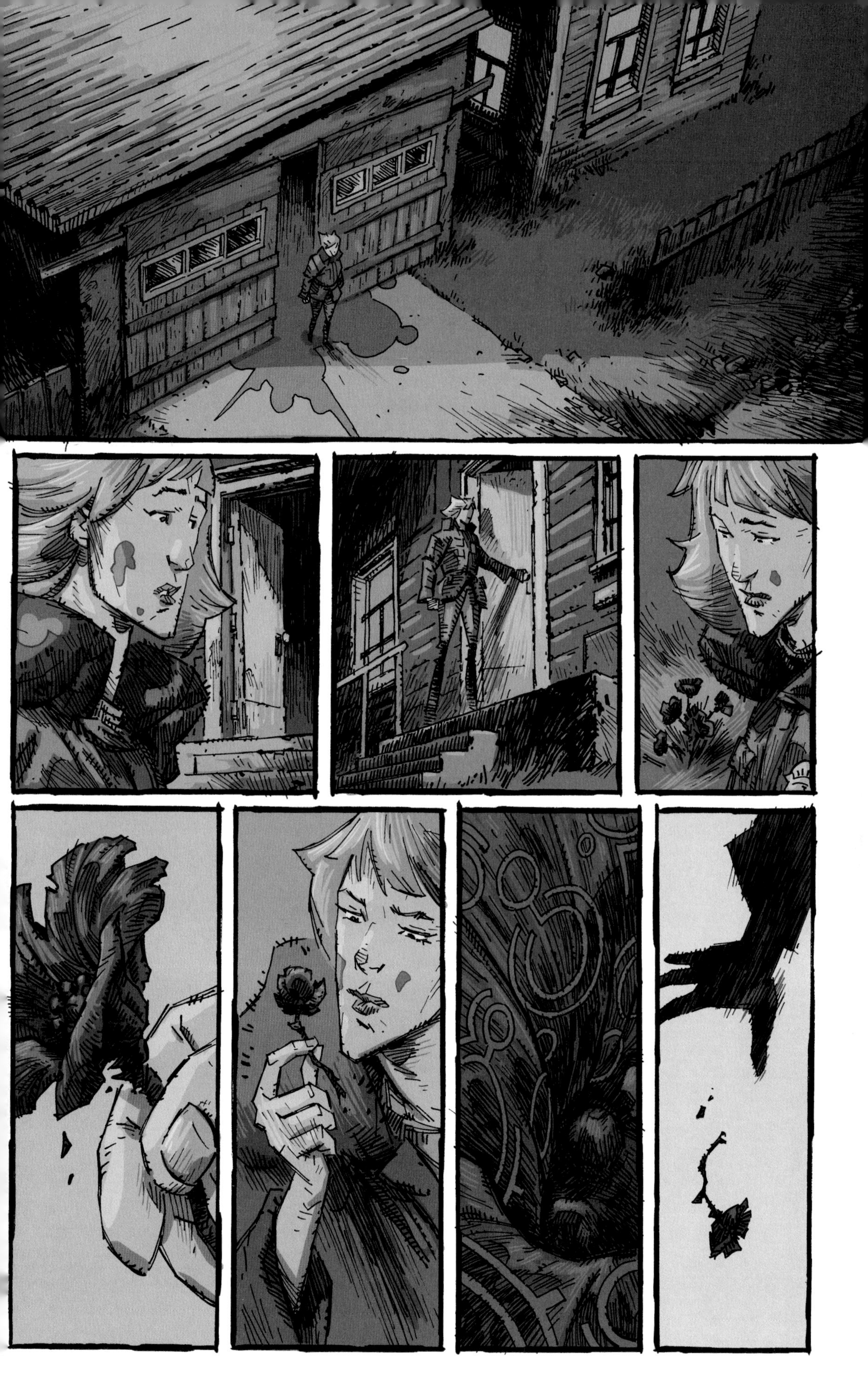

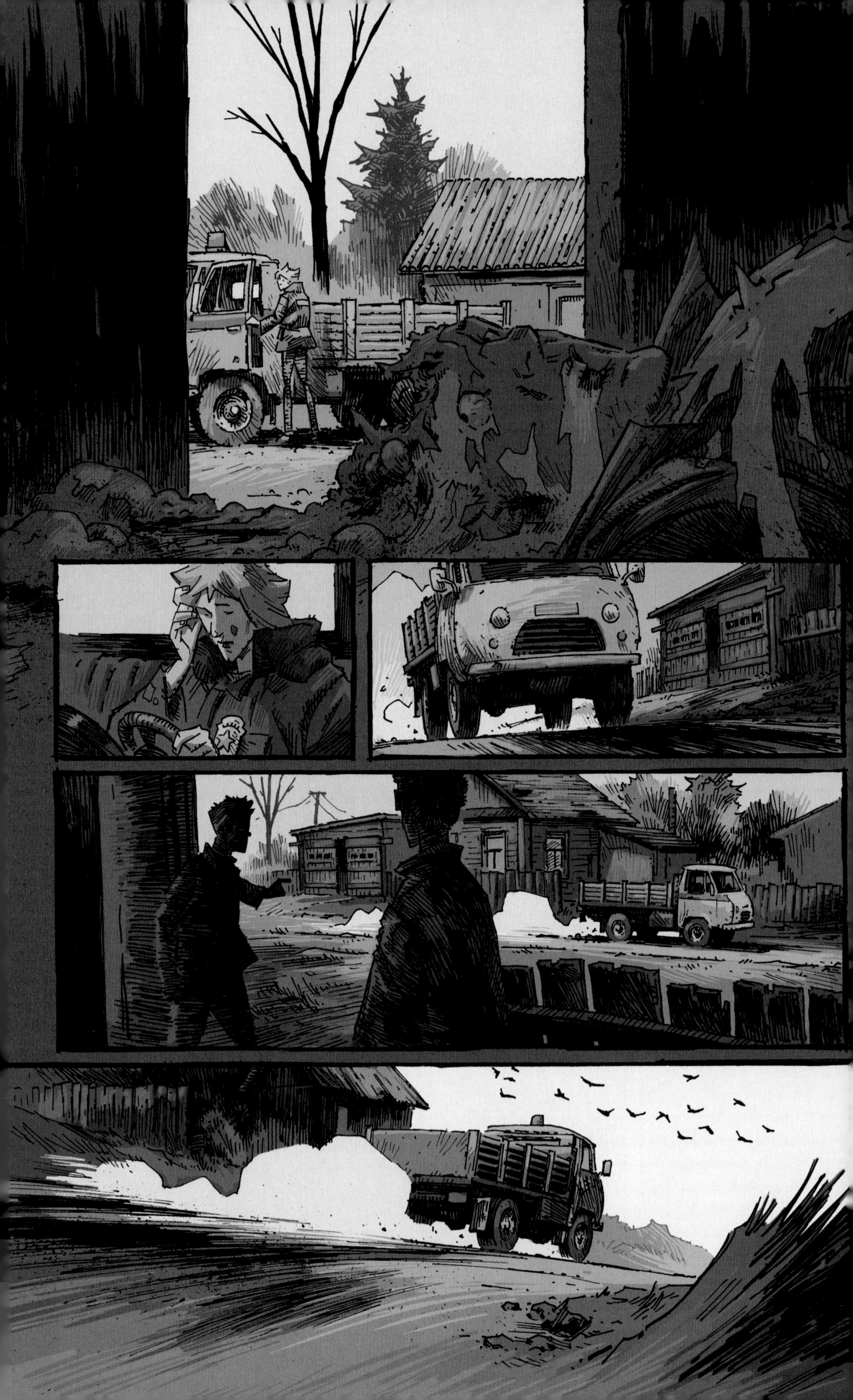

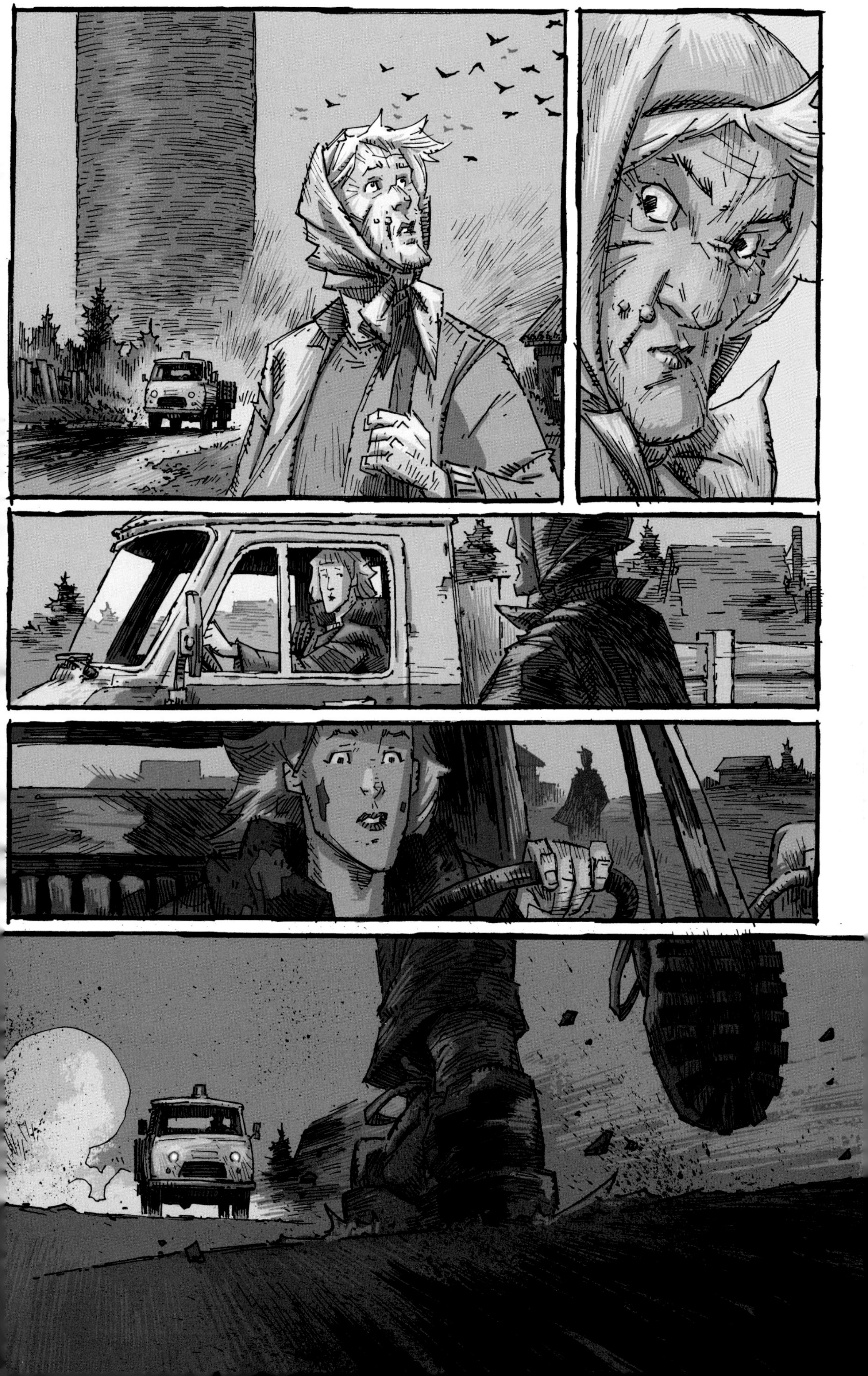

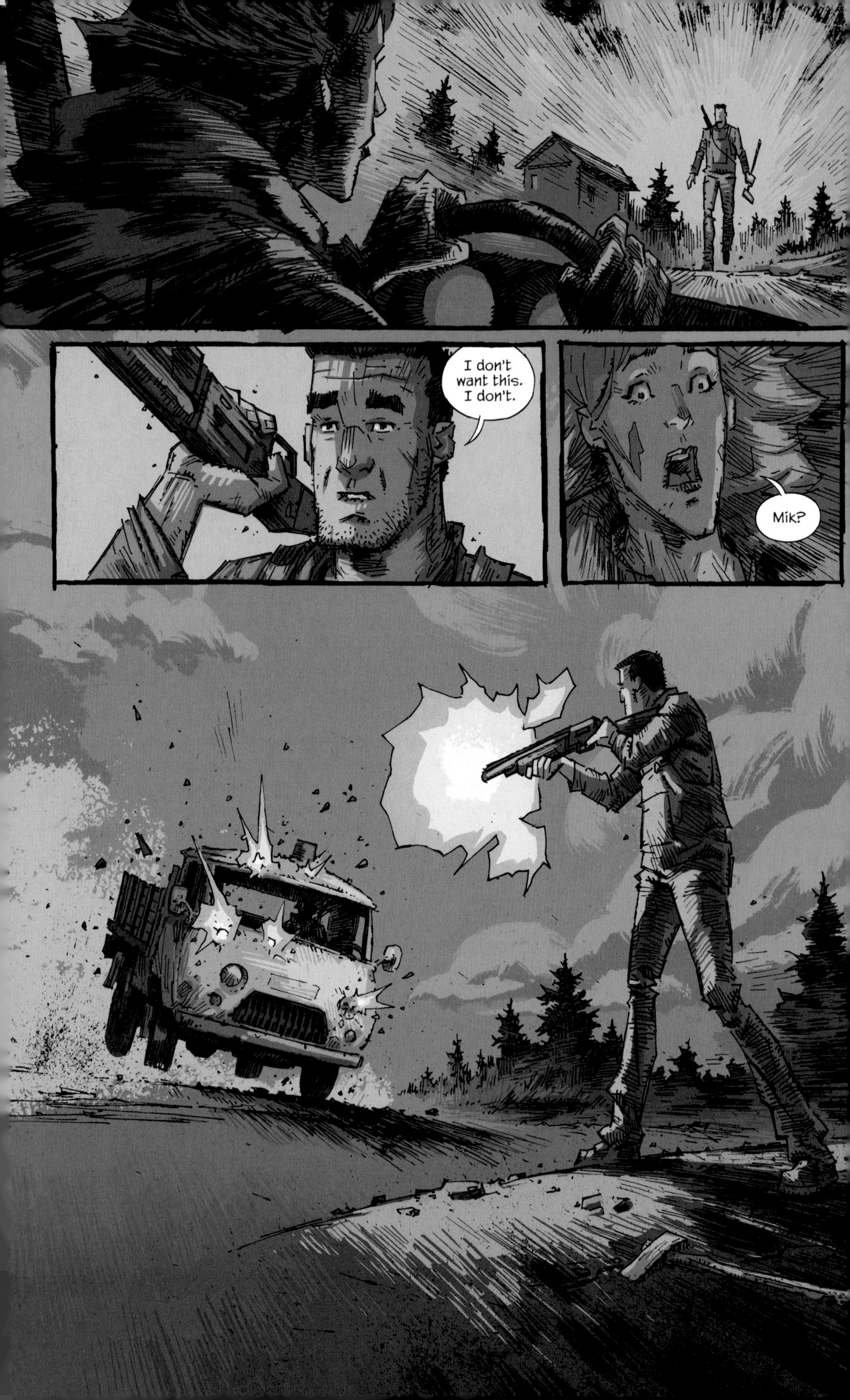
I don't want this. I don't.
Mik?

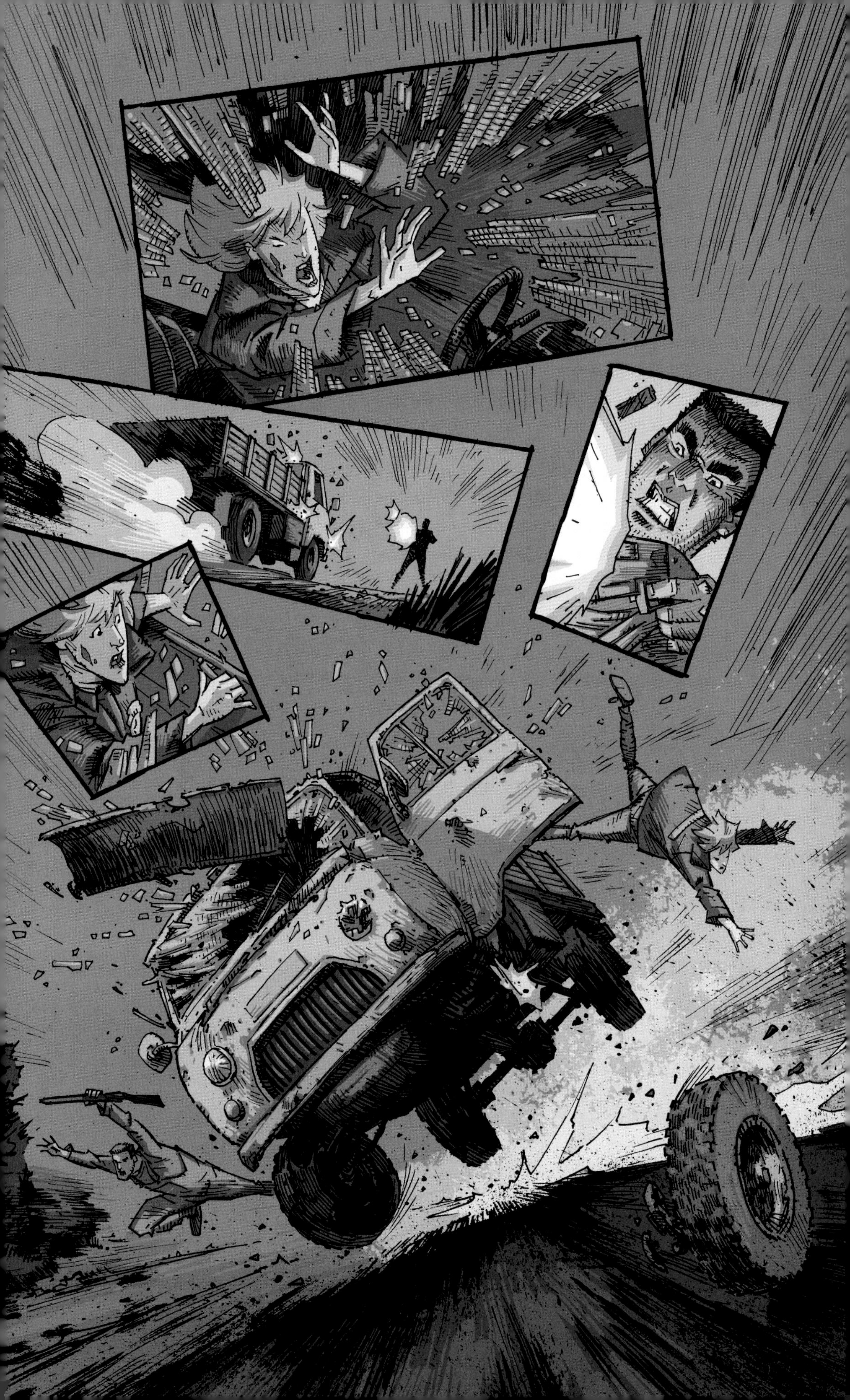

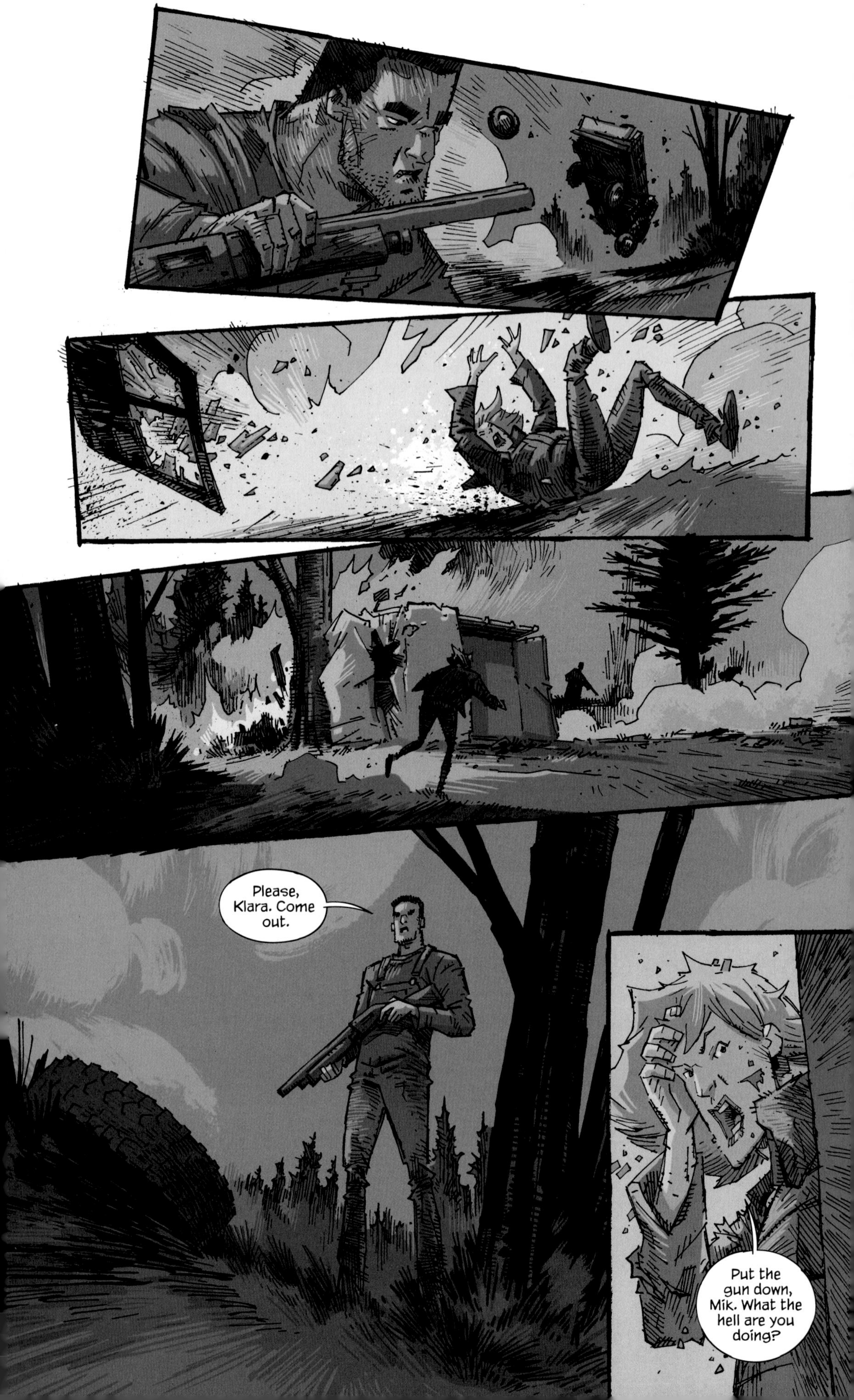
Please, Klara. Come out.
Put the gun down, Mik. What the hell are you doing?

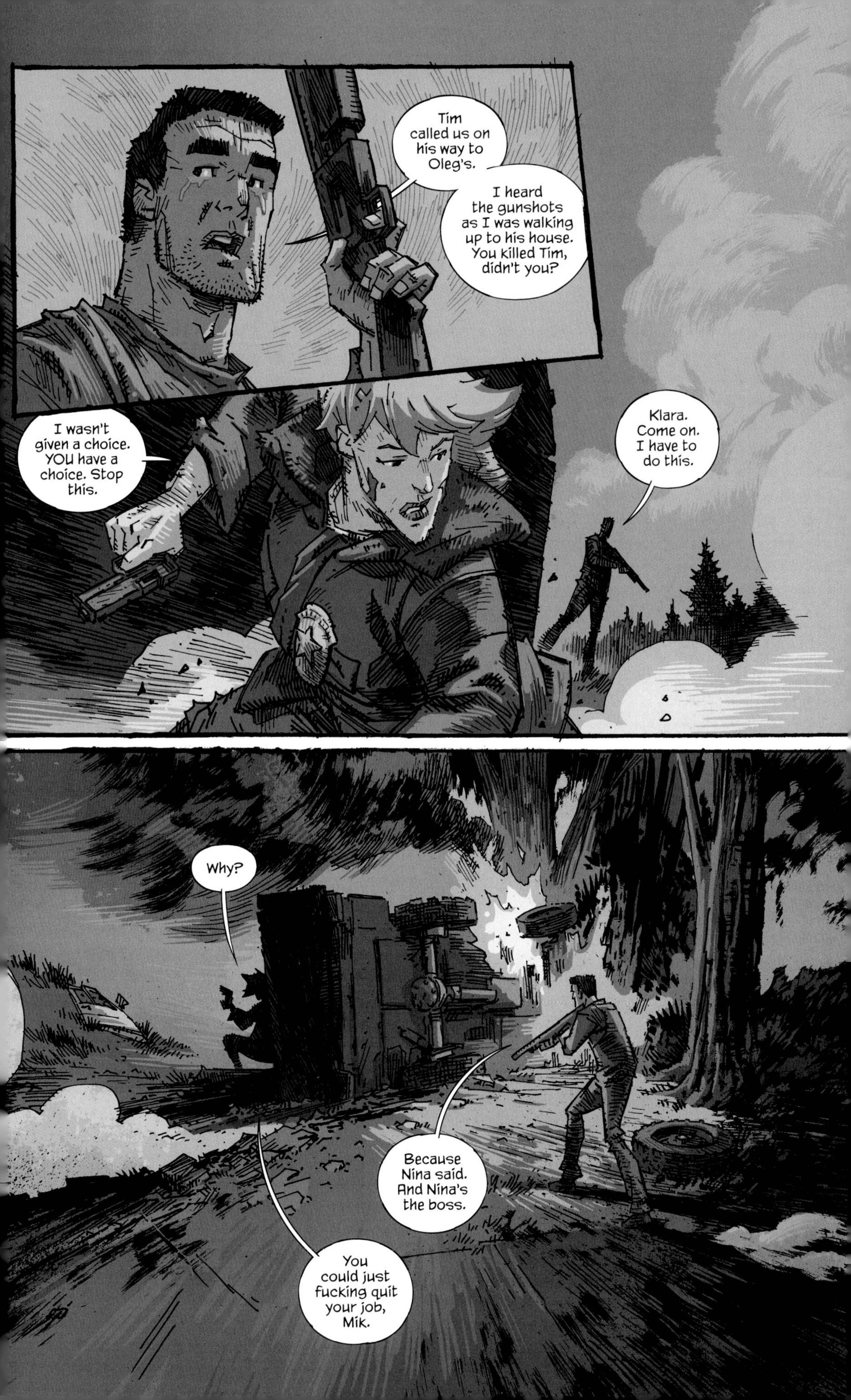
Tim called us on his way to Oleg's.
I heard the gunshots as I was walking up to his house. You killed Tim, didn't you?
I wasn't given a choice. YOU have a choice. Stop this.
Klara. Come on. I have to do this.
Why?
Because Nina said. And Nina's the boss.
You could just fucking quit your job, Mik.

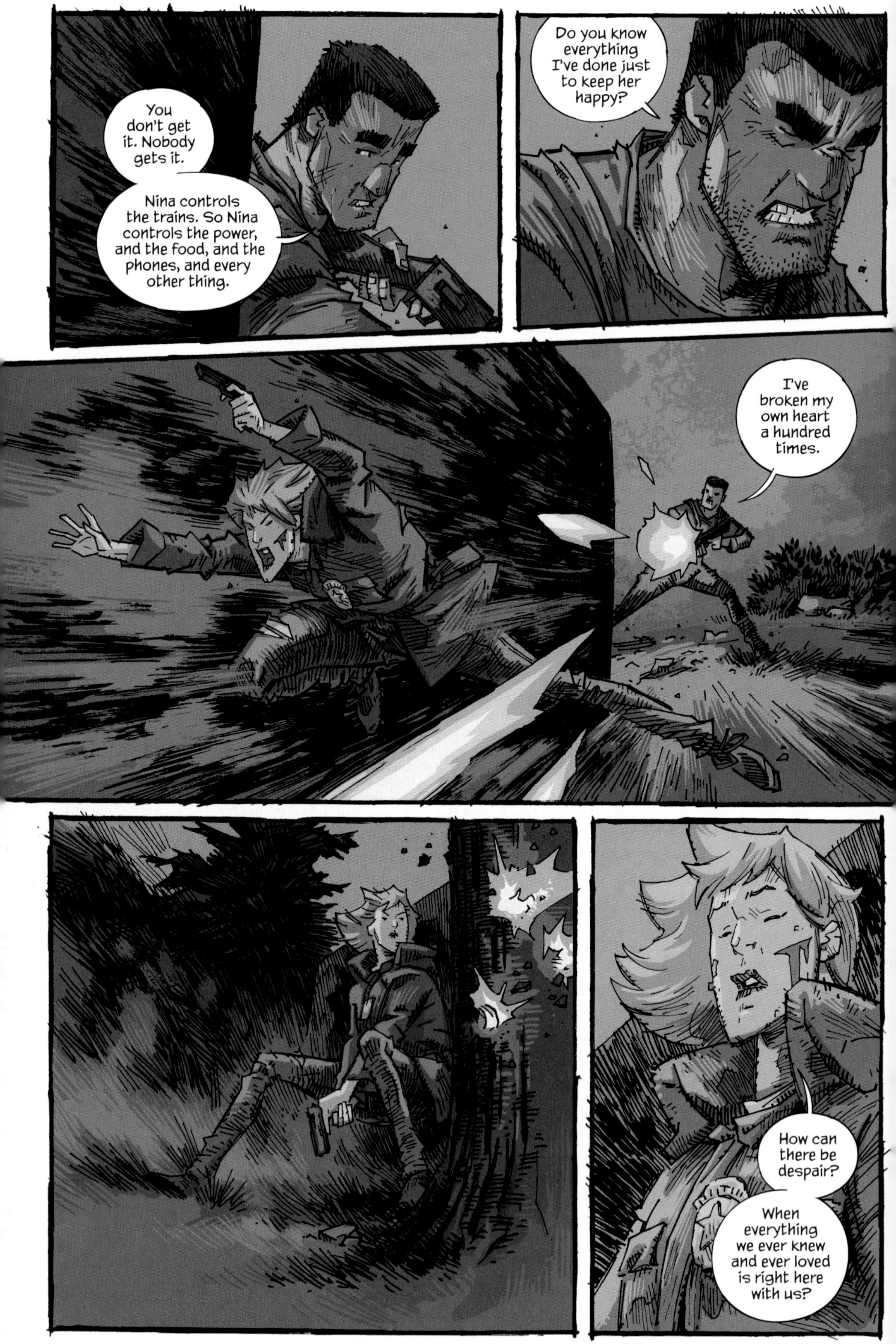
You don't get it. Nobody gets it.
Nina controls the trains. So Nina controls the power, and the food, and the phones, and every other thing.
Do you know everything I've done just to keep her happy?
I've broken my own heart a hundred times.
How can there be despair?
When everything we ever knew and ever loved is right here with us?

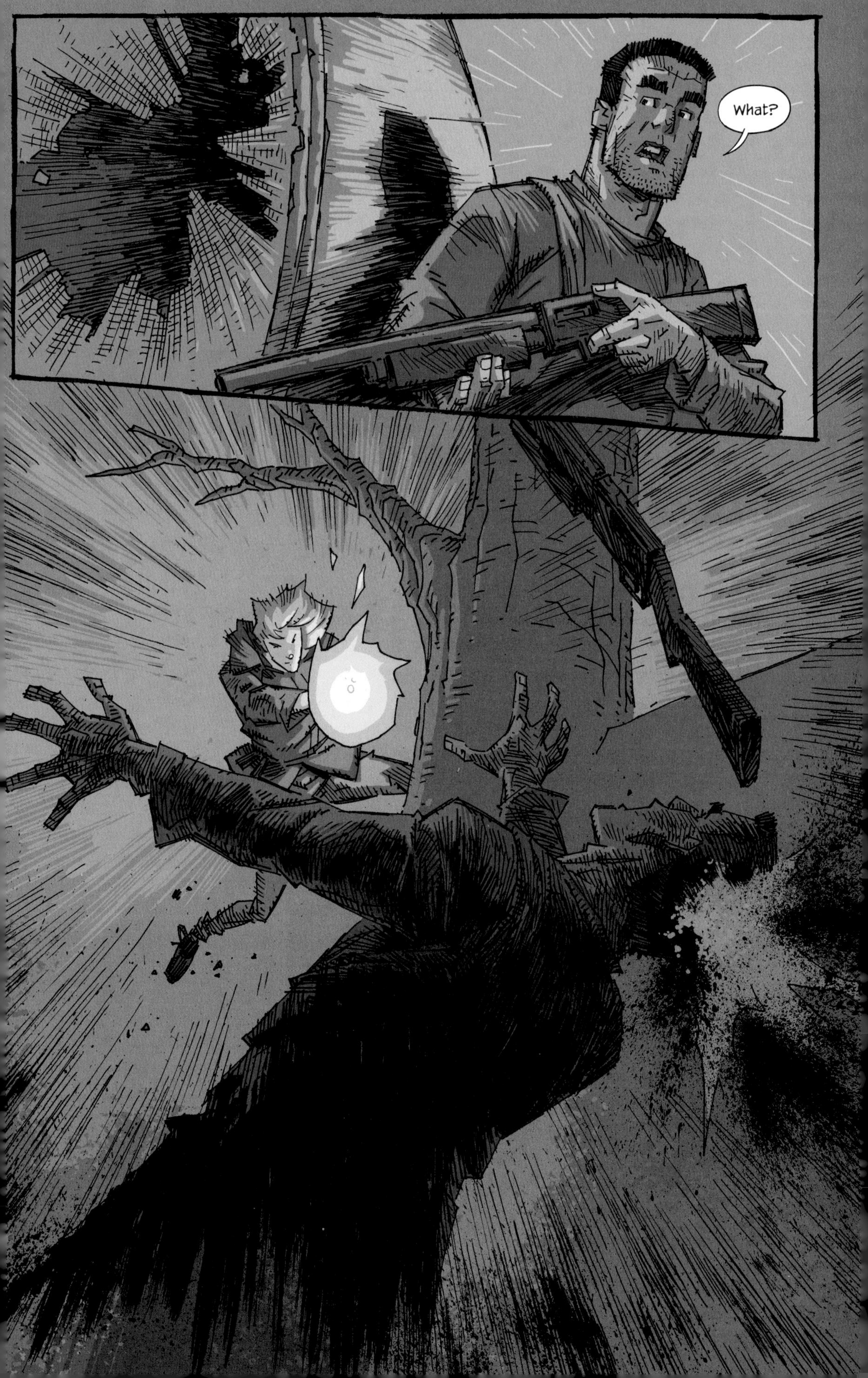
What?

AAAAAAAAAa

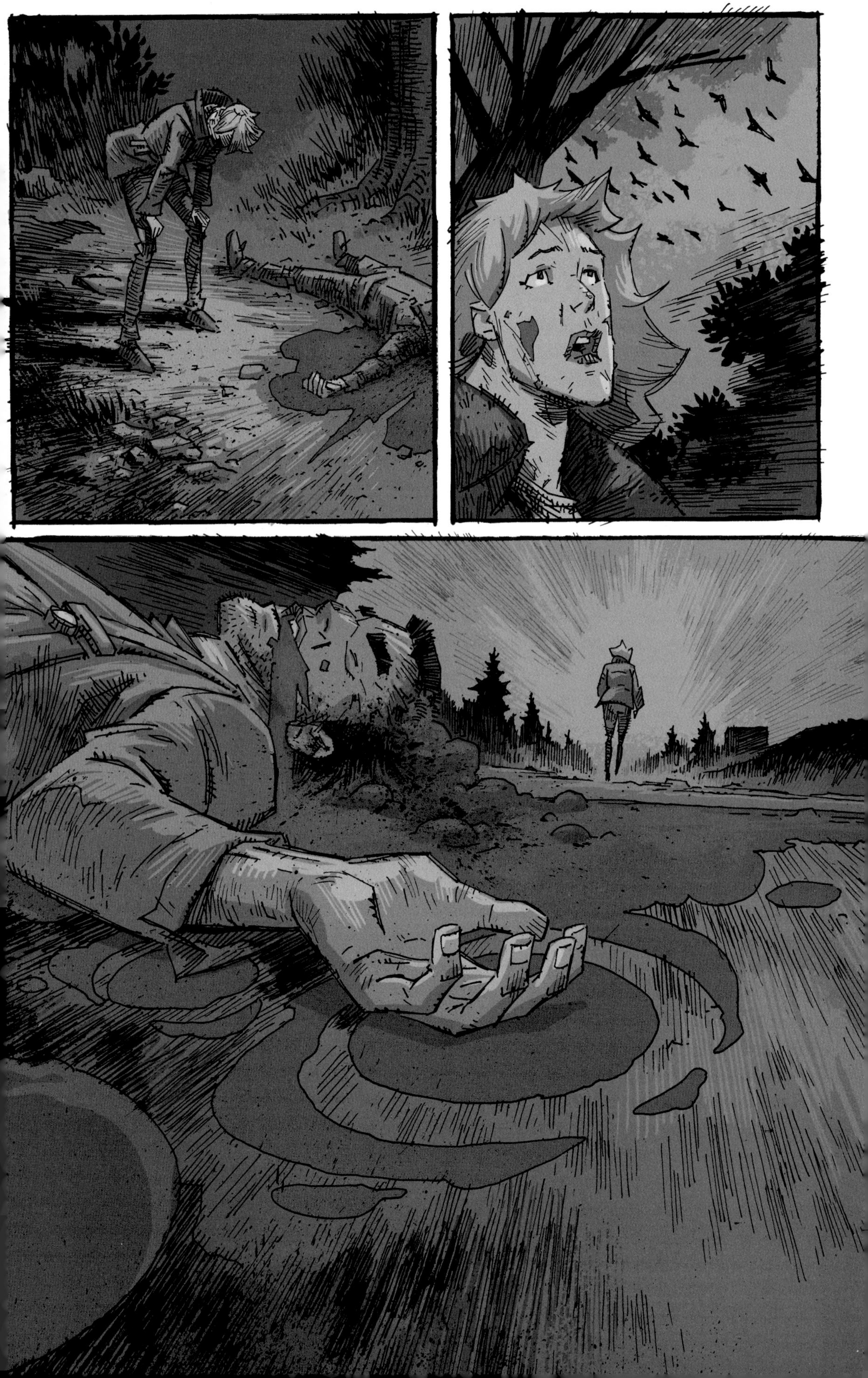

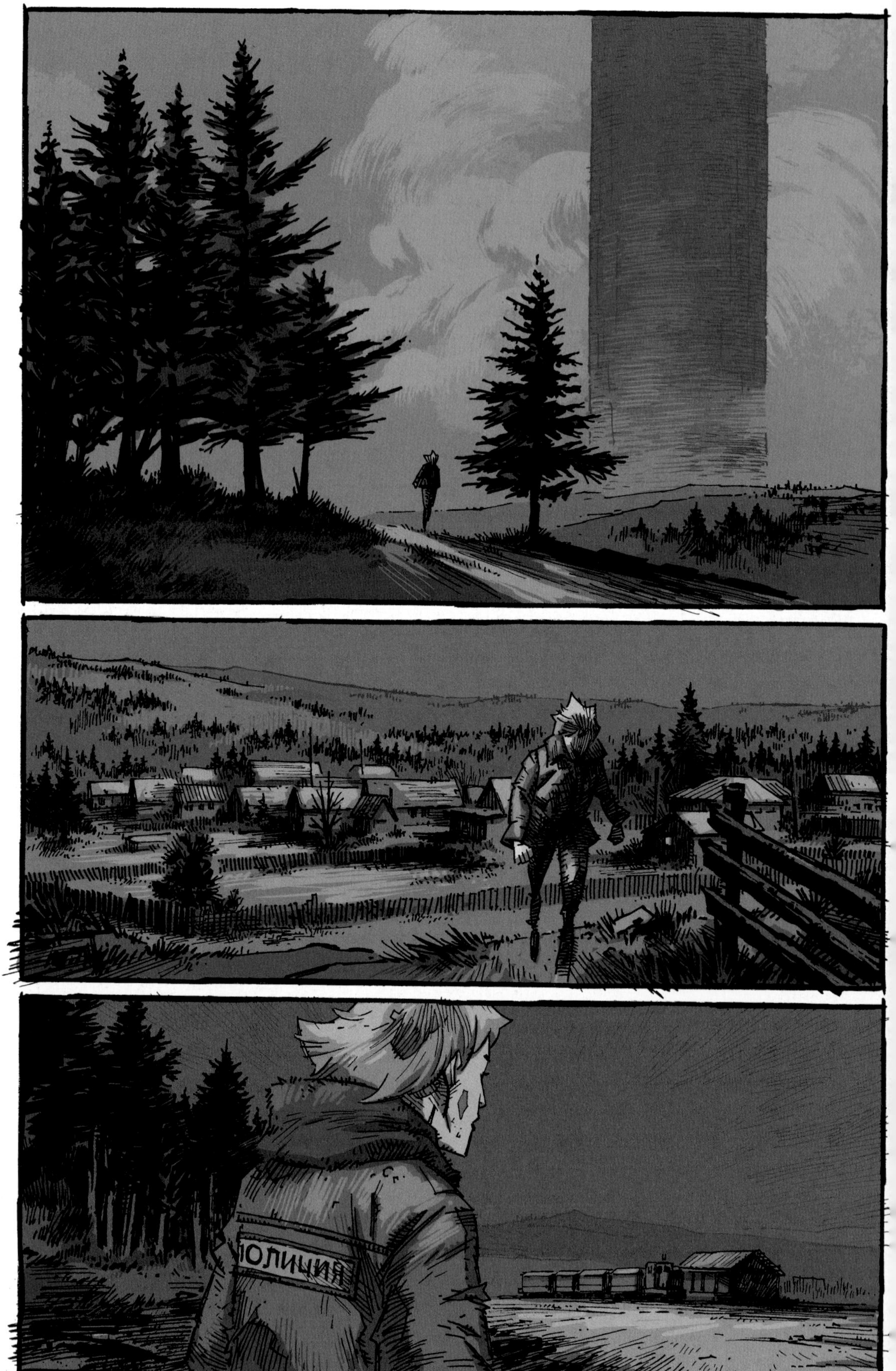

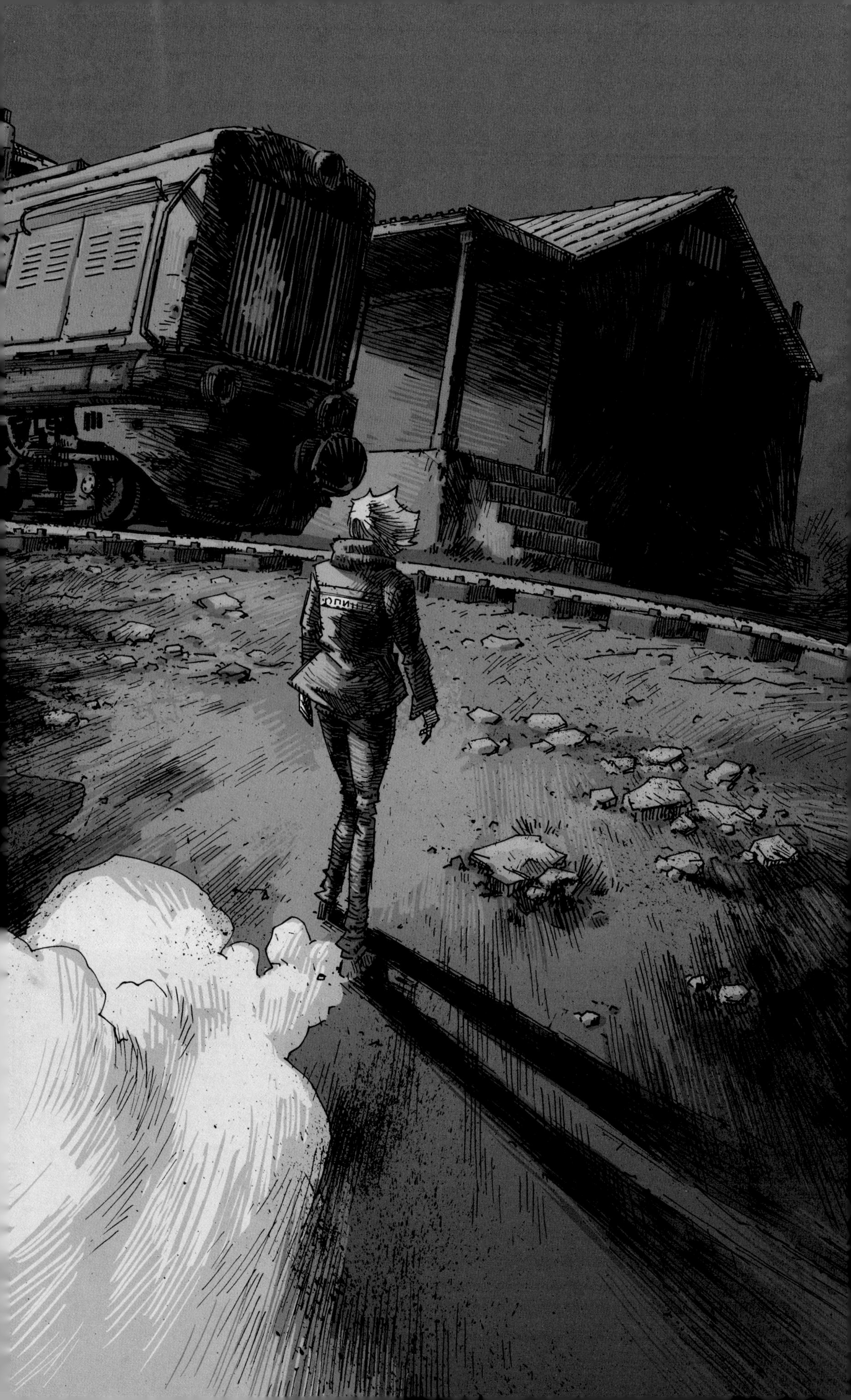

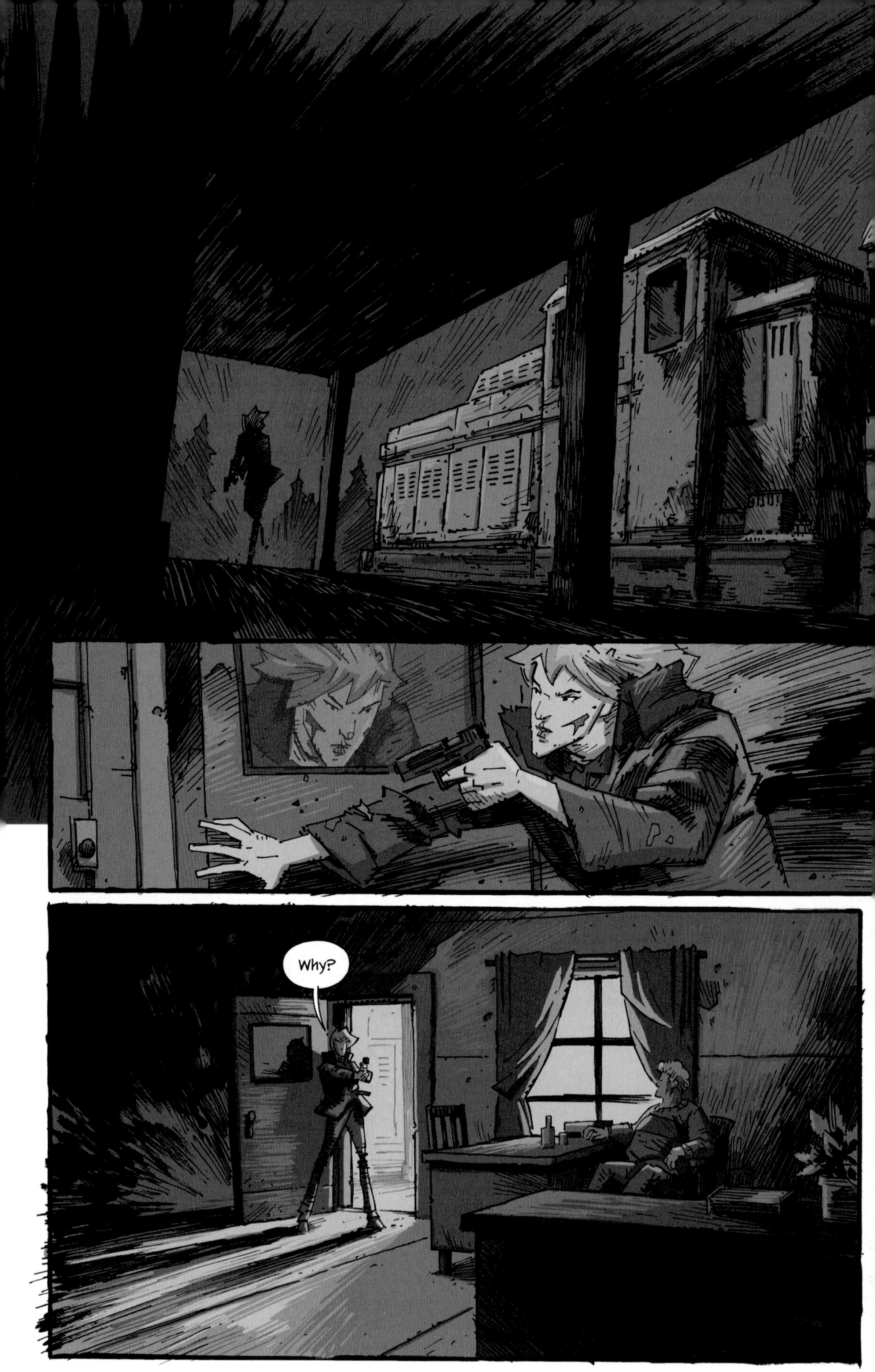
Why?

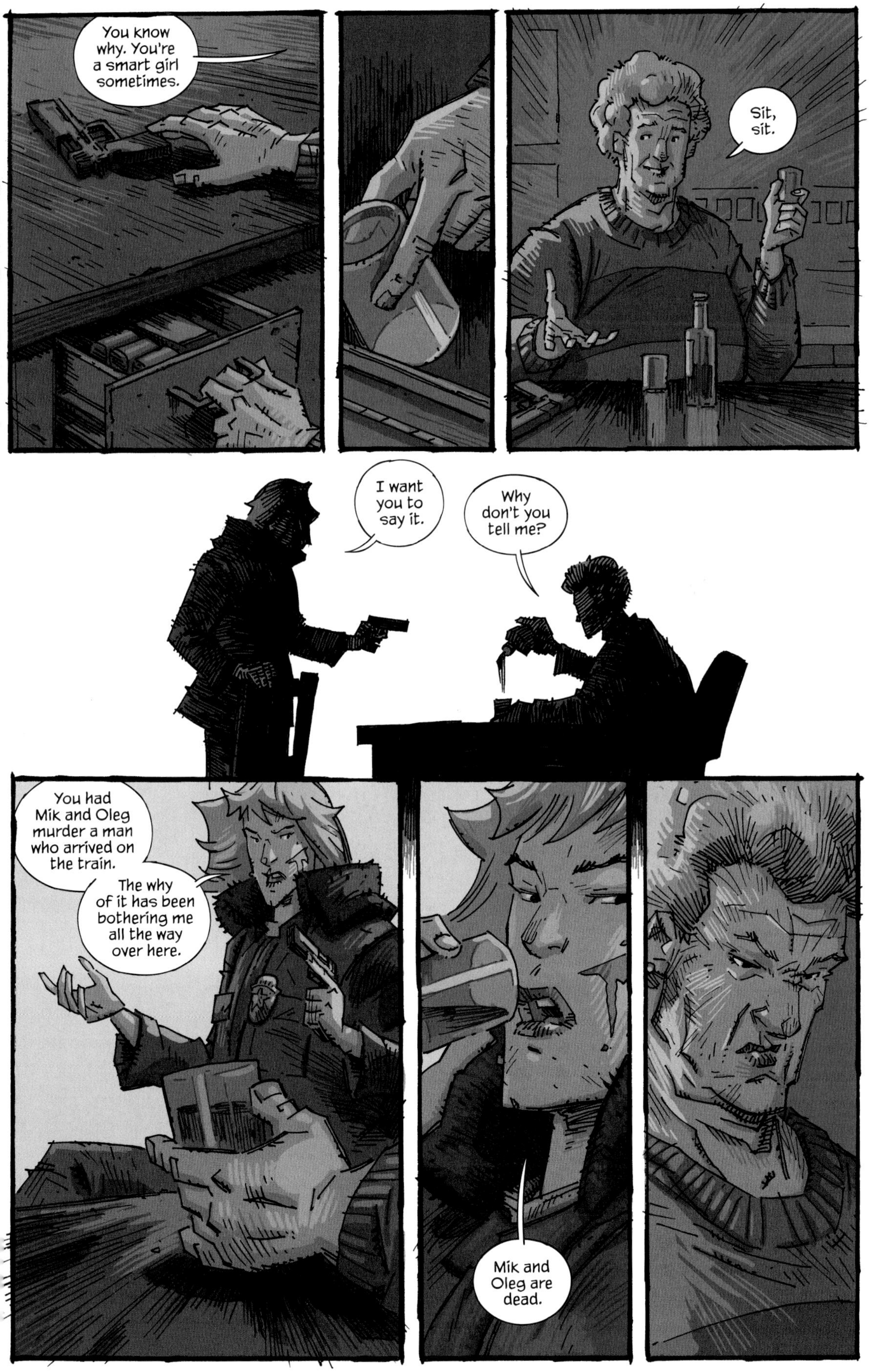
You know why. You're a smart girl sometimes.
Sit, sit.
I want you to say it.
Why don't you tell me?
You had Mik and Oleg murder a man who arrived on the train.
The why of it has been bothering me all the way over here.
Mik and Oleg are dead.

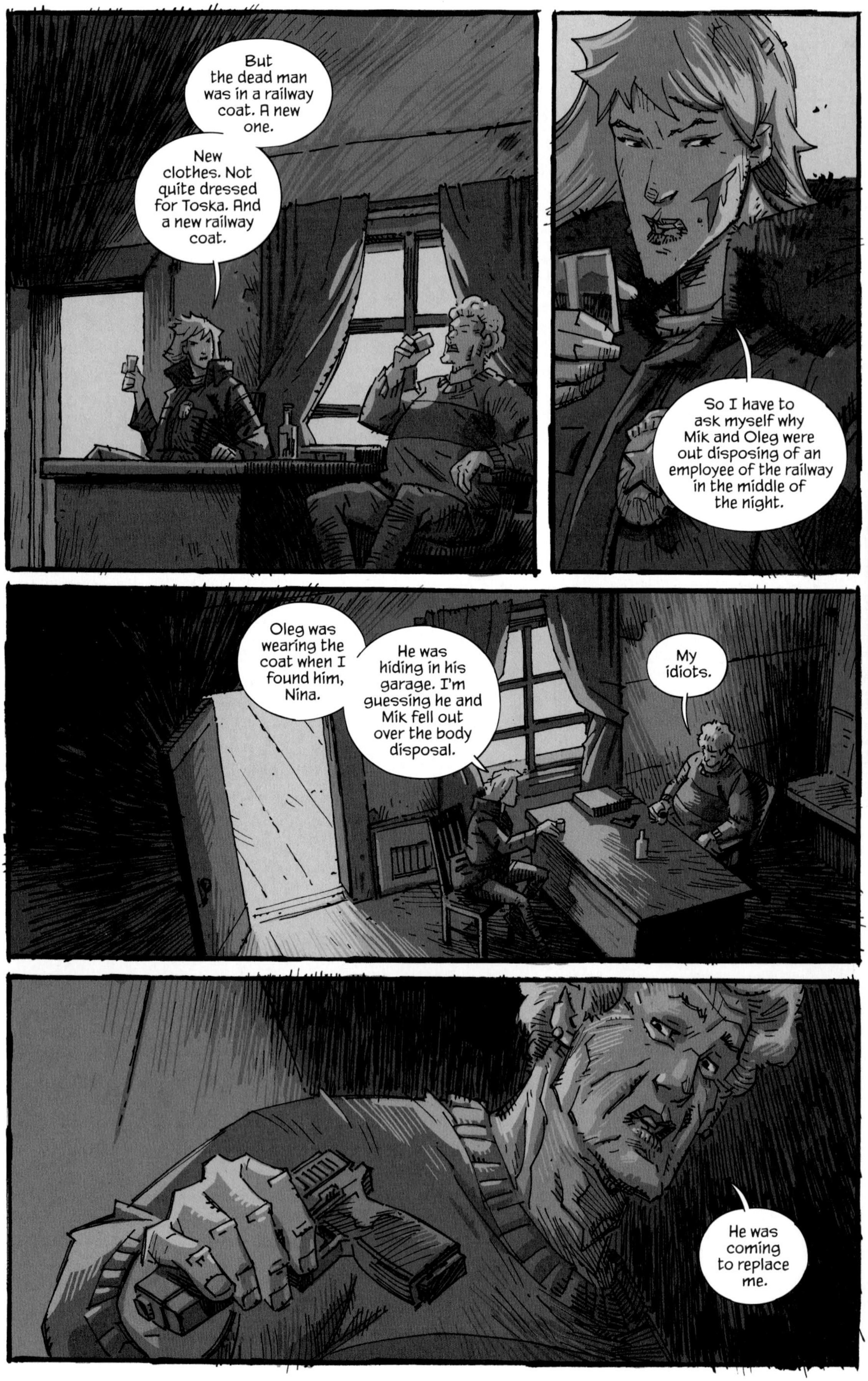
But the dead man was in a railway coat. A new one.
New clothes. Not quite dressed for Toska. And a new railway coat.
So I have to ask myself why Mik and Oleg were out disposing of an employee of the railway in the middle of the night.
Oleg was wearing the coat when I found him, Nina.
He was hiding in his garage. I'm guessing he and Mik fell out over the body disposal.
My idiots.
He was coming to replace me.

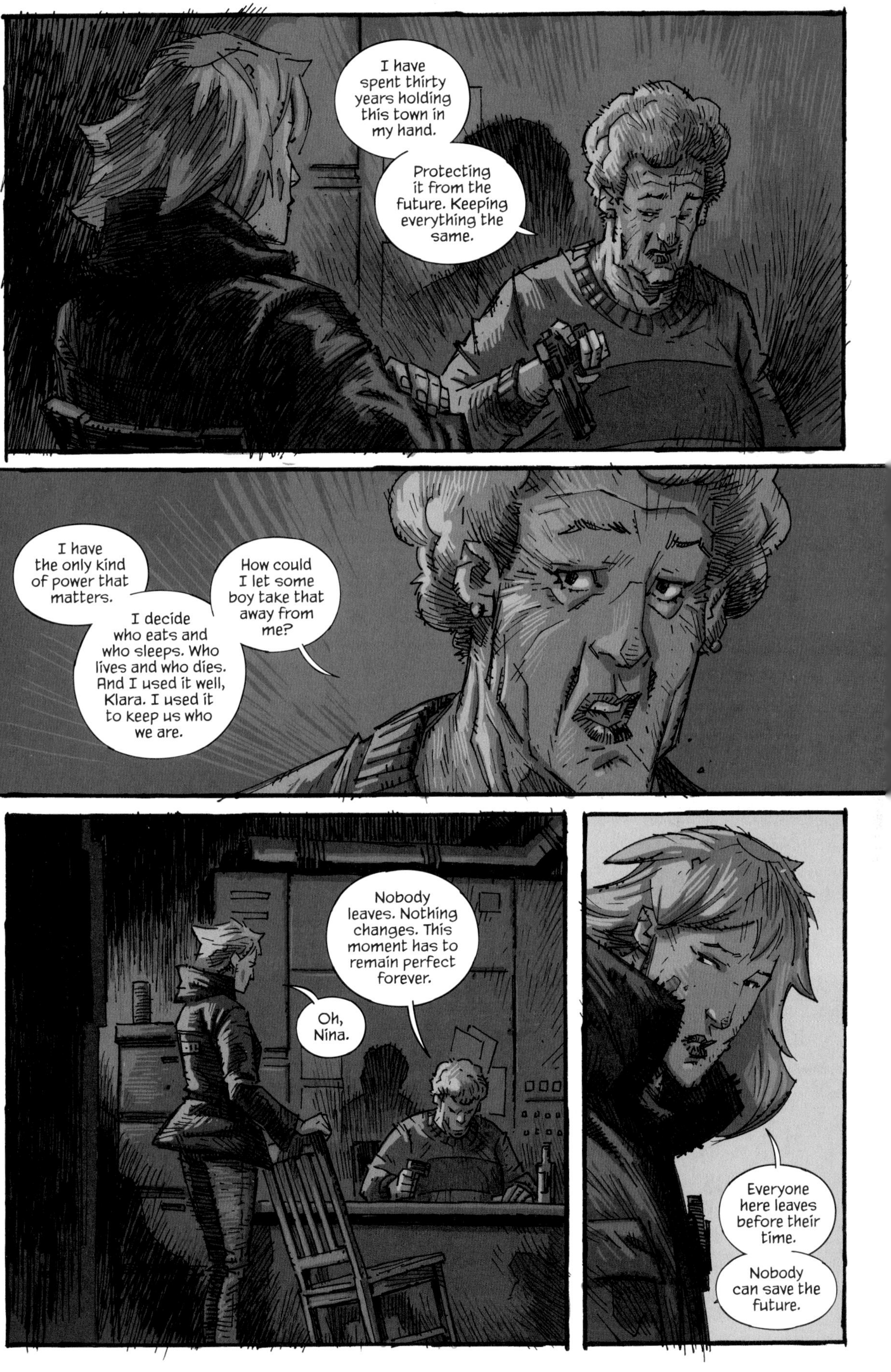
I have spent thirty years holding this town in my hand.
Protecting it from the future. Keeping everything the same.
I have the only kind of power that matters.
I decide who eats and who sleeps. Who lives and who dies. And I used it well, Klara. I used it to keep us who we are.
How could I let some boy take that away from me?
Nobody leaves. Nothing changes. This moment has to remain perfect forever.
Oh, Nina.
Everyone here leaves before their time.
Nobody can save the future.

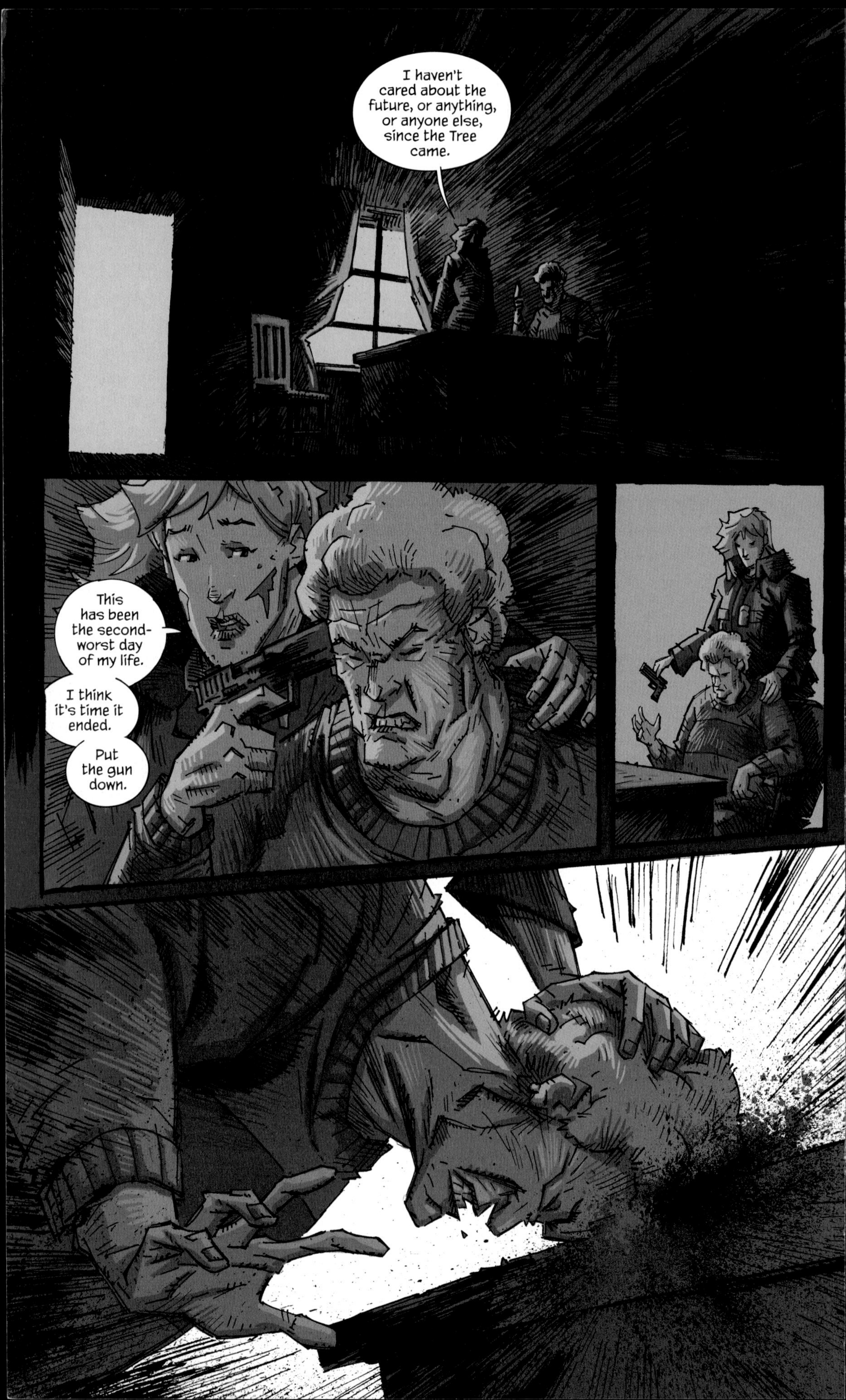
I haven't cared about the future, or anything, or anyone else, since the Tree came.
This has been the second-worst day of my life.
I think it's time it ended.
Put the gun down.

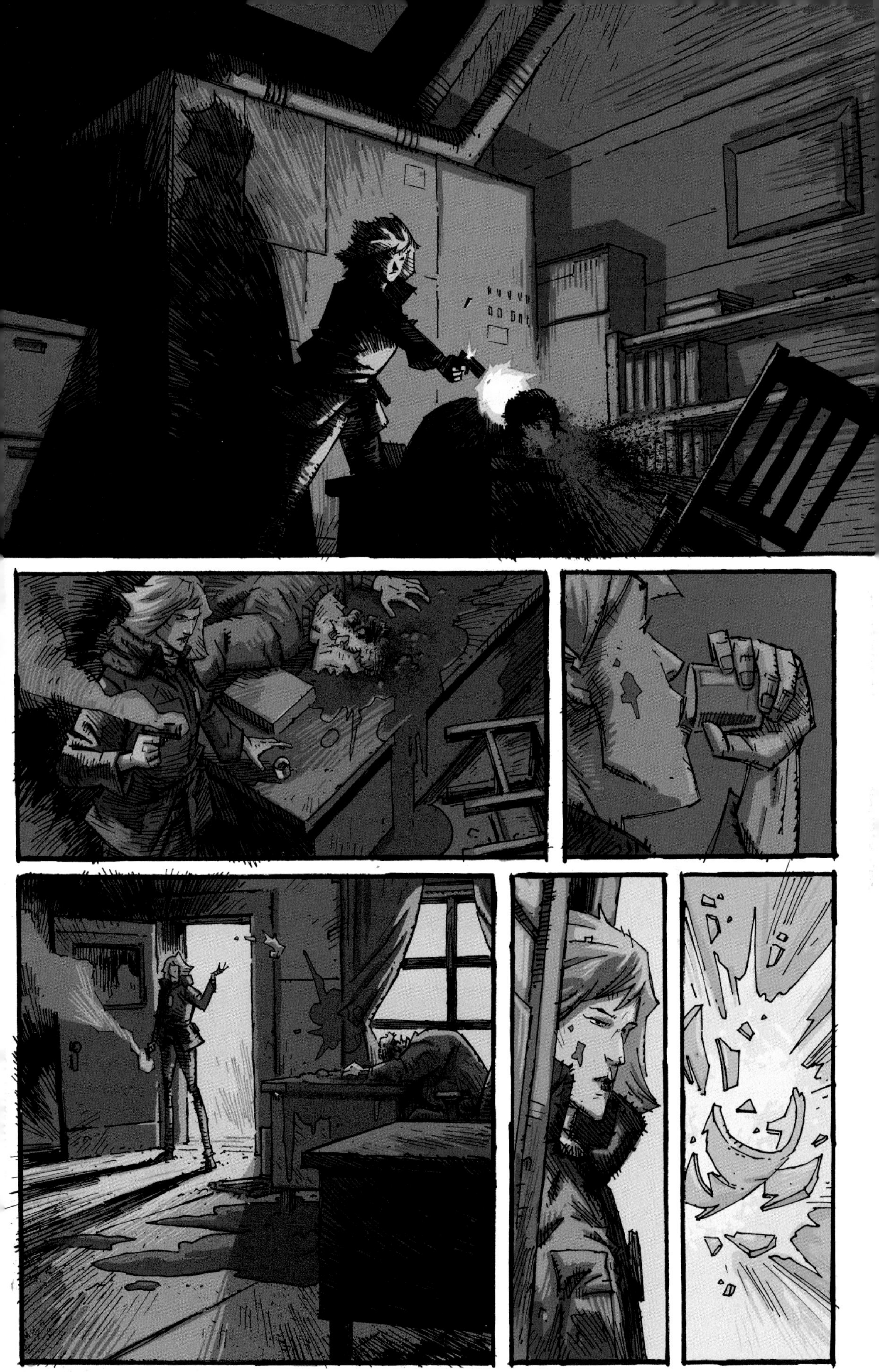

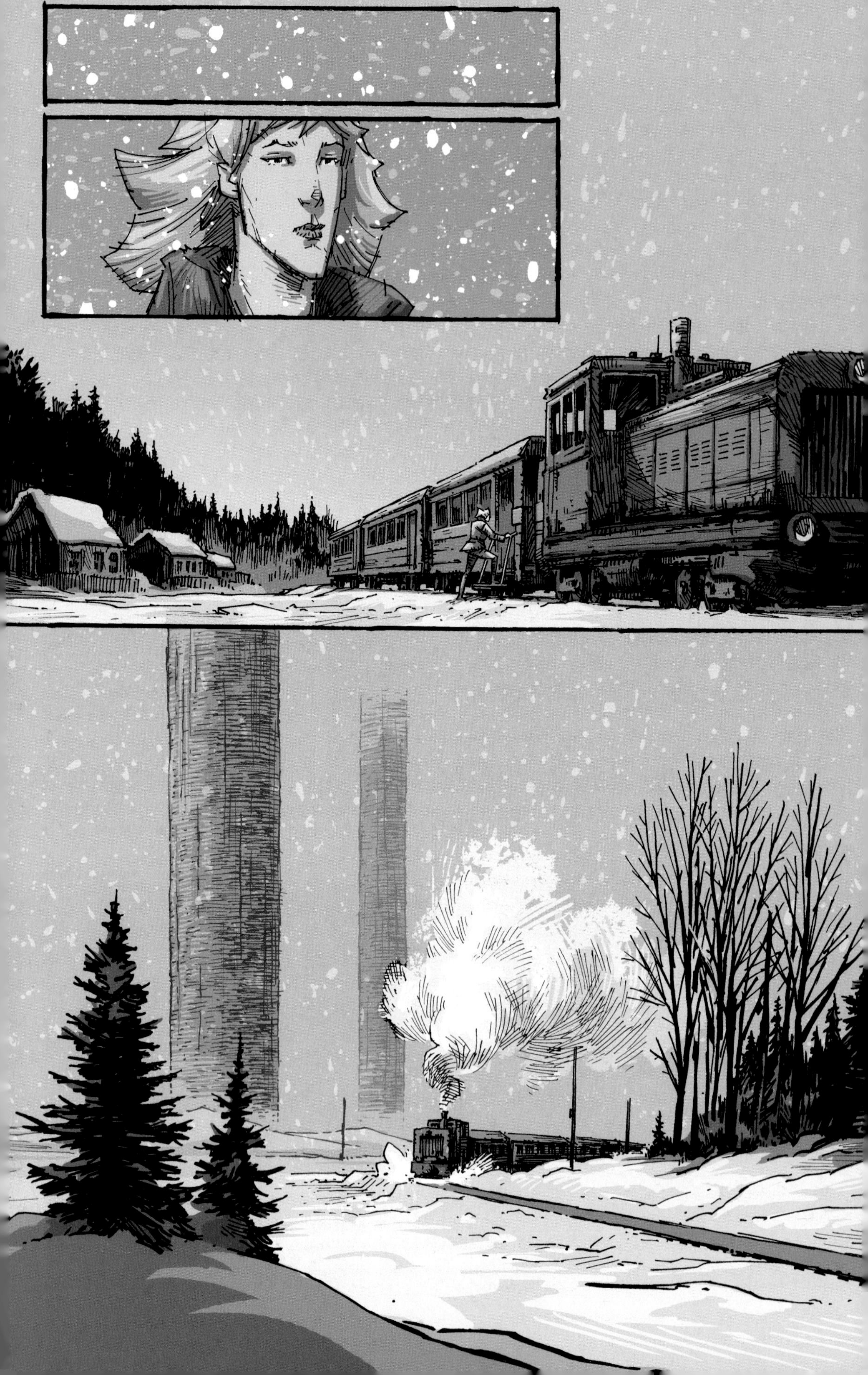

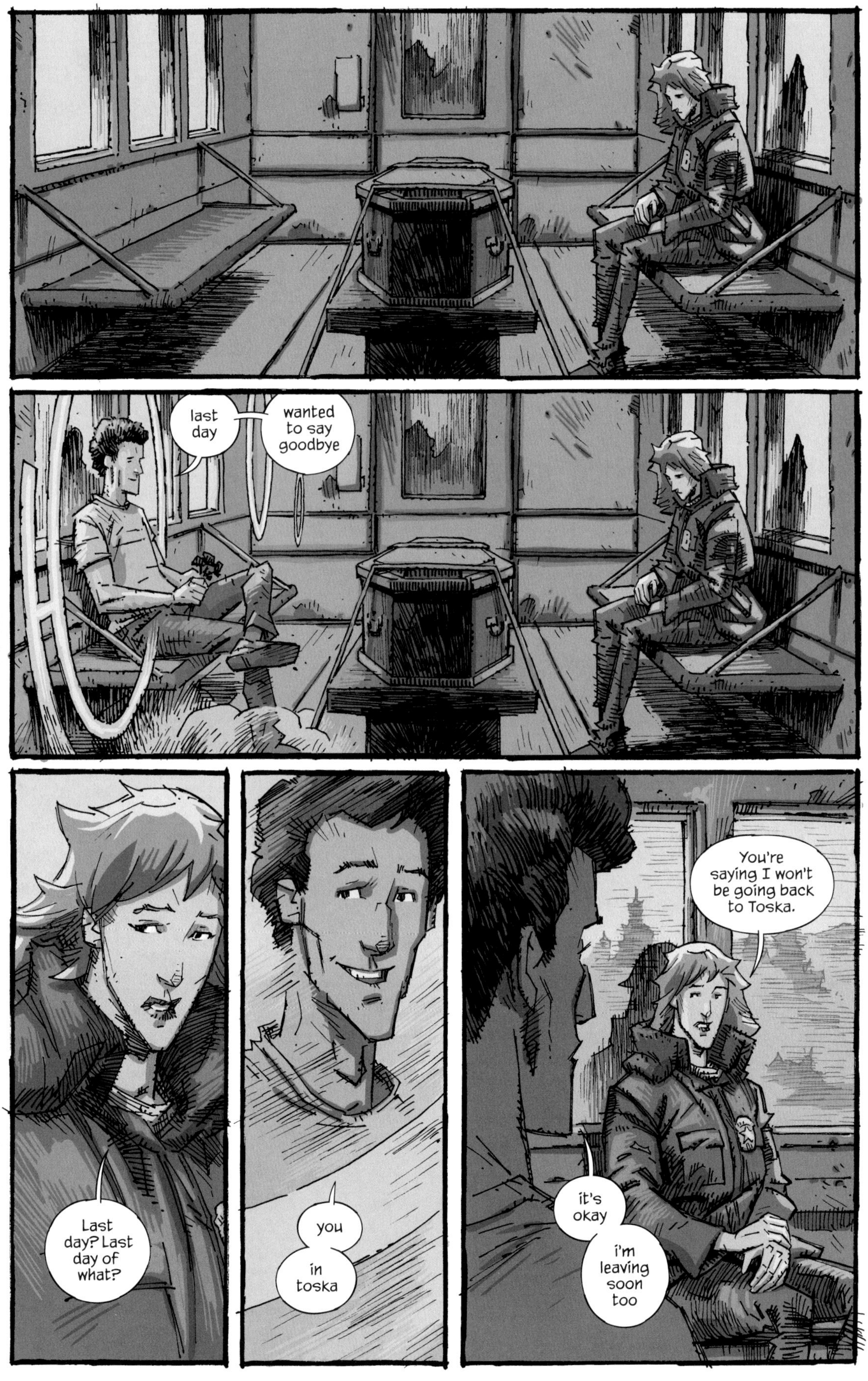
last day
wanted to say goodbye
Last day? Last day of what?
you
in toska
You're saying I won't be going back to Toska.
it's okay
i'm leaving soon too

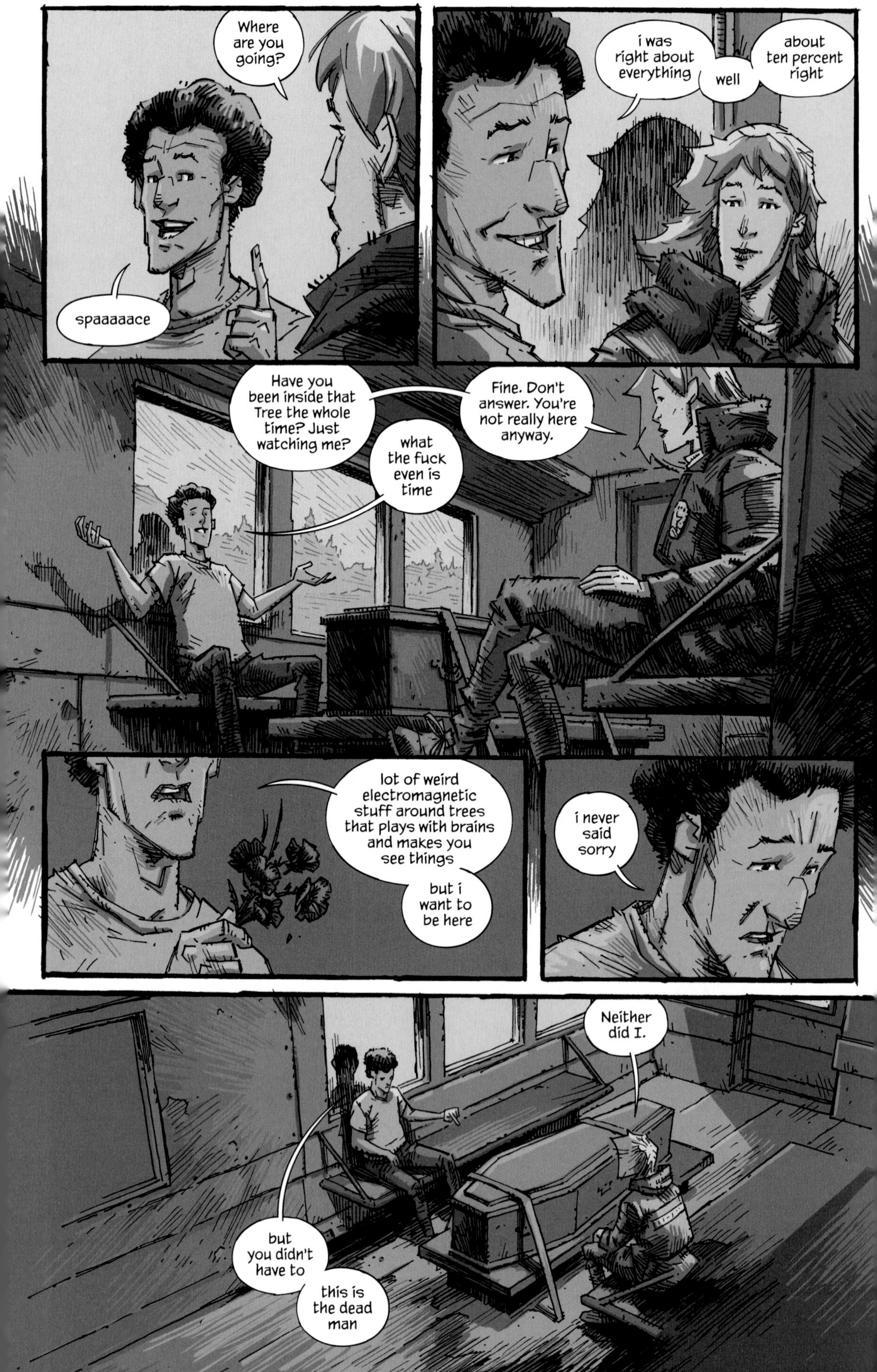
Where are you going?
spaaaaace
i was right about everything
well
about ten percent right
Have you been inside that Tree the whole time? Just watching me?
Fine. Don't answer. You're not really here anyway.
what the fuck even is time
lot of weird electromagnetic stuff around trees that plays with brains and makes you see things
but i want to be here
i never said sorry
Neither did I.
but you didn't have to
this is the dead man

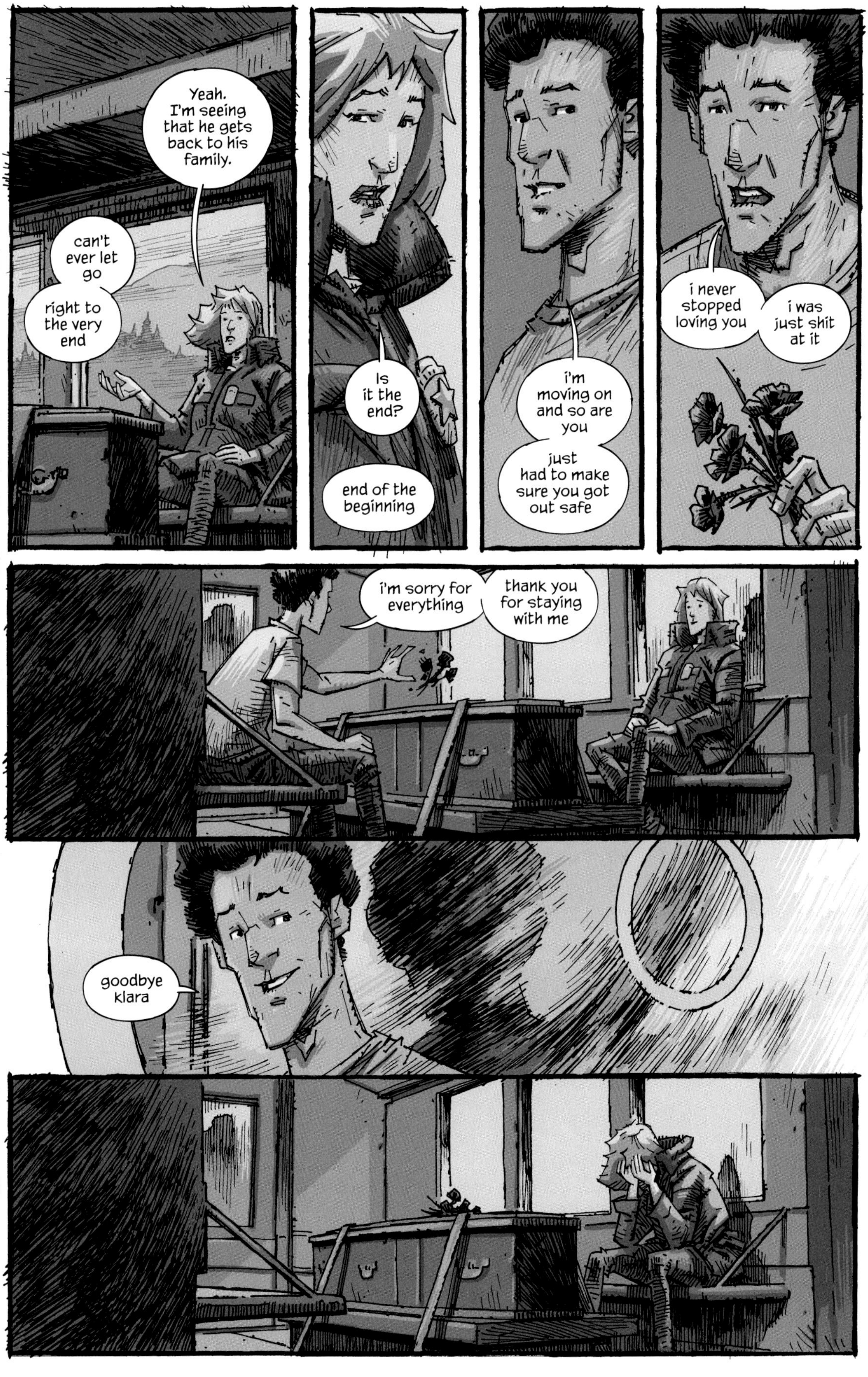
Yeah. I'm seeing that he gets back to his family.
can't ever let go
right to the very end
Is it the end?
end of the beginning
i'm moving on and so are you
just had to make sure you got out safe
i never stopped loving you
i was just shit at it
i'm sorry for everything
thank you for staying with me
goodbye klara

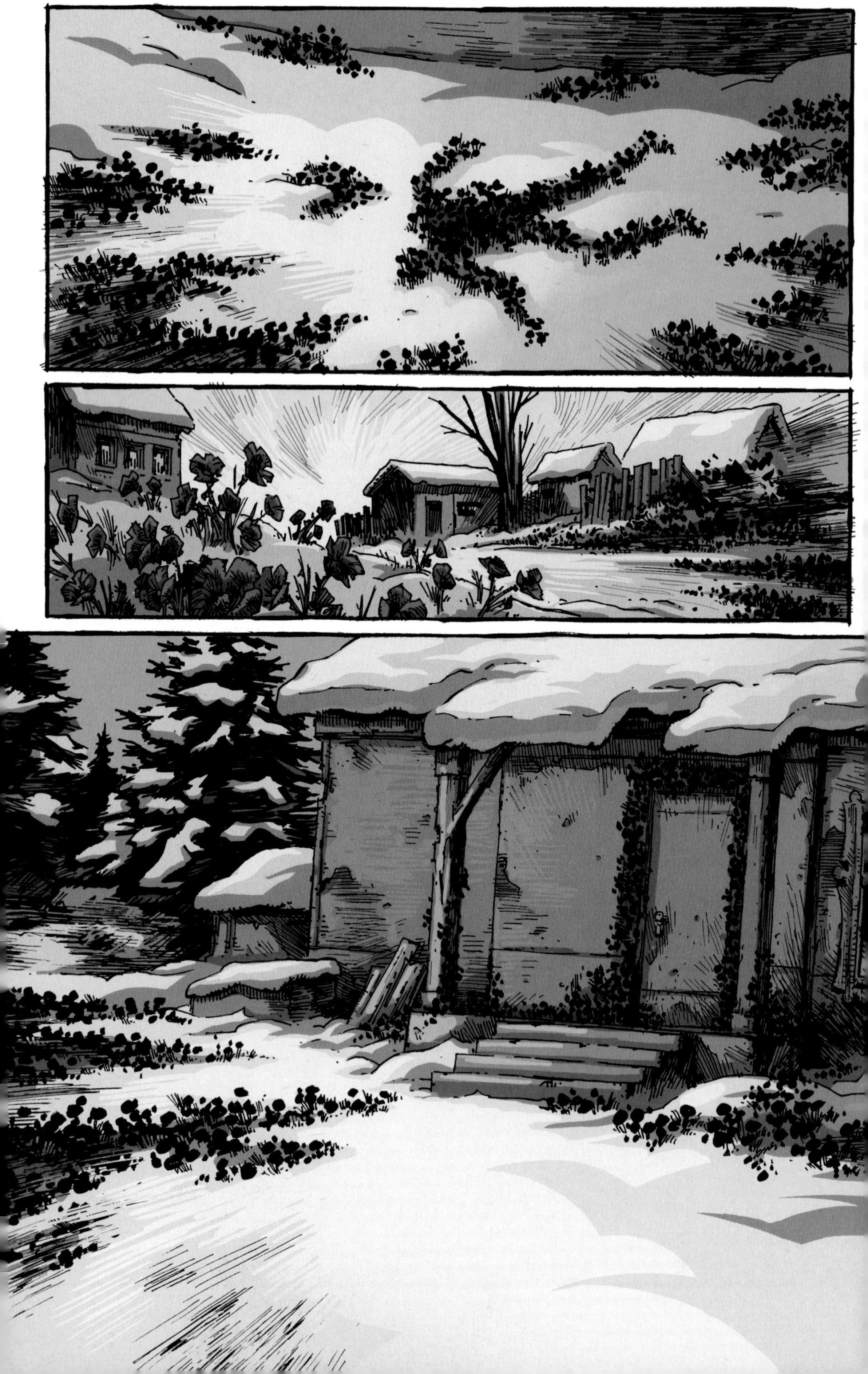

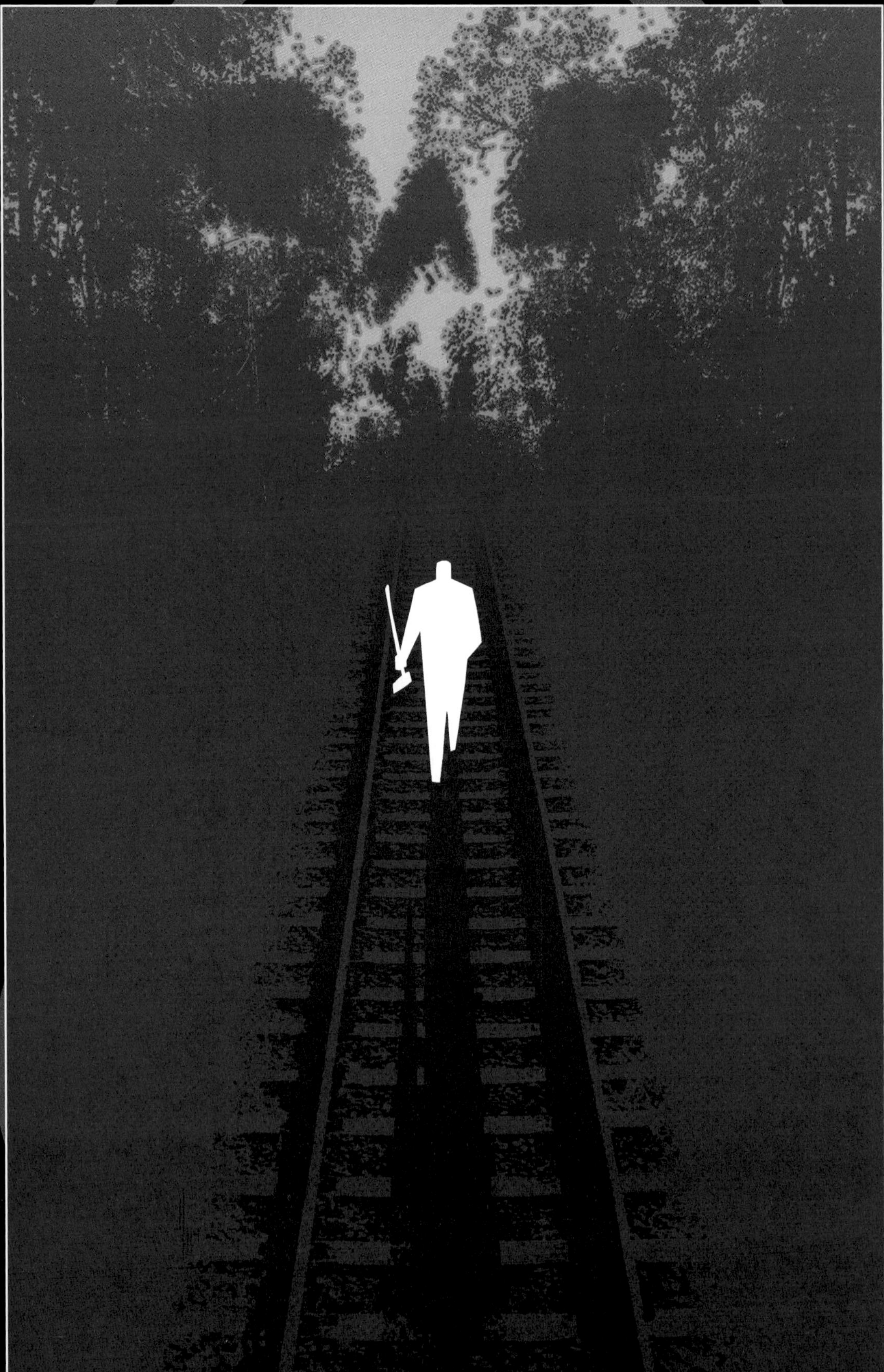

TREES: THREE FATES #1

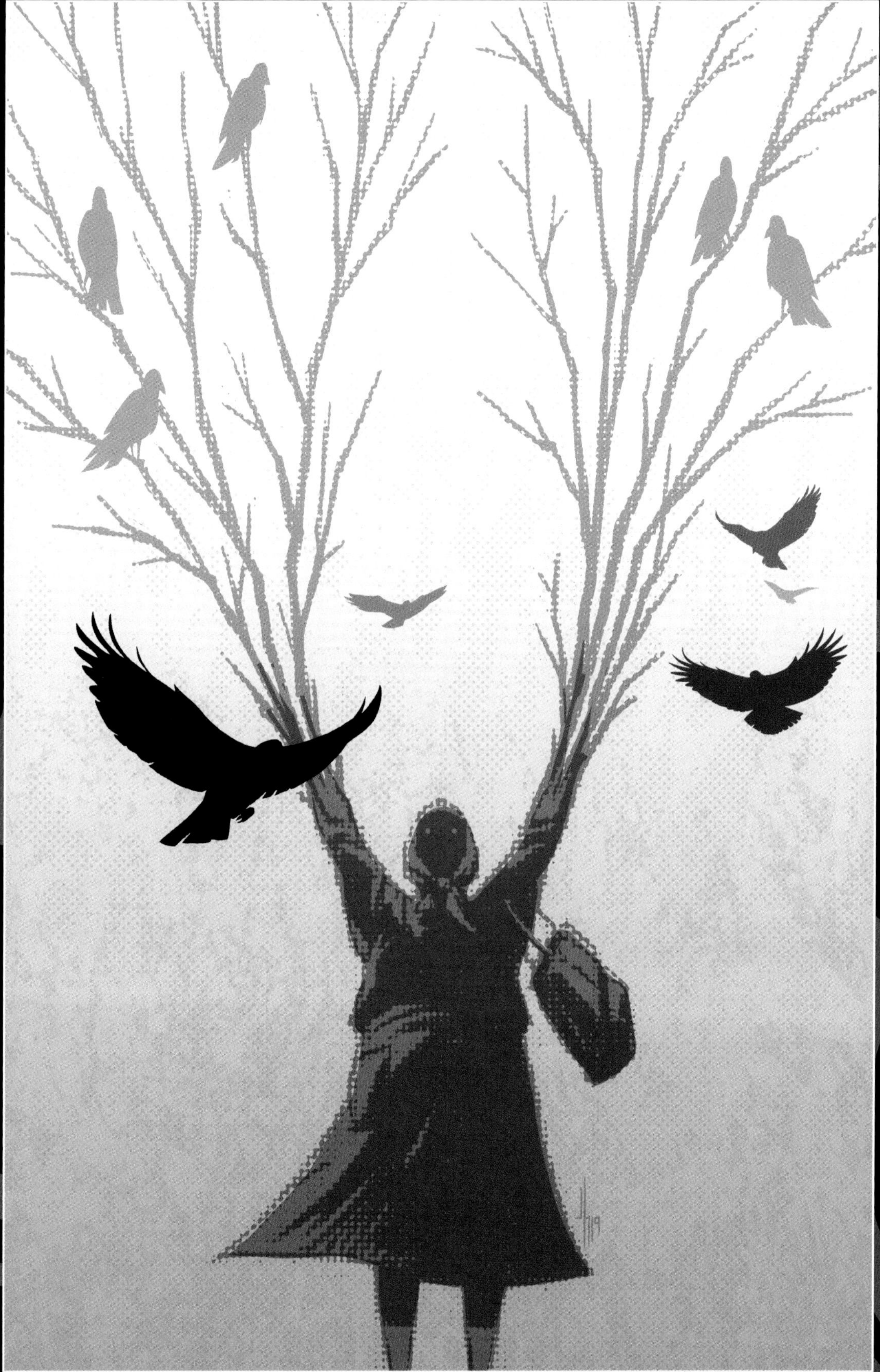

TREES: THREE FATES #2

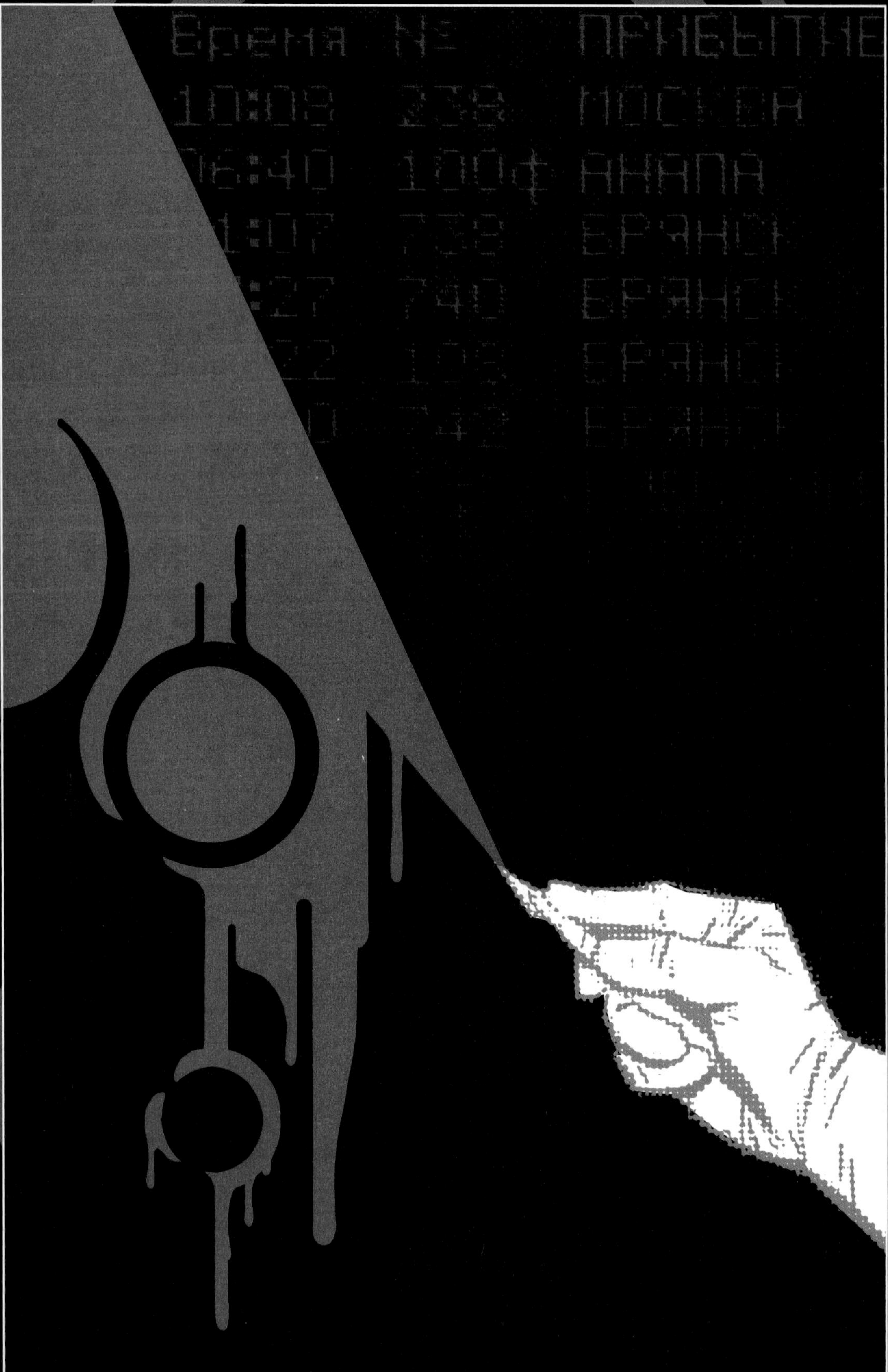

TREES: THREE FATES #3

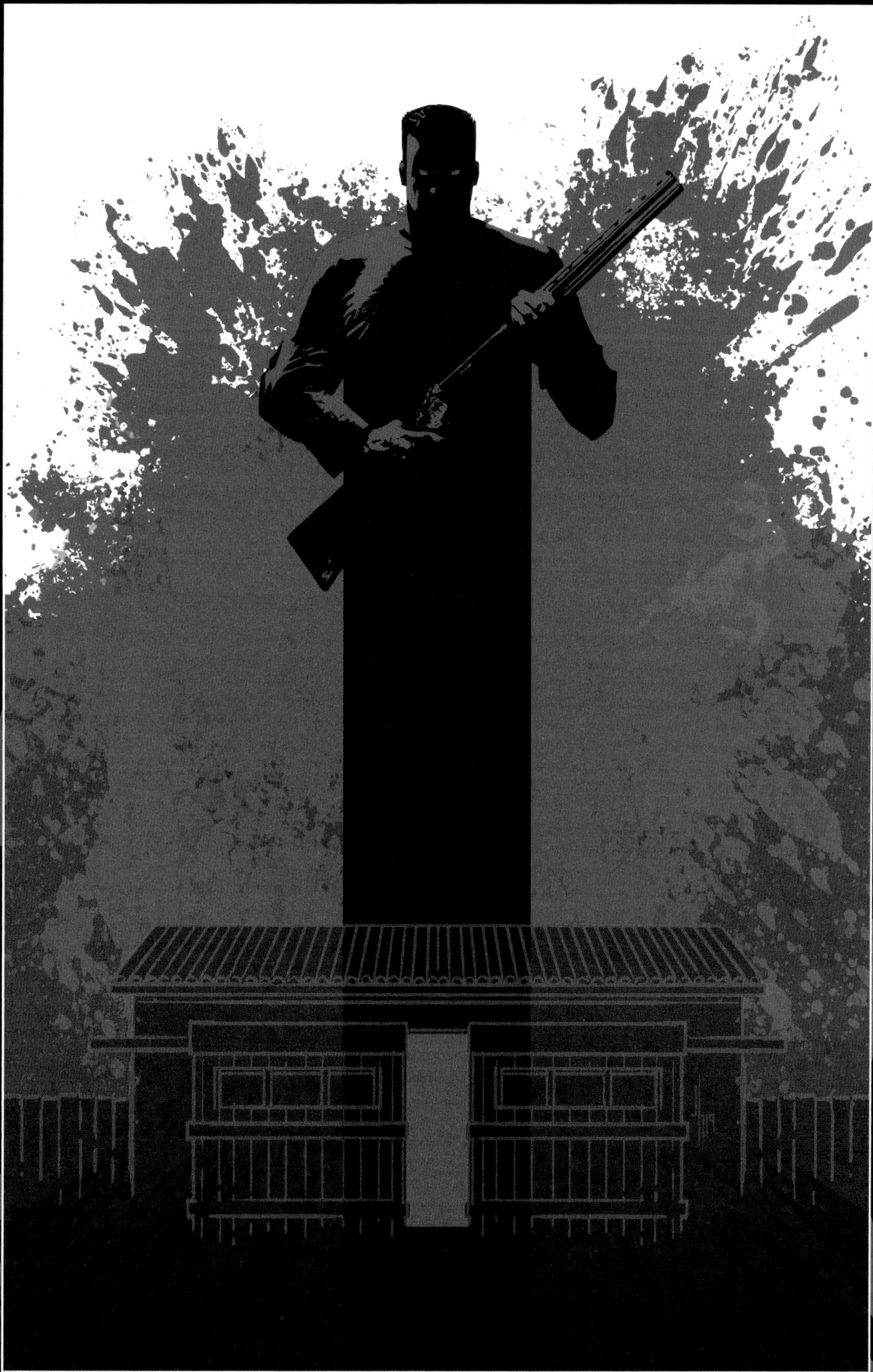

TREES: THREE FATES #4

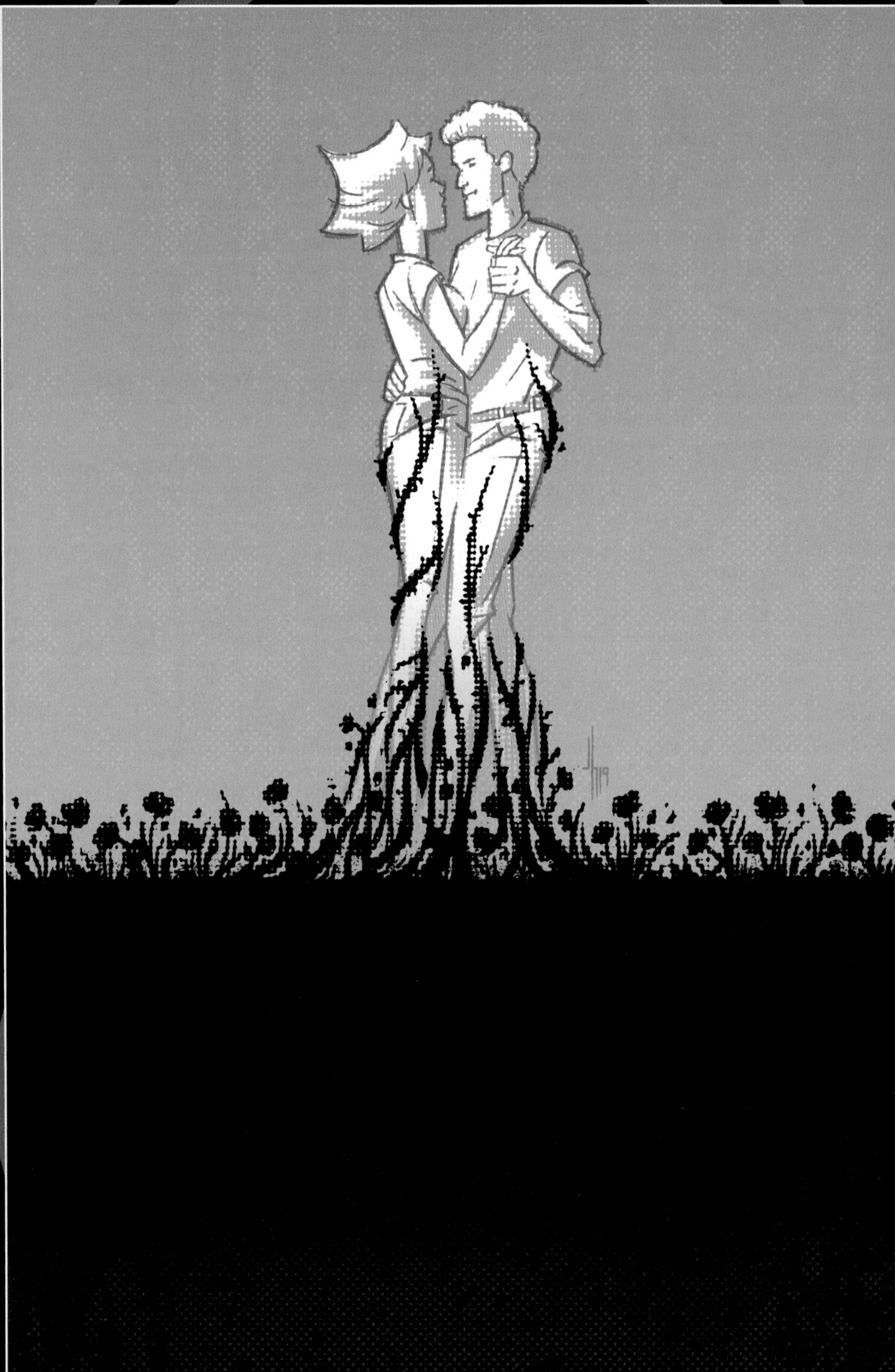

TREES: THREE FATES #5

WARREN ELLIS is the *New York Times*-bestselling author of *Gun Machine* and *Normal*, and the award-winning graphic novelist of *Transmetropolitan*, *Planetary*, CEMETERY BEACH, and RED, which was adapted for films starring Bruce Willis and Helen Mirren. He is the creator, writer and producer of the Netflix series *Castlevania* and *Heaven's Forest*.

JASON HOWARD is an American comic book artist, known for co-creating and illustrating the comic book series TREES and CEMETERY BEACH with writer Warren Ellis (*Transmetropolitan*), and SUPER DINOSAUR and THE ASTOUNDING WOLF-MAN with writer Robert Kirkman (THE WALKING DEAD). Jason also worked on the SUPER DINOSAUR animated series currently airing on Amazon Prime Video in the US.

DEE CUNNIFFE is an award-winning Irish designer who worked for over a decade in publishing and advertising. He gave it all up to pursue his love of comics. He has colored *The Paybacks* and *Interceptor* at Heavy Metal, *Her Infernal Descent*, *The Replacer* and *Stronghold* at Aftershock, Marvel's *Runaways*, DC's *Lucifer*, and REDNECK at Skybound.

FONOGRAFIKS is the banner name for the awarding-winning comics work of designer Steven Finch, which includes the Image Comics series NOWHERE MEN, INJECTION, MAESTROS, and the multi-award-winning SAGA. He lives and works, surrounded by far too many books, in the north east of England.